Reading the past

Current approaches to interpretation in archaeology

Third edition

Ian Hodder

and

Scott Hutson

CAMBRIDGE
UNIVERSITY PRESS

PUBLISHED BY THE PRESS SYNDICATE OF THE UNIVERSITY OF CAMBRIDGE
The Pitt Building, Trumpington Street, Cambridge, United Kingdom

CAMBRIDGE UNIVERSITY PRESS
The Edinburgh Building, Cambridge CB2 2RU, UK
40 West 20th Street, New York, NY 10011–4211, USA
477 Williamstown Road, Port Melbourne, VIC 3207, Australia
Ruiz de Alarcón 13, 28014 Madrid, Spain
Dock House, The Waterfront, Cape Town 8001, South Africa

http://www.cambridge.org

First published 1986
Reprinted 1987, 1988, 1989
Second edition 1991
Reprinted 1992, 1993, 1994, 1995, 1997, 1999, 2001
Third edition 2003

Printed in the United Kingdom at the University Press, Cambridge

British Library Cataloguing in Publication data
Hodder, Ian and Hutson, Scott
Reading the past: current approaches to interpretation in archaeology. – 3rd edn
1. Archaeology
I. Title
930.1

Library of Congress Cataloguing in Publication data
Hodder, Ian and Hutson, Scott
Reading the past: current approaches to interpretation in archaeology /
Ian Hodder and Hutson, Scott. – 3rd edn
   p.   cm.
Includes bibliographical references and index.
ISBN 0 521 82132 0 (hardback)   ISBN 0 521 52884 4 (paperback)
1. Archaeology–Philosophy.   2. Archaeology–Methodology.   I. Title.
CC72.H62 1991
930.1′01–dc20 90-40406 CIP

ISBN 0 521 82132 0 hardback
ISBN 0 521 52884 4 paperback

To Meg

Contents

Contents

Contents

Preface to the first edition

In some ways I am surprised that a book of this nature, discussing widely varying theoretical approaches to the past, can be written. In an important article, David Clarke (1973) suggested that archaeology was losing its innocence because it was embracing, in the 1960s and 1970s, a rigorous scientific approach, with agreed sets of procedures, models and theories. The age of unreflecting speculation was over.

However, archaeologists have always claimed to be rigorously scientific. Indeed, I argued (Hodder 1981) that archaeology would remain immature as long as it refused to debate and experiment with a wide range of approaches to the past. In grasping positivism, functionalism, systems theory and so on, and setting itself against alternative perspectives, archaeology remained narrow and out-of-date in comparison with related disciplines.

But over recent years, alternatives have emerged, largely from the European scene (Renfrew 1982), and one can now talk of Marxist and structuralist archaeology, as well as of processual, positivist approaches. Certainly such alternatives existed before, on the fringe, but they did not constitute a distinctive approach with a body of practitioners. The older normative and culture-historical schools also continue to thrive today. While many of these developments, and the erosion of the old 'New Archaeology' debates, have far to go, archaeology is now beginning to lose its innocence and is gaining maturity by being fully integrated into wider contemporary debates. This book seeks to capture this new spirit of debate and to contribute to it from a particular point of view.

At the same time, it seems to me that far from becoming submerged within other disciplines, archaeology has, through the wider debate, become better able to define itself as a distinct and productive area of study. The debate picks out the differences from other disciplines as well as the similarities.

Archaeology is neither 'historical' nor 'anthropological'. It is not even science or art. Archaeology's increasing maturity allows it to claim an independent personality with distinctive qualities to contribute.

Archaeology no longer has to be 'new' and unidirectional, presenting a unified front. It has the maturity to allow diversity, controversy and uncertainty. From catastrophe theory to sociobiology, it is all being applied to the archaeological past. But through this onslaught a more reasoned genre emerges, recapturing the old and redefining the new to form a distinctive archaeological enquiry.

It has become difficult for any one person to grasp the variety of approaches now present in the discipline, and this is my excuse for the inadequacies in my own account. In particular this difficulty contributes to the limited coverage given here of the approaches offered by ecology or palaeoeconomy. Ecological approaches are examined here in relation to systems theory in chapter 2, but for wider-ranging discussion the reader is advised to turn to the excellent accounts provided, for example, by Bailey (1983) and Butzer (1982). I have necessarily adopted a particular standpoint from which to view archaeology. This position is outlined in chapter 1, which concentrates on the nature of cultural meanings and on material culture as meaningfully constituted. Where ecological paradigms have contributed to this debate they have been discussed, but the majority of the work which might fall under that heading is outside the scope of this volume.

That this book is possible is due to the explanatory efforts of numerous researchers, some of whose work I have tried to capture and summarize here. I can only thank them for their inspiration and apologize in advance for any inadequacies of understanding on my part. The criticisms that I have made of their work will, I am sure, be returned in good measure.

While some of the ideas described in this volume were aired to a generation of Cambridge undergraduates, the text initially took form as the content of a graduate seminar course at the State University of New York, Binghamton, in the spring of 1984. The group of students and staff was lively, critical and keen to contribute. The text owes much to the members of the seminar. It was tried out on them and it took shape through their enthusiasm. I thank them, and particularly Meg, for the opportunity and the stimulation.

The final writing was possible while I was a Visiting Lecturer at the University of Paris 1–Sorbonne in 1985. The congenial environment and the critical comments of my friends and colleagues there were invaluable in the preparation of the final manuscript. In particular I wish to thank Serge Cleuziou, Anick Coudart, Jean-Paul Demoule, Mike Illett, Pierre Lemonnier and Alain Schnapp.

Preface to the second edition

The first edition was written as a personal account in an uncertain world in which post-processual approaches had hardly had any impact. It represented my musings in the dark. Since that time there has been so much other publication (especially the books by Shanks and Tilley 1987a and b, Leone and Potter 1988, Gero and Conkey 1990, Tilley 1990a and b, Bapty and Yates 1990) and so much evaluation in relation to processual archaeology (e.g. the debate in *Norwegian Archaeological Review* 1989, Watson 1986, Earle and Preucel 1987, Preucel 1990) that the book needed to be brought up to date and my views tempered with the opinions presented in the literature.

The book still falls short of presenting a unified post-processual position since there are many diverging points of view now being expressed in theoretical archaeology. Initially post-processual archaeology was held together in the critique of processual approaches. This critique is now well established and post-processual archaeologists have turned more to the construction of the past. In doing so differences have become more stark but the discipline has been enlivened by the variety of perspectives. Nevertheless, the number of substantive post-processual interpretations of the past remains relatively small although several are about to appear (e.g. Hodder 1990a; Tilley 1990b). As more work is done so the differences and arguments will be brought into focus.

In the 1980s archaeology saw the gradual emergence of studies concerned with interpreting past cultural meanings in relation to such issues as power and domination, history and gender. In this move archaeology was taking part in wider changes in the humanities and social sciences. As Trigger (1989, p. 776) has noted, 'in anthropology and the other social sciences there has been during the 1980s a renewed appreciation of the complexity of behaviour and an increasing

interest in the idiosyncratic, the particular, and the contingent'. Archaeology is involved in this new contextualism and
such developments are likely to increase in the 1990s (Watson
1986). Yet we have not escaped the 'colossal, polyhyphen-
ated, multi-systemic monsters' (Ingold 1986) which stalked
the pages of processual archaeological writing. The attractions
of a distanced, number-crunching method brought us first
catastrophe and then chaos theories. Science-based funding
of archaeology threatens to nudge archaeology not towards a
fruitful integration with science (see chapter 9) but towards a
narrow scientism. Nevertheless such trends are increasingly
being countered by integration of science, humanism and critique, by a vibrancy and variety of theoretical position and
by social engagement.

People have often asked me the meaning of the pictures
on the front cover and frontispiece of this book. Perhaps
it is best to leave the pictures open to multiple readings in
the way described in chapter 8. But my own comments may
serve to open up the meanings rather than to close them. I
was attracted to the Mags Harries work partly for reasons
described at the end of chapter 9, and partly for superficial
reasons like the newspaper embedded in the pavement – a pun
for 'reading the past'. Also, the scatter of artifacts, durable
on the pavement, seemed an appropriate metaphor for an
archaeology brought into the present and made active. But
somehow it was the fleeting foot that was most evocative,
like Magritte's feet which are set below a poster on the fence,
amongst stones and dirt, but uncertain and in the process of
transformation. The boots of the archaeologist, feet of clay,
often appear bogged down in the reality of the past. Would
that foot simply pass by leaving an empty trace or would the
boots be filled with the person of the archaeologist and with
the meaning of the past? It is my hope that the archaeology
of the 1990s will grasp the issue of interpretation more fully
and more critically, and this book is my contribution to that
task.

Preface to the third edition

In this second revision we have decided to make major changes, removing some chapters, adding new ones, and completely revising others. In reading through the text published in 1986 and revised with minor changes for the 1991 edition, it was clear that the book no longer adequately discussed the contemporary theoretical field in archaeology. There have been so many changes that we felt that substantial revisions were needed in a book which attempts to comment on theory in archaeology from a particular point of view. There has been a burgeoning in the discipline of discussions of post-structuralism, agency theory and neo-evolutionary theory, and whole new branches of theory such as phenomenology have emerged. It seemed necessary to cover and comment on these areas of debate, as well as to respond to the many changes and developments in debate within feminist archaeology (third-wave feminism), historical approaches (such as cultural history), theories of discourse and signs (semiotics, dialogical models) and so on. The book is now longer and covers more ground. It thus can still be used as an introduction to archaeological theory in general terms. But it retains a distinctive position, based on a commitment to meaning, agency and history, and it reviews the theoretical debates from that position.

The book has always catered to a rather hybrid audience and we have sought to rewrite so as to respond to a number of different interest groups. On the one hand, we have tried to write for undergraduates in archaeology and anthropology, and we believe that the book offers a still relatively short and understandable account at that level. We have also continued to provide a wide range of examples for students in different parts of the world. On the other hand, the book seeks to contribute to theoretical debate by arguing from a particular position, and it thus also talks to those directly engaged in theoretical research.

For the new cover illustration we have again turned to Magritte. *L'art de la conversation* seems full of ambiguity – it needs a careful reading and it can be read in various ways. Is the conversation between the two figures, or is it with the monument, Stonehenge-like, that hides words in its stones? Is the past, the words set in stone, to be read, and is reading like a conversation? The figures seem dwarfed and yet they stand there, trying to work it out. In this book we too have tried to work out how to make sense of the monuments and artifacts that survive from the enormity of the past. We have tried to contribute to the conversation.

We would like to thank Cambridge University Press for its continued belief in this book. Scott Hutson would like to acknowledge conversations with Byron Hamann, Arthur Joyce, Rosemary Joyce and Lisa Stevenson that have contributed to some of the perspectives in this third edition.

1 The problem

Many people are becoming increasingly aware that the so-called New Archaeology of the 60s and early 70s was flawed. Though the New Archaeology met resistance from its inception, a tradition of substantial epistemological critique began more than thirty years ago (Bayard 1969; Kushner 1970; Levin 1973; Morgan 1973; Tuggle *et al.* 1972). However there is little consensus as to the nature and scale of these flaws. It can be claimed that the New Archaeology actually inhibited the development of archaeology itself by trying to subsume it within other realms of study, such as anthropology and the natural sciences. In fact, within anthropology, the type of materialist, neo-evolutionary approach from which New Archaeologists drew inspiration had already lost much of its ground to interpretive, symbolic and structural approaches. Despite David Clarke's insistence on 'archaeology is archaeology is archaeology' (1968), his own approach, based on the importation of ideas from statistics, geography and the information sciences, has not led to a viable and distinctive archaeology.

Despite the great methodological contribution of the New Archaeology, many of the central concerns of the pre-New Archaeology era need to be rediscovered if an adequate *archaeological* discussion is to take place. Of course, the traditional approaches themselves had flaws, and these have to be dealt with. But the older approaches do not have to be thrown out totally, in the way that the New Archaeology sometimes rejected 'normative' archaeology (Flannery 1967; Binford 1962; 1965).

Our own route to this viewpoint was substantially drawn by the ethnoarchaeological fieldwork reported in *Symbols in Action* (Hodder 1982a). The three main ideas which developed out of that work, all of which have parallels in pre-New Archaeology, were (1) that material culture was meaningfully constituted, (2) that agency needed to be part of theories of material culture and social change, and (3) that despite the independent existence of archaeology, its closest ties were with history. We wish now to summarize these three 'problems'.

Cultural meanings and context

Schiffer (1976; 1987) has already argued that cultural transforms affect the relationship between material residues and the behaviour of the people who produced them. *Symbols in Action* showed further the importance of these 'c-transforms', as Schiffer called them.

At first sight such realization offers no threat to archaeology as a generalizing scientific discipline. Schiffer showed how one could generalize about c-transforms. For example, it can be shown that as the duration and intensity of use of a site increase, so there is more organization and secondary movement of refuse away from activity areas. In Hodder's work in Baringo it became clear that material culture was often *not* a direct reflection of human behaviour; rather it was a transformation of that behaviour.

For example, it had earlier been suggested that the stylistic similarity between objects increased as interaction between people increased. In fact, at the borders between ethnic groups in Baringo, the more interaction between people, the less the stylistic similarity. But, again, such findings can be incorporated within New Archaeology because it is possible to generalize and state the 'law' that material culture distinctiveness is correlated with the degree of negative reciprocity between groups (Hodder 1979). So the more competition between groups the more marked the material culture boundaries between them.

Another case in which it became clear that material culture was neither a simple nor a direct reflection of human behaviour was burial. Binford (1971) had suggested a general correlation between the complexity of mortuary ceremonialism and the complexity of social organization. As Parker

The problem

Pearson (1982) elegantly showed, in a study of modern and recent burial practices in Cambridge, such generalizations failed to take into account the cultural transformation of the relationship between burials and people. Even a highly differentiated society of the type found in Cambridge today might choose to bury its dead in an 'egalitarian' fashion.

Once again such work does not necessarily result in the final spanner being thrown in the works of New Archaeology. It might be possible to find some law-like generalizations about why societies represent and express themselves differently in burial customs. For example, at early stages in the development of a more highly ranked society, social status might be exaggerated and 'naturalized' in death, while at later stages the social ranking might be 'denied' in burial variability.

But in the case of burial practices, such generalizations are unconvincing and the force of the notion that material culture is an *indirect* reflection of human society becomes clear. Moreover, if we conceive of material culture as active – and the grounds for doing so are strong, as we will argue later – then the term 'reflection' misrepresents the relation between material culture and society. Rather, material culture and society mutually constitute each other within historically and culturally specific sets of ideas, beliefs and meanings. Thus, the relation between burial and society clearly depends on attitudes to death.

Much the same can be said of cultural boundaries and refuse deposition. Whether a particular artifact type does or does not express the boundary of an ethnic group depends on the ideas people in that society have about different artifacts and what is an appropriate artifact for ethnic group marking. The relationship between refuse and social organization depends on attitudes to dirt. Thus even short-term camps may have highly organized rubbish and long-term camps may allow refuse build-up of a type that we today would find abhorrent and unhygienic.

These cultural attitudes and meanings about material culture seemed to frustrate the generalizing aims of the New Archaeology, since all material culture could now be seen to be meaningfully constituted. If material culture, all of it, has a symbolic dimension such that the relationship between people and things is affected, then *all* of archaeology, economic and social, is implicated.

The problem then becomes, not 'how do we study symbolism in the past?', but 'how do we do archaeology at all?'. Within New Archaeology the methodology to be employed in interpreting the past was 'hard' and universal. Simplistically put, one could correlate material culture patterning with human patterning, and 'read off' the latter from the former by applying general laws and Middle Range Theory. Ultimately material culture could be seen as the product of adaptation with the environment, both physical and social. So, if one kept asking *why* the material culture patterning is as it is, one was always taken back to questions of material survival. With such a 'reductionist' approach one can always predict what the material culture means, what it reflects, in any environmental context.

But to claim that culture is meaningfully constituted is ultimately to claim that aspects of culture are *irreducible*. The relationship between material culture and human organization is partly social, as we shall see below. But it is also dependent on a set of cultural attitudes which cannot be predicted from or reduced to an environment. The cultural relationships are not caused by anything else outside themselves. They just are. The task of archaeologists is to interpret this irreducible component of culture so that the society behind the material evidence can be 'read'.

How does one go about such 'reading'? It is often claimed that material objects are mute, that they do not speak, so how can one understand them? Certainly an object from the past does not say anything of itself. Handed an object from an unknown culture archaeologists will often have difficulties in providing an interpretation. But to look at objects by themselves is really not archaeology at all. Archaeology is concerned with finding objects in layers and other contexts (rooms, sites, pits, burials) so that their date and meaning can be interpreted.

The problem

As soon as the context of an object is known it is no longer totally mute. Clues as to its meaning are given by its context. Artifacts are found in graves around the necks of the skeletons and are interpreted as necklaces. Objects found in elaborate non-settlement contexts are termed ritual. Clearly we cannot claim that, even in context, objects tell us their cultural meaning, but on the other hand they are not totally mute. The interpretation of meaning is constrained by the interpretation of context.

In *Symbols in Action*, the emphasis on context led to discussion of burial, style, exchange, refuse discard, settlement organization. All these realms of material culture could now be seen as different contexts in relation to each other. Artifacts might mean different things in these different contexts, but the meanings from one realm might be related, in a distorted way, to the meanings in other realms. The 'reading' of the archaeological record had to take such cultural transformations into account.

A number of problems and questions arose from such a viewpoint. First, what *is* the context? Context itself has to be interpreted in the data, and the definition of context is a matter for debate. Is the context of a particular artifact type found in cemeteries a part of the body, the grave, a group of graves, the cemetery, the region, or what? How does one decide on the boundary which defines the context?

Second, even assuming we can construct meanings from contextual associations, similarities and differences, are these cultural meanings in people's minds? Certainly much of the cultural meaning of material objects is not conscious. Few of us are aware of the full range of reasons which lead us to choose a particular item of dress as appropriate for a given context. But do we need to get at the conscious and subconscious meanings in people's minds, or are there simply cultural rules and practices which can be observed from the outside? Do we simply have to describe the unconscious cultural rules of a society or do we have to get at people's perceptions of those rules? For example, is it enough to say that in a particular cultural tradition burial variability correlates with social variability or that burial is organized by a culture/nature transform, or do we need to understand people's attitudes to death, getting 'inside their minds'?

The third question has already been touched upon. To what extent can we generalize about ideas in people's minds? Certain general principles concerning the relationships between structural oppositions, associations, similarities, contexts and meanings are used in interpreting the past and the world around us today. Even the notion that meaning derives from contextual associations is a general theory. To what extent are such generalizations valid? And further, what is the aim of archaeology? Is it to provide generalizations? If we say that meanings are context dependent, then all we can do is come to an understanding of each cultural context in its own right, as a unique set of cultural dispositions and practices. We cannot generalize from one culture to another. Even if there are some general propositions we need to use in interpreting the past, these are, by their very general nature, trivial – hardly the focus for scientific enquiry. To what extent can we generalize about unique cultural contexts, and why should we want to generalize in any case?

These questions are also relevant in relation to the second problem that derived from *Symbols in Action*.

Individuals and agents

Material culture does not just exist. It is made by someone. It is produced to do something. Therefore it does not passively *reflect* society – rather, it creates society through the acts of social agents.

The question of agency arises from an older dialogue about the place of the individual in society. On the one hand we have John Donne's famous words, 'No man is an island, entire of itself, every man is a piece of the continent, a part of the main.' We concur and stress that we need to explore how society affects the individual. Yet Donne's view ultimately says that individuals are of little significance in the tide of human history. On the other hand J. S. Mill, a classical individualist, said 'Men are not, when brought together, converted into another kind of substance.'

In the New Archaeology, the possibility of agency was avoided, argued out of social theory. As Flannery noted (1967), the aim was not to reach the individual Indian behind the artifact, but the system behind both Indian and artifact. It is argued by the processual school in archaeology that there are systems so basic in nature that culture and individuals are powerless to divert them. This is a trend towards determinism – theory building is seen as being concerned with discovering deterministic causal relationships. There is a close link here between discarding notions of cultural belief and of agency. Both are seen as being unassailable through archaeological evidence, and both are unpredictable and inhibit generalization.

In the 1980s, a number of authors reacted against the trend towards determinism in the New Archaeology (Hodder 1986; Shanks and Tilley 1987a, b). However, in their passion to re-construct the relation between structure and agency, some writers uncritically erected a particular version of agency that privileged only a certain form of agent, namely, the individual. Critical and philosophical scholarship has documented that the 'individual' is a very recent construct, tied closely to the development of modernity in the West (Foucault 1970; Handsman and Leone 1989). People in other cultures and at other times may be constructed in a very different way from the individual subjects of our own society, which means that the notion of agency should not be restricted to 'the individual'.

By emphasizing agency in social theory we do not mean to suggest that we should identify 'great men' and 'great women'; but that each archaeological object is produced by an individual (or a group of individuals), not by a social system. Each pot is made by specific actors forming the shape, inscribing the design. Archaeology thus raises in acute form the problem of the relationship between agency and society. What is the relationship between the individual pot and the society as a whole?

Within the New Archaeology this central question was simply bypassed. Individual pots were examined solely as passive reflections of the socio-cultural system. Each pot, each artifact could be examined to see how it functioned for the system as a whole. For example, the pot reflected status and thus helped to regulate the flow of energy and resources within the system. In addition, the system was seen as developing 'over the long term'. Thus individual instances of variability which did not act for the good of the system as a whole would be of no significance for the long-term survival of the system and would in any case hardly be visible archaeologically.

These two notions – the overall adaptive system and the long term – led to a rejection of the individual in archaeological theory. As a result, material culture became a passive reflection of the social system. Whatever agents had in their heads when they made a pot, the only thing that was important was how that pot functioned in the social system. What the individual was trying to do with the object became irrelevant.

The ethnographic work reported in *Symbols in Action* showed the inadequacy of this view. For example, in a Lozi village, pottery similarities did not passively reflect learning networks and interaction frequency. Rather the pottery style was used to create social differences and allegiances within the village; it was produced to have an active role. Similarly, some artifacts indicate social boundaries in Baringo, in Kenya, but spears, for example, do not. This is because spear styles are used by young men to disrupt the authority of older men. They play an active role.

That material culture can act back and affect the society and behaviour which produced it can readily be accepted within processual archaeology (Rathje 1978, p. 52). In particular, town and house architecture clearly channels and acts upon later behaviour. On the other hand, material culture cannot of itself do anything: if it does 'act back' on society it must do so within the frameworks of meaning within the society itself. The way in which material culture acts on people is social; the action can only exist within a social framework of beliefs, concepts and dispositions.

Material culture and its associated meanings are played out as parts of social strategies. Agents do not simply fill predetermined roles, acting out their scripts. If they did, there would be little need for the active use of material culture in order to negotiate social position and create social change. We are not simply pawns in a game, determined by a system – rather, we use a myriad of means, including material culture symbolism, to create new roles, to redefine existing ones and to deny the existence of others.

It could be argued that processual archaeology is indeed concerned with individual variability. After all, did it not react against normative approaches and emphasize the importance of situational adaptive behaviour? The question of whether processual archaeology escaped a normative position will be discussed throughout this volume. For the moment it is necessary to set the scene by clarifying some of the meanings given to the term normative in archaeology. First, it is often used to refer to the culture-historical approach. In this context it sometimes has pejorative connotations; it refers to descriptive culture history. This is not the sense in which we will use the term in this volume. Second, 'normative' refers to the notion that culture is made up of a set of shared beliefs. The implication is sometimes present that the shared ideas (the norms) hinder situational variability. Third, there is a prescriptive component to norms – they indicate what should be done. In this sense norms refer to rules of behaviour. Of course one can be critical of the normative approach (in the first sense) while still being interested in norms in the second and third senses, but both these latter meanings of the word give little in the way of a role to individuals as social actors. A more general critique of normative positions will be required in this volume.

The renewed emphasis on agency in archaeological interpretation is not designed to argue that prehistoric change was the result of 'free will' or that particular individuals in the past can or should be identified. Rather, the aim is to integrate both meaning and agency into archaeological theory. Our interpretations of the past need to incorporate cultural meanings, intentions and purposes (see above). Societies are not purposive (Shanks and Tilley 1987a, p. 124), but individual agents are. It is certainly possible to argue that the purposes, meanings and intentions are themselves always already structured within historical trajectories, but the notion of agency allows for the ability of individuals to transform the structures in concrete situations. Positioned subjects manipulate material culture as a resource and as a sign system in order to create and transform relations of power and domination. Determinism is avoided since it is recognized that in concrete situations contingent situations are found and structures of meaning and of domination are gradually restructured (Giddens 1979; Bourdieu 1977). Johnson (1989) has provided a constructive critique of discussions of the dialectical relationship between structure and agency in recent archaeological writing. He notes that theoretical accounts have not been backed up by applications which include a truly reflexive relationship between social structure and human agency. (In chapter 5 we will discuss structure and agency in greater detail.) Detailed small-scale studies of variability are needed in order to examine the link between individual, meaningfully constituted events and long-term structures. Johnson's own example derives from historical archaeology and is part of a wider trend towards small-scale historical studies (e.g. Ladurie 1980; Le Goff 1985; Duby 1980; see also chapter 7) but similar small-scale methodologies are relevant in prehistoric contexts (Hodder 1987a and b) where the opposition between individual event and long term structure is accentuated.

Historical context

In the reaction against culture history and normative archaeology, processual archaeologists turned to anthropology.

Ultimately the main reason why the New Archaeology never really took hold in Europe to the extent that it did in America may be that in Europe archaeology is intellectually and administratively (in universities) closely linked to history, not anthropology. In American processual archaeology, the new approach was to be cross-cultural, looking at systems in relation to their environments and producing universal statements. In effect a timeless past was produced. System trajectories were examined, but time was sliced into segments and attention was focussed on the cross-cultural regularities in changes from type *a* to type *b* (for example from mobile hunter-gatherers to settled farmers).

While the discussion so far in this chapter has implied that cross-cultural laws which are more than trivial are unlikely to exist, what is the possibility of historical laws – that is generalizations valid through time in a particular context? Since action in the world partly depends on concepts, and since concepts are learnt through experience in the world, in which one is brought up and lives, it is feasible that long-term continuities in cultural traditions exist, continually being renegotiated and transformed, but nevertheless generated from within. Part of the aim of archaeology may be to identify whether such long-term continuities exist, and how they are transformed and changed.

It was noted earlier that an emphasis on cultural meanings is here taken to imply that culture is not reducible to material effects. In explaining why a cultural form has a specific meaning and use, it is necessary to examine its previous associations and contexts, its diffusion and sequence. While diffusion and cultural continuity are social processes, the pre-existing cultural form also influences what comes after. This is because human beings can only perceive and act through a cultural medium which they both create and live within. As Childe (1936) put it, man creates traditions, but traditions make the man – man makes himself.

It might be thought that there is a danger here of a new type of reductionism. Rather than reducing cultural behaviour to survival, there is the possibility of an infinite regress as cultural forms are interpreted in terms of previous cultural forms, backwards until we get to the first stone-tool ever made, in the temporal mists of the Palaeolithic. While it will rarely be necessary to go to such historical lengths, it is difficult to see why one should want to deny the importance of culture-historical work. There is something in all of us of the decisions made in the flaking of the very first hand-axe. Only archaeology can achieve this grand design. But even when we get to the origin of some idea it is not reduced to something outside itself. The cultural form remains created, specific and irreducible.

While it may ultimately be desirable to trace the creation of the present out of the distant past, the transformations of meaning over such time periods are considerable. More frequently we can gain adequate insight into cultural meanings by examining the more immediate historical context.

It *is* important, therefore, to examine where things come from. This was the focus of culture history within traditional archaeology. We now have to see the diffusion of traits as a social and meaningful process; the associations of an item in another or in a previous cultural context affect the use of that item within a new context. Diffusion is thus explanatory, not descriptive, as is so often claimed.

While placing an emphasis on cultural meaning and the simultaneous maintenance and active 'invention' (Hobsbawn and Ranger 1984) of cultural traditions we do not wish to argue that history consists only of conceptual structures and we do not wish to claim an idealist history (see p. 20 and chapter 7). Environmental and technological constraints and social relations of production also structure change. They contribute to the historical potential for social transformation and they provide the resources with which change can be built. The split between the ideal and the material is best seen as an historical dialect in which the material resources and relations are meaningfully embedded so that neither the ideal nor the material are privileged.

While it is argued that archaeology should reassert its European ties with history, it is also important to see the differences between archaeology and history. To the extent that historical explanation can be defined by its reference to antecedent contexts and events (an inadequate or incomplete description, as we will argue in chapter 7), archaeology is part of history. Yet archaeology is about material culture not documents. The writing of ink on paper is itself one type of material culture, and the inference of meaning from such evidence is equivalent to that for material objects in general. In this sense, history is part of archaeology. Even though historical documents contain considerably more contextual information when we recognize the language they are written in, the process of inference is still one of giving meaning to the past material world. Of course, in those cases where texts are readable, the archaeological record should not be considered impoverished in comparison with the historical record. Texts record the voices of select segments of the population, depending on the (often low) rates of literacy in the past, therefore putting the archaeologist in an excellent and sometimes unique position to uncover the actions of the less powerful (Deetz 1977).

This archaeological approach has become influential in a number of disciplines. Prompted by, among other things, the recognition of ruptures between self and other, whether the other is conceived of as cultural, psychological or historical, a wide variety of writers, including Freud, Foucault, Lacan and Benjamin, have claimed an affinity towards 'archaeological' approaches or expressed their methods using archaeological metaphors (see also Shanks 2001).

Conclusion

In the course of this volume we hope to discuss the problems raised in this first chapter. The aim is to meet the challenges posed to archaeology by a recognition of the importance of cultural meaning, agency and history. In summary, we can see that such recognition has effects in the three central areas of archaeological debate. These are (1) the relationship between material culture and society – how material culture relates to people, (2) the causes of change – what causes social, economic and cultural change, and (3) epistemology and inference – how archaeologists interpret the past.

1 *Behaviour–material culture*

It has always been recognized that the relationship between behaviour and material culture is the central difficulty to be resolved in archaeology. The problems in this relationship were early recognized in the only partial correspondence discovered between material 'cultures' and 'peoples' (Childe 1951).

The contribution of processual archaeology was an attempt to think systematically about the relationship between behaviour and material culture. In much early work the dominant theme was: behaviour → material culture. Material culture was the passive by-product of human behaviour. This view is seen in the matrilocal residence hypothesis (Longacre 1970) and in theories about the relationship between population and settlement area (Naroll 1962) and between style and interaction (Plog 1978). The attempt by Binford (1983) to identify Middle Range Theory, insofar as this can be applied to cultural processes, recaptures the same desire for secure, unambiguous relationships, essentially equivalent to Schiffer's (1976) laws, between material culture and human behaviour. More recently, as was shown above, this cross-cultural approach has been extended (Rathje 1978) to include the notion that material culture acts back upon society, forming a two-way relationship: behaviour ↔ material culture.

In this book we wish to go further and argue that the relationship between behaviour and material culture depends on the actions of people within particular culture-historical contexts.

$$\text{behaviour} \longleftrightarrow \text{material culture}$$
$$\uparrow$$
$$\text{agency,}$$
$$\text{culture,}$$
$$\text{history}$$

The problem

There is thus no direct, universal cross-cultural relationship between behaviour and material culture. Frameworks of meaning intervene and these have to be interpreted by the archaeologist. This endeavour must be undertaken by all of those who want to examine the past as archaeologists, even if we are mainly interested in economics and social organization rather than symbolism. Even if we want to say that the economy at a particular site was based on hunting many wild animals because of the high percentage of wild animal bones on the site, we need to make some assumptions about attitudes towards animals, bones, and waste. For example, we need to assume that people ate, or discarded the residues from the animals they ate, on sites (rather than eating and discarding off sites, throwing bones in rivers where they would not survive archaeologically, or burning the bones to ash). Whatever we want to say about human behaviour in the past, cultural meanings need to be assumed. In chapter 9, we will discuss the suggestion, grounded in phenomenology and psychology, that material culture plays such a fundamental role in constituting culture, agency and history that our existence as subjects cannot be intelligibly disentangled from the material world in which our behaviour is embedded.

2 Cause–effect

The second major area of research is the causes of social change. Again, simple notions of cause → effect (technological change leads to population increase, for example) have been replaced by cause ↔ effect relationships through the introduction of systems, feedback loops, multiplier effects and multiple causality. Most archaeologists today would accept that the causes of social change are complex, involving many different factors – economic, social and ideological – and there have recently been many interesting attempts to relate these factors into complex interlocking systems (chapter 2).

Within such work, however, there remains the notion that causes have effects which are to some degree universal and predictable. On the other hand, the central importance of the individual perception of causes leads to a different view.

$$\text{cause} \longleftrightarrow \text{effect}$$
$$\uparrow$$
$$\text{agency,}$$
$$\text{culture,}$$
$$\text{history}$$

Causes in the form of events, conditions and consequences (intended and unintended) in the world cannot have social effects except via human perception and evaluation of them. Thus land erosion may be a *cause* with the *effect* that people abandon their village and disperse. But the fact of land erosion does not by itself determine any particular response because there are many ways of dealing with or avoiding or preventing land erosion. How land erosion or its effects are perceived, and how the possible responses are evaluated, depend on how land erosion is involved in individual social strategies within particular culture-historical contexts.

This is saying more than that ideology is important in human adaptation and that it functions in various ways. Within most archaeological discussion of ideology, the belief system is seen as a predictable response of the adaptive system (chapter 2); it is claimed here, however, that the particular content of the postures and practices that are constructed within historical channels is the medium through which adaptation occurs. Thus causes (social or physical) do not have social effects; rather, an historical tradition reproduces itself in relation to events in the world.

3 Fact–theory

Through much of the early development of archaeology an empiricist stance was maintained, in which the facts were seen to speak for themselves – 'let the pots speak'. Thus Colt Hoare, a British archaeologist writing in the 18th century, said that we speak from facts not theory. It was held that by staying close to the facts certain things, though by no means all things, could be known with security. As we shall see later, this is a simplification of a complex set of beliefs held by archaeologists prior to the emergence of processual archaeology (Wylie 1989a, b; 1993). But in general, inference could be seen as following the design: data → theory.

More recently an alternative view has been emphasized, in which data are collected in relation to a theory. The hypothetico-deductive approach involved deducing from a theory various implications, and testing these implications against the data. Binford's (1967) smudge-pit example provides a good illustration of this procedure. Renfrew (1982) has depicted the relationship between theory and data as data ↔ theory. Fact and theory confront each other but each changes in relation to the other (Wylie 1993).

Binford and Sabloff (1982) have in fact suggested that the relationship between theory and data is so close that data are observed within theory, and that therefore observational data are really theories (in Binford and Sabloff's terms the observational data are paradigm dependent). Thus, while all the approaches mentioned above would argue that the real world exists separate from our observations of it, more and more of the observational process is seen as being theory dependent. The bare bones that are left are the facts in the real world which we can never observe.

The problems of observation raised by post-positivist philosophy can be exemplified in the diagrams shown in Fig. 1. Before we can measure and compare such objects we have to decide what they are. For example, if we decide to measure the front faces of all such boxes, which is the front face? Or if we decide to measure the length of the rabbit's ears, we have to be able to differentiate between rabbits and ducks.

Such problems are particularly acute in the study of prehistoric art, but they pose a major difficulty for all archaeology since before one can measure or count, compare or contrast, one has to form categories (types of pots, contexts, cultures and so on). These categories are formed through the process of perception.

The solution followed by Binford and Sabloff (1982) is to invoke Middle Range Theory. They argue that independent instruments of measurement can be brought in to test the relationship between material culture and the society which

Fig. 1. The relationship between data and theory. (A) Which is the front edge of the box? (B) Is this an image of a duck or a rabbit? (C) Do you see a face or a person playing a horn? B and C from *Mind Sights* by Roger Shepard, © 1990 by Roger Shepard. Reprinted by permission of Henry Holt and Company, LLC.

produced it, and that in this way one can 'objectively' test between paradigms. This answer is inadequate (a) because what one measures depends on perception and categorization, and (b) because there can be no *independent* instruments of measurement since methodology is itself theory dependent.

Although it will be argued in this volume that the real world does constrain what we can say about it, it is also clear that the concept of 'data' involves both the real world and our theories about it (see chapter 8 for discussions of objectivity and relativism). As a result, the theories one espouses about the past depend very much on one's own social and cultural context. Trigger (1980), Leone (1978) and others (see also Arnold 1990; Conkey 1997; Handsman and Leone 1989;

The problem

Kehoe 1998; McCafferty and McCafferty 1994; Tilley 1989b) have shown with great effect how changing interpretations of the past depend on changing social and cultural contexts in the present. Individuals within society today use the past within social strategies. In other words, the data–theory relationship is conceived and manipulated within cultural and historical contexts.

$$\text{Fact} \longleftrightarrow \text{theory}$$
$$\uparrow$$
agency,
culture,
history

Towards the end of this volume we wish to examine the varied implications of the realization that there can be no 'testing' of theory against data, no independent measuring devices and no secure knowledge about the past. It seems to us that most archaeologists have shied away from these problems since at first sight they seem destructive: the whole fabric of archaeology as a scientific discipline, accepted since the early development of archaeology, is threatened. We wish to argue that the problems need to be faced if archaeology is to remain a rigorous discipline and if archaeologists are to be socially responsible.

2 Processual and systems approaches

In chapter 1 the question was posed: how do we infer cultural meanings in material remains from the past? In this and the following chapters various approaches to achieving this end will be discussed. The search is for an approach that takes adequate account of agency in an historical and cultural context.

It is necessary first to make a distinction between two broad classes of approach followed by archaeologists, which we shall term materialist and idealist. We shall see later that these terms have numerous senses within different schools of thought; for the moment we wish to give them provisional but precise meanings.

For Kohl (1981, p. 89) materialism 'accords greater causal weight to a society's behaviour than to its thoughts, reflections, or justifications for its behaviour'. This kind of materialism is considered 'vulgar' because thoughts, reflections and justifications – the 'superstructure' – are said to be wholly determined by the productive economic behaviour that forms the 'base' of society. In the materialist scheme, productive capacity and behaviour is influenced only by technology and environmental limitations (see chapter 4 for other forms of materialism). This definition needs to be extended to include the nature of inference within materialist approaches. In this book we mean by materialist approaches those that infer cultural meanings from the relationships between people and their environment. Within such a framework the ideas in people's minds can be predicted from their economy, technology, social and material production. Given a way of organizing matter and energy, an appropriate ideological framework can be predicted.

By idealist we mean any approach which accepts that there is some component of human action which is not predictable from a material base, but which comes from the human mind or from culture in some sense. In chapter 1, we referred to the viewpoint that culture was not entirely reducible to other variables, that to some extent culture is what culture is. In inferring cultural meanings in the past, there is no necessary relationship between social and material organization of resources on the one hand and cultural ideas and values on the other.

The distinction made above is equivalent to Gellner's (1982) identification of 'covering law' and 'emanationist' conceptions of causation. The former limits itself to the world of experience and seeks causality in the pattern of similar experiences, the regular associations, the observed laws; the latter, on the other hand, postulates inner essences, normally hidden from view, which lie behind and bind together visible phenomena.

In this chapter, we wish to examine some recent approaches to recovering past cultural meanings which in our view are often materialist, and 'covering law' in nature. They are all 'processual' in that they claim to view culture not as normative, but as an adaptive process. Processual archaeology, though deriving from the New Archaeology of the 1960s and 1970s, has spawned various offspring or reactions termed neo-evolutionary, behavioural and cognitive processual archaeology. These approaches will be evaluated in terms of their approach to cultural meanings. But we wish to focus first on one approach that has long been of interest to processual archaeologists – the use of systemic adaptive theory. Kohl (1981, p. 95) argues that there is no necessary relationship between materialism and systems analysis. In practice, however, systems analysis has been the vehicle for the application of models emphasizing ecology and economy, based on predictable law-like relationships. We intend to illustrate these points by taking a number of representative examples. It must be emphasized that these examples are chosen precisely because they are good examples within the framework used. In criticizing them we do not criticize the authors and their work, only the framework which they have adopted (for other examples see Conrad and Demarest 1984; Earle 1990; Jochim 1983; Braun and Plog 1982).

The article by Trubitt (2000) on changes in economy and society at Cahokia in the Mississippi River Valley in the 12th and 13th centuries A.D. is our first example of the way in which systemic approaches incorporate the ideational subsystem, including ritual and monumental architecture. Demarrais *et al.* (1996) also show the ways ideologies change through time in relation to other subsystems. They examine sequences of change in Neolithic and Bronze Age chiefdoms in Thy, Denmark, in the Moche state of north coastal Peru, and in the Inka empire of Andean South America.

Much recent work on symbolism and style has as its starting point an article by Wobst (1977). This important and creative work shows the way in which style can be linked to processes of information exchange, and Wobst relates the information exchange sub-system to flows of matter and energy. Wobst explains style by its functioning in relation to other variables, and we will therefore describe his approach as systemic.

An equally important and influential article is that by Flannery and Marcus (1976) in which ideology is seen to play a part in regulating the social and economic sub-systems throughout long periods in the Oaxaca valley, Mexico. They show the way in which the Zapotec cosmology can be seen as a means of organizing information about the world.

A materialist approach to culture?

On the surface, the two recent articles (Trubitt 2000 and Demarrais *et al.* 1996) seem to diverge from the older studies (Wobst 1977 and Flannery and Marcus 1976). Whereas the earlier cases see style, symbolism, ideology and cultural meaning as conferring adaptive advantage, the later articles focus explicitly on strategies of political actors. In fact, the 'dual-processual' approach favoured by Trubitt was offered in direct contrast to neo-evolutionary theory (Blanton *et al.* 1996, p. 1). However, all four cases retain a systemic, materialist approach, and, when pressed, will reduce cultural meaning to adaptive considerations. Trubitt attributes a decrease in monumental construction and an increase in status differentiation and craft production at Cahokia to a switch from corporate political strategies, in which social inequality is downplayed, power is corporate and ritual activity expresses communal goals and ideologies, to network political strategies, in which individual leaders monopolise power and build networks of support through prestige goods exchange. In this model (see also Blanton *et al.* 1996), both the form (collective representations at massive, collectively built monuments) and the content (themes of fertility, renewal and cosmic order) of ritual are precipitates of the political strategy. The political strategies themselves are in most cases determined by material conditions. Trubitt's goal is not to determine what may have motivated the change from corporate to network strategies at Cahokia, but in passing she notes that declines in population may have caused this shift, forcing leaders to try new strategies to gain followers. Likewise, though Blanton *et al.* declare that the dual-processual approach transcends the materialism/idealism divide, old-time materialist factors such as population size ('scale limitations') and environmental factors predict, in most cases, which of the two strategies will be pursued.

A similar pattern is seen in Demarrais *et al.*'s example. Their three case studies in the materialisation of ideology span the upper rungs of the neo-evolutionary ladder (chiefdom, state, empire) and each of the three culture's locations on the ladder in part determines the nature of ideological strategies (Demarrais *et al.* 1996, pp. 19–20). The authors envision ideology as a central element of cultural systems (p. 15), though in their case studies, ideology responds rather directly to environmental and political factors. For example, in Thy, changes in ideology were determined by local environmental factors and external technological factors. During the Pastoral Warrior Period (2600–1800 B.C.) the lack of a local material resource that could be monopolised prevented early strong warriors from building chiefdoms. The development of warrior chiefdoms and their associated ideology depended upon the non-local development of bronze technology and its introduction to Denmark (copper and tin were not locally available). Bronze-working was sufficiently difficult to prevent all but ambitious chiefs and their attached artisans from mastering it. In the Inka case, ideological strategies were a direct adaptation to the problems of communication and the challenge of establishing authority over geographically dispersed and culturally, linguistically distinct subjects (p. 27). Demarrais *et al.* attend to the specific contents and meanings of these different ideologies to some degree, but by casting ideology as an adaptive strategy, they reduce ritual and meaning to a mere function of other subsystems.

Wobst clearly states that he is concerned not with the production of artifacts but with their use lives. He is concerned with the adaptive advantage that artifacts provide in information exchange. 'Learned behaviour and symbolizing ability greatly increase the capacity of human operators to interact with their environment through the medium of artifacts. This capacity . . . improves their ability to harness and process energy and matter' (p. 320). In looking at the adaptive advantage style may convey, Wobst suggests a number of cross-cultural generalizations. For example, artifact style gains in value if the potential receivership is neither too close socially (since emitter and receiver will be acquainted) nor too distant (since decoding of the message is unreliable). Thus, as the size of social units increases so that there is more interaction with socially intermediate receivers, artifact stylistic behaviour will increase. Another generalization is that 'the less an artifact is visible to members of a given group, the less appropriate it is to carry stylistic messages of any kind' (p. 328).

Such work concentrates on material functions and reduces symbolic behaviour to utility and adaptation. General statements are derived suggesting predictable relationships between economy and society: for example Hodder suggested (1979) that material culture boundaries are more marked where there is increased negative reciprocity between groups. In the same vein Wobst suggests in relation to Yugoslavian folk costume that 'in areas of strong inter-group competition one would expect a higher proportion of people wearing hats that signal group affiliation than in areas with relatively stable homogeneous populations' (p. 333).

Flannery and Marcus (1976) suggest a broader context for such generalizations. They show the way symbolism and ritual can be seen as part of human ecology, following the ecological stance of Rappaport (1971). Their concern is with the way ritual regulates the relationship between people and environment; the Zapotec cosmology is seen as a way of giving order to and regulating natural events. Ritual blood-letting, using sting-ray spines, shows to other members of a community that a farmer is making a loss and needs the support of gifts of maize. Human ecosystems involve the exchange of matter, energy and information.

To what extent can these materialist systemic approaches explain cultural meaning, ideology and ritual? The first point to be made is that they are not intended to explain the 'becoming' of cultural production. As Wobst clearly states, his interest is in the use and functions of artifact styles, not their production. This is a difficulty of all functional, adaptive explanations, where the 'cause' of an event is also its 'effect'. Thus in explaining how something like sting-ray spine blood-letting came about, we refer to a later effect, the regulation of resources. This temporal inversion is, however, recognized by most systems theorists, and answered by saying that archaeologists can only look at adaptive advantage over the long term, at what is selected for survival. Within this view there is little concern with why something was produced.

Thus, almost by definition, most of the cultural variability dug up by archaeologists is ruled out of the court of explanation. We cannot explain why a sting-ray spine is used, why blood-letting is used rather than other artifacts and rituals. Reference is made only to gross characteristics of cultural behaviour – Trubitt's monumental mounds, Wobst's increases and decreases of stylistic behaviour. In most cases we cannot explain why a particular ritual, or why a ritual at all, is used for a particular function, since other things could presumably have done the same job equally well. The difficulty is made clear if we start, not from the adaptive functional end, but from the decoration, the particular squiggle painted on a pot. We can hardly say that squiggles on pots are determined by adaptive advantage. There is a poverty to systemic arguments which do not allow us to explain specific cultural variability. A great amount is left unaccounted for.

How are the ideational meanings assigned in these studies? Is the imputation of meaning achieved critically? Many archaeologists retain an empiricist view and are sceptical of the ideational realm, which is often equated with the speculative and non-scientific, and prefer to talk of material functions rather than ideas which were in people's minds in the past. However, in our view it is impossible to discuss function to the exclusion of the ideational realm, for at least three reasons.

First, the notion of 'function' assumes some 'end', or several 'ends' which are in some way ranked in order of importance. For example, if one is discussing whether barbed or unbarbed arrowpoints are more efficient in fulfilling their function(s), one has also to discuss what these functions were, and their relative importance. Such 'ends' might be to wound or kill a person or animal, from near or far, quickly or slowly, with or without the possibility of reuse of the same implement, and so on. And of course the implement may have important symbolic meanings which could affect its use and killing potential. These various 'ends' are produced within a matrix of cultural meanings.

Second, before we can talk of the functions of an object, we normally produce categories of objects – points, barbed points, pots and so on. However, in producing these categories, the archaeologist automatically embeds them with meaning. In so far as they are always in at least partial conformity to our current linguistic and perceptual codes, categorisation schemes inevitably carry with them a contemporary and contingent sense of order (often a far cry from notions of meaning and order shared in the past; Shanks and Tilley 1987, pp. 16–18). For example, from the 17th century to the present, dramatic shifts in the way in which species were classified were contingent not upon new discoveries, but upon mutations in the meaning of history: each mutation caused natural historians to see the objects of classification differently. For instance, when a 17th-century notion of history as visibility was replaced by a 19th-century notion which prioritised the hidden and the invisible, dissections gained importance and classification was reorientated towards internal anatomy as opposed to external structure (Foucault 1970 [1966], pp. 125–38). Thus, the ways in which we classify are fully constituted by the system of meaning through which we relate to the artifacts. Systems of meaning in modern western archaeology tend to privilege form/shape as a basis for classification (Miller 1985b, pp. 51–74). Dunnell (1986, p. 158) speculates that this is so because 'shape seems a natural descriptive dimension, one that does not have to be rationalized to English speakers'. Even when we attempt to expunge such a 'bias' from the process of classification by deploying sophisticated statistical methods such as numerical taxonomy, our own systems of meaning intervene because we still select the 'appropriate' variables and statistical algorithms (Dunnell 1986, p. 184; Hutson and Markens, in press; Read 1989, p. 184). Even the order in which artifact classes are listed in catalogues may contain hidden narratives about which functions are perceived to be the most important (Spector 1993; Hodder 1999a, p. 53). In sum, as an artifact's function is a product of its position within a classification, that function is already laden with the structures of meaning that underlie the logic of that particular classification system.

Third, the hypothesis concerning function is always based on an assumption about the meaning of an object. Even to call an object an axe is to assume that people in the past saw it in the same light as we do today – as an object used to cut down trees. Function and meaning are inextricably linked; this is particularly clear when we discuss the social functions of objects. Such social functions depend on a conceptual meaning which we often impose covertly and uncritically.

For example, Demarrais *et al.* claim that burial monuments communicate social identity. In their Early Farmer Period, communal burials are said to emphasise group identity. In the subsequent Pastoral Warrior Period, a shift to low burial mounds that mark the graves of individual men and women is said to emphasise individual identity (pp. 20–1; see also Tilley 1984). Then, in the Early Bronze Age, the tradition of individual burial mounds established in the prior period continues, but now these mounds have the added function of dividing the landscape into cultural regions owned by local chiefs (p. 22). Beyond a consideration of Hodder's analogy of burial mounds and houses (1990a), there is little attempt to understand attitudes to death. Burials may have communicated social identity, but they may have had other meanings: whatever conclusion we make involves an attempt, sometimes unacknowledged, to 'think ourselves into' prehistoric attitudes to burials. In looking at other contexts of the Thy archaeological record as presented in Demarrais *et al.* we notice that the switch to individual graves coincides with the beginning of a tradition of burying men with weapons of destruction (daggers, swords, battle axes) as opposed to agricultural tools such as axes for clearing forests. The use of individual graves and weapons as burial offerings continues into the Early Bronze Age despite discontinuities such as the appearance of chiefs, which triggered differentiation in the size of graves, and change in the material used for weapons (metal replaces stone). In the face of these discontinuities, the continuity of single graves with weapons suggests long-term historical meanings that could be taken into account when discussing how weapons or graves functioned to consolidate chiefdoms. As a further example of this point we can return to Wobst's Yugoslavian head-dresses. He uses these to support the general statement that more visible cultural items carry messages to larger social units – the head-gear is highly visible. But there are many visible ways of using the body to show social group allegiance at a distance, particularly, for example, posture, trousers, coats etc. Wobst may be correct in his reconstruction, but if he is it is because he has correctly hypothesized the indigenous perceptions concerning which aspects of the body are important in marking social affiliation. The head-dress may be highly visible but it may not have been perceived as highly visible, or it may have been perceived to have meanings not primarily related to identity display.

Hodder (1984a) made a related point about the megaliths of Europe. These monumental burial mounds have been widely accepted as territorial or group markers (Renfrew 1976), legitimating competition over resources by reference to the ancestors. Now while this may seem perfectly reasonable, it is important to recognize that the theory about the social functions (competition, legitimation) is based on a theory about what the tombs meant (ancestors, the past). Clearly, they *could* have been perceived in a different way, in which case their social function might have been different. An apparently materialist, covering law argument is based on the imputation of perceptions inside the culture. A similar point can be made about the archaeological identification of 'prestige' items.

Within the covering law, systemic approach, cultural meanings are imposed, but always from the outside, without adequate consideration. The assignment of cultural meanings is normally based on Western attitudes, which are implicit and undiscussed. It is assumed that burials, rituals, head-gear and pot decoration have universal social functions, linked to their universal meanings; objects are wrenched out of their context and explained cross-culturally.

The partition of cultural systems into various sub-systems, which is the starting point for all systemic analyses, is itself based on a Western view of the world. The divisions made between subsistence, trade, society, symbolism may not be appropriate for past societies. The division, based itself on a covering law, may appear to give equal weight to all the sub-systems, but in practice, as we have seen, the 'material' sub-systems are given dominance. Flannery and Marcus try to give a more important role to ideology, arguing that systems must be seen to work *within* a cosmology, bracketed by and organized by a set of cultural beliefs. But even here the ideology has a passive regulative role, working for the good of the system as a whole, and over the long term. Any systems analysis involves making assumptions about cultural meanings, and we have seen that in archaeology these assumptions are often materialist in character.

We have argued so far that ecosystemic approaches are inadequate partly because they do not give sufficient weight to non-material forces and to particular historical meanings. But we should equally eschew idealist accounts which give little significance to material forces. The symbolism of a sign derives partly from its relationships to other signs in a structure (Shanks and Tilley 1987b, p. 74). All meaning, therefore, has as abstract, conceptual component. But in practice, in concrete situations, signs can come to have new meanings. The material, external world impinges on symbolic structures in a number of ways (Hodder 1989a). Material objects derive their functional meanings largely from such factors as weight, hardness, friability, distribution and ease of access. The objects which are used for particular tasks depend on these factors as well as on technological and ecological processes and structures. Much material culture meaning comes about pragmatically through use and experience, always embedded within and helping to constitute the structured systems of signs. Artifacts embody the dialectic between the material and the ideal. Systems applications in archaeology have not provided a balanced probing of this dialectic.

Agency

As a result of the passive view of ideology within most systems analyses, agents play little part in the theories – they only appear as predictable automata, driven by covering laws. In the examples discussed, individuals appear controlled by rituals according to universal expectations; there is no sense in which they actively manipulate and negotiate ideologies.

This point is evident in relation to style. Wobst concentrates on style and information exchange: the only thing that matters is whether a message is emitted and received efficiently. Certainly the organization of information as studied by Wobst could be said to be active in that the information aids the organization of energy and resources, but since there is no interest in such work in the production of style, one is left with the impression that agents are situated passively in pre-existing roles and that the material symbols simply allow such roles to be organized efficiently. There is little idea here that agents have to create roles in action and in the competent manipulation of the symbolic world – one has the impression that 'other things being equal' it is simply a matter of following the rules. Active people play a minor part in such theories.

Another aspect of the systemic approach to ideology is that individuals appear to be easily fooled. They are easily duped by the dominant ideology, and they easily accept the legitimation of control. Rituals appear which legitimate control within groups. Presumably everybody is duped by, or at least accepts, the new ideology without being able to penetrate its *raison d'être*.

It is perhaps surprising that, although the whole of the New Archaeology or processual archaeology was based on the rejection of normative archaeology, the systemic covering law approach is itself normative, in the sense that the beliefs and rituals, the meaning of style, are all rules shared by members of social communities. There is little indication that different people or sub-sections in society might view the same thing (a ritual such as blood-letting, or burial display) differently. Wobst in particular discusses the way in which style allows members of a group to evaluate how closely a given individual is subscribing to the behavioural norms of the group. Head-dresses are seen as having a common significance throughout the society in which they are worn.

History and time

If, within the systems approach, each society has a set of norms which regulate relationships with the environment, how does social change occur? The way in which time is treated is distinctive. Cultural development is broken up into temporal phases, and adaptation with the environment is assessed for each phase separately. The difficulty thus becomes one of explaining the move from phase *a* to phase *b*. This may be done by arguing for a new environmental, economic context necessitating social and ideological change, or by arguing for internal problems and pathologies leading to change, but it is unclear how a *particular* resolution to the new problems is found. Of all the choices available, including retraction and stability as opposed to growth, how is one choice made? Systems theory in archaeology has been concerned to examine the functions of things which already exist. By disregarding production, creation and innovation, by only looking at the adaptive qualities of a system, we cannot explain how that system developed; neither can we explain how people come to accept the new system. How did the new ideational system, the social legitimation, come about? Where did the new system of beliefs come from and why did people accept them?

In order to explain system change, it thus becomes necessary to see how phase *b* is generated out of phase *a*. If we can understand the social and ideological structures in phase *a*, then we can begin to examine how the change to phase *b* was produced and given meaning. Our analysis of systemic changes must thus take historical meanings into account. The choices about system trajectory are formulated within a pre-existing but changing cultural framework. The systemic analysis which most closely meets these requirements is that of Flannery and Marcus, who achieve an interpretation which, despite the shortcomings mentioned above, has many contextual components. The Zapotec cosmology is understood as being unique and historically particular. Rather than imposing modern Western notions of satisfying or maximizing strategies, Flannery and Marcus suggest the Zapotec had a 'harmonizing ethic' in which a particular relationship with the cosmos underlay ritual, society and economy.

> The Zapotec world was an orderly place in which human actions were based on empirical observations, interpreted in the light of a coherent body of logic. Once that logic is understood, all Zapotec behaviour – whether economic,

political or religious – makes sense as a series of related and internally consistent responses based on the same set of underlying principles. In other words, one very non-Western metaphysic regulated exchanges of matter, energy and information. (p. 383)

While this view is highly normative, it certainly defines a framework within which social and economic change can be explained and understood. The Zapotec metaphysic is the medium for social change in relation to a changing human and physical environment.

Behavioural archaeology

One of the outgrowths of processual archaeology that did not adopt a systemic approach is behavioural archaeology. Behavioural archaeologists 'seek to explain variability and change in human behavior by emphasizing the study of relationships between people and their artifacts' (Schiffer 1996, p. 644). This explicit interest in people and material culture is strengthened by a careful attention to the relational and spatial context of artifacts and an ambitious commitment to the entire range of human activities, including communication, ritual and religion (Rathje and Schiffer 1982; Walker 1998). Despite such promising goals, the behavioural approach, like the systemic and materialist approaches documented thus far, falls short of recognising the importance of meaning, history and the active potential of material culture.

The chief flaw of behavioural archaeology is its failure to recognise that material culture is meaningfully constituted. For example, the regularities that behavioural archaeologists have found in people–artifact interactions silently contain modern western assumptions about the meaning of artifacts. These assumptions ignore the possibility that these artifacts may have had different meanings for people in the past. Thus the McKellar hypothesis, which states that when an activity area is frequently cleaned, only the smallest refuse from that activity will remain (McKellar 1983), works only if the meaning of refuse and the meaning of cleaning are the same for both the archaeologist and the people in prehistory conducting the activities.

The confusion over meaning may reside in the refusal to conceive of culture as a causal agent in the explanation of variation and change (Schiffer 1996, p. 647). By 'culture' Schiffer means learned behaviour: that which is the object of cultural transmission. In practice, behaviourists occasionally do conceive of culture as a causal agent. For example, with reference to pottery production, Schiffer and Skibo (1997, pp. 33–4) state that the community in which 'the artisan learned the potter's craft' influences the technical choices of production. Despite such examples, most variation in material culture is said to result from attempts to achieve high values on behaviourally relevant performance characteristics (Schiffer and Skibo 1997). Though Schiffer (1999) claims to have renounced a definition of performance that includes optimisation, the discussion of the potter's decision-making process is fraught with maximisation and rationality. The potter is seen as a tinkerer, experimenting with various alternatives, settling on whatever combination will solve the most problems (Schiffer and Skibo 1997, p. 40). This approach reduces the artisan's final product to a mere reflection of the functional expectations – or 'situational factors' – of its consumers. Material culture is thus a passive 'effect'. While admirable in its recognition of the agency of the potter as a tinkerer, this approach goes too far in that direction, giving the potter total and unrestricted latitude for experimentation. In responding to a particular technical problem, the potter does not possess in her cognitive repertoire the entire universe of alternative solutions. Rather, in any particular place and time, only some solutions populate the realm of what is thinkable; many choices are settled unconsciously by the potter's learned dispositions and thus do not even present themselves as 'choices'. The specificity of each choice and the specific nature of each artifact is a product of a long history of meaningful perception.

Processual and systems approaches

The behavioural approach declares itself to be sympathetic to history and idiographic studies (Schiffer 1996, p. 644). However, Schiffer's diachronic study of radio technology treats history as a series of causes and effects. It may be true that progress in the development of radio technology at the turn of the century was caused by a need for longer-distance ship to shore radio communication, but until it is made clear why the desired distance of ship to shore communication changed and why this particular solution for adapting to the new distance was chosen over others, little has been explained. Schiffer's diachronic study of radios also falls prey to the same weaknesses as his consideration of the causes of variation in pottery form. The replacement of the vacuum tube radio by the more expensive transistor radio in the 1950s is explained by its performance characteristics (better battery economy), but also by a conspicuously cultural phenomenon – 'the cachet of "modernity"' – that Schiffer's own cultureless, meaningless, approach forbids him to explore. Finally, the insistence that all inference must be grounded in already known interactions between people and objects (Walker 1998, p. 250) denies the possibility of historical particularity and the prospect that the past can be unique.

The difficulty with ignoring meaning is clearest in behavioural archaeology's approach to the study of ritual behaviour. Walker (1998) states that archaeologists should avoid attending to symbolic evidence and symbolic variability when exploring 'ritual prehistory'. Artifacts thus have no meaning beyond their physical interactions with people. However, Walker attempts to show that certain artifact deposits in the American Southwest are the remains of ritualised violence against witches. Such a claim relies on exceptionally meaningful Pueblo worldviews regarding witchcraft, its connections with death and environmental problems, and a logic of retribution through ritualised violence. Even the smallest of Walker's interpretations, such as designating an archaeological object as 'ritual' or 'sacred', impute symbolic meaning. In fact, symbolic meaning, as we shall later argue, imbues every artifact and every activity. Rather than deny the importance of symbols and meaning yet, like Walker, surreptitiously attribute meaning in the same breath, we need to make symbolism and meaning a conscious subject of inquiry. If Walker is correct in his identification of ritual violence, then the physical residues of this violence would have communicated strong values about witchcraft, yet values lie outside the purview of behavioural archaeology.

Measuring and predicting mind: cognitive processual archaeology

Flannery and Marcus derive the Zapotec metaphysic from historical and ethnographic sources. How is this to be done for prehistoric societies for which there is no cultural continuity into the present? As implied by Gellner's description of the covering law approach, the methods most closely linked to systems archaeology are modelled on the natural sciences. Ritual, social organization and ideology are seen as having universal cross-cultural relationships with the material, observable world; we can therefore infer the ideology from measurable archaeological data, and we can do this with security.

A different perspective on ancient mind has been articulated by Renfrew (1983b; 1993; 1994a) in his attempts to develop a cognitive processual archaeology. Renfrew sets out to examine the ways in which symbols were used, rather than search for the meaning or metaphysics of past symbolic systems. As much as Renfrew seeks to avoid intuitive leaps towards meaning, ascertaining the function of symbols necessarily involves assumptions about their meanings. As we commented above, the ends towards which symbols – or any other 'tool' for that matter – function are always produced within a matrix of cultural meanings. For example, Renfrew's claim that the system of weights found at Mohenjodaro shows a notion of equivalence of materials (1983b, pp. 13–14), or that an Upper Palaeolithic burial communicates with the supernatural (1994a, p. 8), can only be correct if we intuitively accept that materials are meant to be understood as commodities and that death means transcendence, neither of which is always the case. More recently, Renfrew (1998) examined the iconography of terrestrial transportation in later European prehistory in order to show how 'cognitive constellations' – symbolic representations of groups of associated ideas and concepts – function to illustrate and reinforce the social ethos. Renfrew succeeds in detecting a number of enduring symbolic associations, not the least of which is the horse and rider, which has survived over two thousand years and is still seen today in Western equestrian statuary. However, to assume that a dominant ethos will be depicted in art is to attribute a certain meaning to the act of representation, namely that representation is reserved only for communicating values. It is quite possible, on the other hand, that in some societies, art is not about communication of an ethos; social values may be reinforced through other media. Furthermore, Renfrew gives no explanation as to why certain symbolic concepts endure for millennia while other concepts or ideas fail even to become 'cognitive constellations'. If we accept that the reproduction of a dominant ethos is never a given, a more compelling treatment of the cognitive constellations that support such an ethos will have to ask what that ethos is and explain the historical contexts and struggles that enable it to endure.

Perhaps the fundamental difficulty underlying Renfrew's cognitive archaeology is his reaffirmation of old dichotomies such as function/symbol, etic/emic and subject/object. Ultimately such dichotomous thinking pervades not just Renfrew's ideas on *what* we can and cannot know about the past, but also his ideas on *how* we claim to know what we do. Despite flirting with the idea that data cannot be fully objective, Renfrew's cognitive processual archaeology regresses to an absolute objectivity: 'The material record of the past, the actual remains, may indeed be claimed as value-free and lacking in observer-induced bias' (Renfrew 1989, p. 39). Ironically, this unreconstructed objectivity 'in which the data have the last word' is nearly inverted in Renfrew's approach to the study of religion (1994b, p. 51), in which he suggests that investigation will be advanced by his own definition of religion, which is claimed to have nearly universal correlates. Elsewhere, Renfrew (1994a, p. 10) claims that his own personal experience does not differ radically from that of other humans. Renfrew's unmitigated objectivity coexists uneasily with his latent subjectivity. Both are undermined by the discussion in chapter 1 of the relation between fact and theory and will be discussed at greater length in chapter 9.

Despite its different goals, Renfrew's cognitive archaeology shares with Flannery and Marcus' approach a systemic understanding of the relationship between mental constructs and the material, observable world. Renfrew suggests six ways in which symbols structure human life and human affairs. The cognitive system thus has functional relationships with a variety of activities – measurement, art, production of architecture – that can be studied through their material remains. To recover cognitive processes from material signatures, Renfrew has repeatedly called for the development of secure networks of inference.

Such a direction appears to imply that there are some universal measurements of mind. The natural science model is clear, but the internal tension within this view is distinctive. On the one hand, Renfrew, here, and Binford and Sabloff (1982), argue for independent yardsticks for measuring the past; on the other hand they accept that the past is perceived within our own social and cultural matrix. Renfrew also claims, in line with Flannery and Marcus, that 'each culture has its own "helix of interaction", its own historical trajectory, to use the terminology of systems thinking' (p. 25). The development of ideas, he claims, will be different in each context; each history will have its own cognitive phylogeny. For Renfrew, 'mind' is the formulated concepts and the shared ways of thought which, within any specific cultural matrix, are the common inheritance of all its citizens as participants (p. 26).

There is an internal contradiction within this natural science-derived *and* historically relative point of view. On the one hand 'we' in the present and 'they' in the past have our own cultural matrices, our different ways of thought within which 'we' and 'they' perceive(d) the world of things and objects. On the other hand there is postulated a universal method and coherent theory which relates ways of thought to material objects. How can my coherent theory and explicit methodology about the relationship between the material and the ideal be applied to another culture with its own cognitive processes and 'cognitive phylogeny'?

There is no problem of inference within the systemic and processual approaches as long as one remains fully materialist. As long as one says, 'I can predict ideas, thought and cognition from the economic base using a covering law, and the economic base can be objectively perceived and measured', there is no difficulty. But as soon as one says this, the lack of humanism is apparent; and in discussing 'mind' Flannery and Marcus and Renfrew have sometimes adopted a normative and partially idealist position within which cognition and perception are not universally determined by the material base, but are partly historically contingent, based on particular cultural phylogenies. As soon as one admits some cultural relativity in this way an insuperable contradiction emerges. It is no longer possible to have a universal natural science theory and method which will allow secure inference and prediction from one historical context to another.

It will be necessary, then, in the quest for an adequate archaeology of mind, to ditch decisively the natural science, covering law approach. We shall see that the inferential procedures followed routinely by archaeologists include reconstructing past cultural matrices 'from the inside'. The implications of the collapse of the natural science model in confrontation with mind will be shown later in this book to be far-reaching.

Neo-evolutionary archaeology and mind

One area far from collapse is evolutionary archaeology. Though most case studies in this area focus on subjects such as tool technology, demography and subsistence, archaeologists have also applied evolutionary approaches to rather 'ideotechnic' domains such as ceremonial architecture, carved monuments, ceramic style and Upper Palaeolithic cave painting (Ames 1996; Bettinger *et al.* 1996; Graves and Ladefoged 1995; Mithen 1996a; Neiman 1995; 1997; Rindos 1986; Shennan and Wilkinson 2001). For example, Shennan has recently attempted to use models of population size and genetic transmission of information to explain Upper Palaeolithic/Late Stone Age cultural innovations such as the emergence of personal adornment, musical instruments, complex forms of art, and new stone, bone, antler and ivory tools. Briefly, Shennan uses simulations to show that cultural innovations result in greater adaptive fitness for individuals in large interacting populations as opposed to small ones. Thus, although the first modern humans were capable of cave painting and musical innovation, these innovations did not 'catch on' (were not successfully transmitted) until the size of interacting populations reached the level at which such innovations became adaptive – approximately 50,000 years ago. Since Shennan treats cultural innovations as mutations, and since mutations are only transmitted to others when the population is large enough, there is no room in his account for intentionality or meaning. Shennan appears to understand that innovations such as musical instruments are not 'adaptive' in a strict biological sense, so he instead uses the term 'attractive'. However, it is difficult to understand what sort of innovation would be considered attractive when these innovations have no meaning.

Evolutionary psychology takes a somewhat different approach. Mithen (1996a, pp. 80–2; 1998a, p. 10) uses a holistic, evolutionary, ecological perspective on the ancient mind. This approach attends to all facts of ancient life – art, religion, economy – and does not divorce cognition from the rest of society. At the centre of Mithen's explanations of past behaviour is a rather progressive understanding of adaptation which takes into account individual decision-making and the importance of creativity (1996a; 1998a). Mithen's interdisciplinary focus has produced a number of ambitious and thoughtful explanations (1996a, b; 1998b). Nevertheless, as seen in a recent analysis of Palaeolithic handaxes, evolutionary psychology falls prey to some of the same problems addressed above.

Kohn and Mithen (1999, p. 524; Mithen 2001) argue that 'handaxes were products of sexual selection: they were used as reliable indicators of a potential mate's quality by those of the opposite sex'. This argument seems to allow for expressions of agency and creativity in the manipulation of material culture, as in Wiessner's 'assertive style' (1983; 1985), but owing to the evolutionary framework the space for agency disappears. Because handaxes are said to be indicators of good genes, individual action is reduced to and determined by genetic makeup. But there is no good explanation as to why handaxes are even tied to genes: those not genetically blessed with extraordinary dexterity might still learn to knap. Nor is there any allowance for the possibility that factors in mate choice are shaped by socially contingent, non-adaptive preferences. Kohn and Mithen's argument accounts for the specificities of many handaxes – elaborately crafted to demonstrate the skill of the knapper, symmetrical because symmetricality is attractive, unwieldy and unused because they function purely as objects of social display – though one may ask why handaxes and not some other shape or type of artifact became the preferred focus of the sexual gaze. The highly developed aesthetics of the handaxes might imply that they have meaning beyond courtship. Finally, unsupported statements like 'males tend toward display, so conspicuously impractical handaxes were most likely made by males' (Kohn and Mithen 1999, p. 523) reveal gender trouble. In our view, the natural science origins of neo-evolutionary archaeology constrain its ability to move beyond measurement and prediction in discussing meaning, agency and history. An adequate account of why some material culture items become 'attractive' and are successfully transmitted takes us into the realms of power, social action, meaning – a world which extends beyond the natural sciences and beyond the covering law inferential procedures most commonly attributed to the natural sciences.

Conclusion

In this chapter we have equated systems theory and processual approaches in archaeology with Gellner's covering law approach. A relationship between systems analysis and law-and-order models has been specifically denied by Flannery (1973), who argues that the analysis of processual inter-relationships does not necessitate the imposition of covering laws.

There is certainly a sense in which systems thinking is contextual. The aim is to examine the way in which a particular set of components is related into a whole. It might be thought that the method, or way of thinking, does not involve any universal laws; however, as with all methodologies, this one is theory-bound. It certainly is difficult to represent other viewpoints, such as Marxist notions of contradiction, conflict and dialectic, within a systems framework. Equally, the method does not allow for a structuralist conception of society of the form culture:nature::male:female.

The very method does assume some specific general principles. In particular it assumes that societies can be divided into sub-systems – separate types of activity. For example, we would find it difficult to decide whether a 'meal' today was in the economic, social or ritual sub-system, or which parts of the 'meal' should be in which sub-system. We would certainly be highly suspicious if it were claimed that 'meals' were in the same sub-system in all societies. In addition it is assumed that explanation of one type of activity (such as ritual) always involves reference to something outside itself (another sub-system such as the social sphere). We explain one thing by its functions in relation to something else. We would again find this unsatisfactory in relation to an English 'meal'. While the utilitarian, social and ideological functions are part of the explanation of the 'meal', it seems to us that the meal must partly be understood as being organized in ways that are not reducible to external functions.

While the notion of functionally related sub-systems is a clear cross-cultural theory, it is not necessarily the case that systems theory is materialist: there is no necessity for the material base to be primary. However, in practice, as we have seen, it does tend to have a dominant role in relation to which society and ideology function. This underlying viewpoint is identical to Hawkes' (1954) ladder of inference. An important aspect of processual theories in archaeology is that they have allowed movement up this ladder in a systematic fashion. For Hawkes, the technology and to a lesser extent the economy of past systems were attainable, but higher up the ladder, social organization and religion were largely beyond reach. Daniel (1962, pp. 134–5) accepted that artifacts are the product of the human mind but said that there is no coincidence between the material and non-material aspects of culture. Systems theory provides a method for bringing the social (Renfrew 1973) and the ideational (Renfrew 1983a) into the domain of feasible study, because systematic links between the material world and these less visible aspects of life could be predicted. For example, links have been demonstrated between subsistence categories and burial practices (Binford 1971), between stress and 'generalized feather-waving' (Johnson 1982, p. 405), and between increased production and increased ritual (Drennan 1976, p. 360).

Systems and processual theories may have bridged the credibility gap in relation to archaeological study of the ideational realm, but in this chapter we have tried to show that they have not taken us very much farther along the road. The approaches are not able to account for the great richness, variability and specificity of cultural production, and agents and their shared thoughts are passive by-products of 'the system'. Human activity is timeless, the product of systemic inter-relationships rather than being historically derived. Above all, the processual approaches have led to an internally self-contradictory epistemology. No wonder alternative approaches are now being sought.

Underlying all the criticisms that have been made of systems and processual analysis in this chapter is the implication that such analysis occurs only at a 'surface' level. The procedures involve measuring directly sizes of settlements, numbers of figurines, population infill and expansion and so on. All these 'observable' data are then inter-related, and in computer simulation a set of mathematical equations may be applied. Abstract theories (such as the primacy of the material base) are of course accommodated to the data, but the impression that is gained is that all is as it seems to be. If the term 'structure' is used at all in such analyses it is equivalent to the term 'system'.

But throughout this chapter there have been intimations of another level of analysis. Why is the system or sub-system the way it is, why the sting-ray spine, why burials and not hoards to display social rivalry, why feather-waving and not pot-smashing, and what structures the 'meal'? There is perhaps an order or structure behind these cultural choices that systems theory is not allowing us to approach.

And we have begun to see the importance of interpreting symbolic meanings rather than just ascribing symbolic functions. For example, we cannot discuss the social functions of tombs without also discussing what they meant. We need, then, to turn to an approach which looks at structure and at the meaning of signs.

3 Structuralist, post-structuralist and semiotic archaeologies

When Edmund Leach (1973) suggested that archaeology would soon turn from functionalism to structuralism, following the path of social anthropology, he was clearly unaware that structuralist archaeology already existed. In particular the work of Leroi-Gourhan (1965), similar in some respects to that of Levi-Strauss, had been widely debated. Certainly structuralism has never dominated the discipline, but its wide-spread attraction cannot be denied (Anati 1994; Bekaert 1998; Bintliff 1984; Campbell 1998; Collet 1993; Deetz 1983; Helskog 1995; Hill 1995; Hingley 1990, 1997; Huffman 1981, 1984; Kent 1984; Lenssen-Erz 1994; Leone 1978; Miller 1982a; Muller 1971; Parker Pearson 1996, 1999; Richard and Thomas 1984; Schnapp 1984; Small 1987; Sørensen 1987; Schmidt 1997; Tilley 1991; Van de Velde 1980; Wright 1995; Yates 1989; Yentsch 1991). These various articles, in addition to those to be discussed in this chapter, suggest that one can now talk of a structuralist archaeology.

Yet why has the analysis of 'structured sets of differences' been so slow to arrive and so slight in impact? Why has structuralism never formed a major coherent alternative in archaeology? The first answer to these questions is that structuralism is not a coherent approach itself, since it covers a great variety of work, from the structural linguistics of Saussure, and the generative grammar of Chomsky, to the developmental psychology of Piaget and the analysis of 'deep' meanings by Levi-Strauss. In archaeology this variety is reflected in the differences between the formal analyses of Washburn (1983) and Hillier *et al.* (1976), the Piagetian accounts of Wynn (1979; and see Paddaya 1981), and the Levi-Strauss type of analyses conducted by Leroi-Gourhan (1965; 1982).

The second answer is that, linked to this variability, some structuralist approaches in archaeology could fit within processual archaeology, almost unnoticed, and working towards the same ends as New Archaeology. Fritz (1978), for example, discusses the adaptive value of spatial and symbolic codes. Indeed there are many close similarities between systems analysis and structuralism, and we shall see below that the criticisms of both run parallel. The most obvious similarity between the two methods is that both are concerned with 'systemness'. The emphasis is on inter-relationships between entities: the aim of both systems and structuralist analysis is to provide some organization which will allow us to fit all the parts into a coherent whole. In systems analysis this structure is a flow diagram, sometimes with mathematical functions describing the relationships between the sub-systems; the system is more than, or larger than, the component parts, but it exists at the same level of analysis. Although in structuralism the structures exist at a deeper level, the parts are again linked to a whole by binary oppositions, generative rules and so on. In both systems and structuralist analysis it is the relationship between parts that is most important.

A further similarity between systems theory and structuralism is that both sometimes claim to involve rigorous analysis of observable data. In some types of structuralist archaeology (particularly that which we shall describe as formal analysis) the structures and conceptual schemes are thought to be empirical and measurable. In systems theory there is a close link to positivism, in that by measuring covariation between variables observable in the real world, the system can be identified and verified. While positivism is an 'ideology' expressed by some structural and formal analysis in archaeology, we shall see that, as in systems analysis, the apparent 'hardness' of the data and rigour of the method are illusory.

A third answer to the question of why structuralism never offered a coherent set of alternatives in archaeology lies in the fact that while some types of structuralism (such as formal analysis) were *perceived* to be rigorous and 'hard', other types (particularly work modelled on that carried out by Levi-Strauss) were *perceived* to be 'soft' and unscientific. In particular, it was thought that it would be impossible to verify hypotheses about structures of meaning, especially since much structuralist analysis outside archaeology has concerned myths. Archaeology, with its dominant perception of itself as positivist and materialist, could scarcely launch itself with any confidence into such an arena. As Wylie (1982) has shown, all types of archaeology involve moving beyond the data in order to interpret them, and structuralism is no different in this respect. Yet the dominant archaeological perspective of science was antithetical to structuralism.

Given these three reasons for a sceptical reaction in archaeology to Leach's claims, the type of structuralism that could most easily be placed within processual archaeology, and which will be discussed first here, was formal analysis, which purports to describe the real world rather than to divine inner essences.

Formal analysis and generative grammars

With the structural linguistics of Saussure, the sign itself is seen as arbitrary and conventional. In other words any symbol (a bead, duck, arrowhead) *could* be used to signify a chief; there is no necessary relationship between the signifier (the bead) and the signified (chiefness). Because of this arbitrariness, Saussure's analysis of meaning concentrates on structured sets of differences. Thus the bead, indicating 'chiefness', is contrasted with the lack of bead, or presence of another item, signifying 'non-chiefness'. Analysis is of *form* not content.

Formal analyses in archaeology are best exemplified by the work of Washburn (1983), who has concentrated on the way symmetry rules can be identified and compared within and between cultures. Examination of pottery designs, for example, can produce classifications not based on design motifs, but on the way the motifs are organized in symmetrical relationships. The main types of symmetry recognized are shown in Fig. 2. The concern is not, then, with whether a comma, triangle or star are used as the design motif, since ethnographic research (cf. Hardin 1970) has shown that design content is

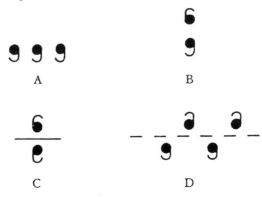

Fig. 2. Types of symmetry and repetition of design. (A) Translation. (B) Bifold rotation. (C) Horizontal mirror reflection. (D) Slide reflection. Source: Washburn 1983.

not a good indicator of group affiliation. Design structure is thought to be a more stable measure of cultural groupings.

Symmetry analysis is in many respects non-generative. It is concerned with examining pattern as it exists, static, on a pot surface, and identifying underlying structure. On the other hand symmetry can be described as a rule which generates patterns. Chomsky emphasized 'rule-governed creativity', and, in an analysis of calabash decoration amongst the Nuba of Sudan, a generative grammar was claimed (Hodder 1982a), following the analyses published by Faris (1972).

To talk of a design grammar or language is to note the origins of structuralist analysis in Saussure's structural linguistics. In the Nuba case the grammar was derived from a cross motif (Fig. 3:1). Both 'words' and 'grammatical rules' were suggested and shown to be able to produce a wide variety of calabash decoration, from highly organized designs (Fig. 3:10) to apparently 'random' designs. Thus, the band of bow-tie motifs in Fig. 3:15 can be produced by taking the triangle 'word', and attaching another at the angle (not at the side): ⋈. This 'bow-tie' motif is then, according to another rule, rotated though units of 90° to produce ⋈⊠⋈ etc. In all the calabash designs depicted in Fig. 3, the rules are kept to: the 'words' join at the angles (not at the sides) and so on.

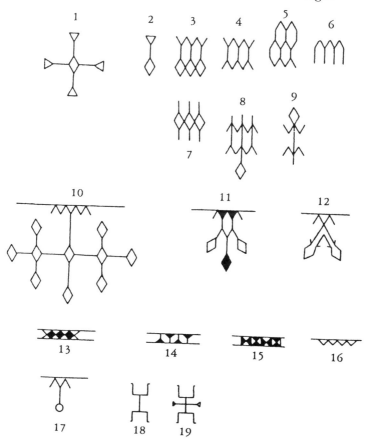

Fig. 3. Nuba designs using a grammar derived from a cross motif (1). The 'words' of the grammar are the triangle, line and diamond in the cross, and the 'rules' include joining words at angles rather than sides, and rotation in units of 90°. Source: Hodder 1982a.

Washburn (1983, p. 138) claims that symmetry analysis allows systematic and objective measurement and comparison of designs through time and across broad areas. Formal analyses of settlement structure (cf. Hillier *et al.* 1976; Fletcher 1977) appear to offer a similar promise. In all these cases it appears that we can describe structures and test them rigorously against the data. Statistical tests can be carried out (Fletcher 1977) and the grammars simulated on a computer

(Hodder 1982a) to see whether they really do generate the observed patterns. Such work, then, appears not to involve risky leaps of faith: apparently no meaning is assigned and there is much scientific rigour. The analysis is purely formal. As a result such work can easily be placed within positivist New Archaeology – it offers no threat, particularly when linked to systems interpretations (see below).

Is it really the case, however, that formal analyses do not involve the imposition of meaning, that they are not concerned with content? Let us take as an example Washburn's analysis of the chevron design <<<<<<. Her concern is to eliminate 'subjective design labels' such as 'chevron' (1983, p. 143), and she prefers instead 'Class 1–110: one dimensional designs generated by horizontal mirror reflection'. Washburn suggests that the chevron design has been generated by placing an horizontal axis through the 'chevrons' and seeing the upper part as a mirror reflection of the bottom part:

$$<<<<<< = - \frac{\mathbf{\varsigma}}{\mathbf{e}} - = \text{horizontal mirror reflection}$$

An alternative analysis would be to take the units of design not as the individual slanting designs but as the chevron:

$$<<<<<< = \mathbf{9} \, \mathbf{9} \, \mathbf{9} \, \mathbf{9} = \text{horizontal mirror reflection}$$

Washburn attempts to avoid such ambiguities by defining the unit of analysis precisely as the smallest asymmetrical element (such as the comma). However, clearly lines and circles cannot be fitted into such a scheme, and the definition is itself arbitrary: while it may assist objective analysis, it may hide other levels of symmetrical relationships as in the chevron example above. Equally, the axis along which symmetry is sought is an interpretation, not a description, of the data. Put another way, the symmetrical analysis is a description within a set of interpretive decisions. Thus, such analyses *do* involve giving meaning to content – they are not just formal descriptions to aid comparison. To perceive a mark on a pot as 'a unit of analysis', or as a 'design motif', is to give meaning to that mark, to interpret its content, and, whether we like it or not, it involves trying to see the design as prehistoric people saw it.

We shall return to this latter point later in this volume, but for the moment it is important to recognize that the subjectivity lying behind Washburn's supposed objectivity in no way detracts from her work. Rather such subjectivity is a necessary component of all archaeological analysis. We have seen the pervasiveness of the problems of perception in post-positivist philosophy (pp. 16 to 19). All archaeological analyses are based on subjective categories (pot types, settlement sites, etc.) and unobservable structural or systemic relationships (positive and negative feedback, exchange relationships and so on). In the imposition of Thiessen polygons on a settlement pattern, for example, we can never be sure that our 'units of analysis' (the sites or nodes in the settlement pattern) are really comparable. We have to give them meaning (as settlement sites, towns, cities) before we can suggest systemic and structural relationships between or behind them.

The 'hard' nature of formal analysis is thus illusory. That symmetry analysis, for example, can be slotted into archaeology without threat is because the whole of archaeology is guided by the same ideology of positivism, as a result of which there has been very little attempt to push beyond the symmetries in pottery decoration to the content of the message(s). The interpretation of symbolic meaning has been minimized in favour of direct links between symmetry and processes of social interaction. For example, Washburn suggests that 'identity in design structure seems to be indicative of homogeneous cultural composition and intensity of cultural interaction' (1983, p. 140). This may well be a fruitful hypothesis, 'tested' within ethnographic interpretations and successfully applied to archaeological data (*ibid.*), but by linking design form to society in this direct way we overlook the very real possibility that design structure may have different meanings in different cultural contexts. To what extent can we assume that subjectively defined design structures will have universal social implications? A properly rigorous and hence scientific analysis needs also to examine the symbolic meanings which mediate between structure (of design) and social functions.

Structuralist analysis

When we ask for the meaning of the symmetries or other formal structures, when we consider whether the symmetries in the pottery decoration are transformations of those in the organization of settlement space, or in burial practices, and when we relate such structures to abstract structures in the mind, we begin to move from formal to structuralist analysis.

It could be argued that the assignment of concepts to parts or wholes of structures, as in the work of Leroi-Gourhan (1965; 1982), differs not at all from the assignment of meaning to marks scratched on pots when defining design motifs. Perhaps the only difference is that the assignment of meaning in the latter type of work, as exemplified by Washburn's careful and persuasive analyses, is masked within objective science. The earlier work of Leroi-Gourhan, on the other hand, involved a self-conscious attempt to assign meaning. At the same time, the Leroi-Gourhan type of work is potentially more 'scientific' in the sense that it does involve bringing one's 'meanings' out into the open rather than applying them covertly.

Too often, however, structures have been identified and compared in archaeology without an adequate consideration of meaning content. This criticism is easily levelled at early structuralist work (e.g. Hodder 1982b), but persists even in highly sophisticated studies that have successfully moved beyond their structuralist beginnings. For example, in his analysis of the Swedish rock carvings at Nämforsen from the 3rd millennium B.C., Tilley (1991, pp. 27–8) identifies seven design classes, one of which is a boat. He proceeds to uncover binary oppositions that structure the patterns in which the seven designs appear; specifically, the opposition between elks and boats represents such dualities as nature:culture, inside:outside and land:water (Tilley 1991, p. 105). In true structuralist fashion, Tilley notes that the specific identity of the designs – the content – is not important because meaning arises from the relationship between designs, not from any specific design in isolation: the relation between a design

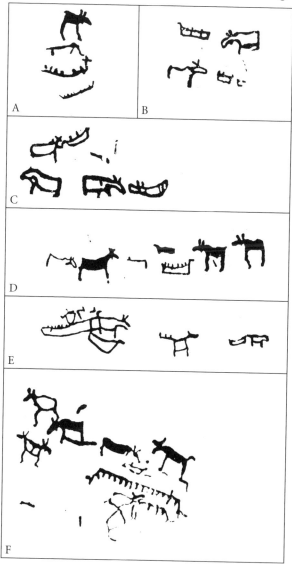

Fig. 4. Types of elk–boat associations from different carving surfaces at Nämforsen on which only elks and boats occur. A: nearity; B and C: opposition; D: linearity and opposition; E: three examples of merging elks and boats taken from different carving surfaces; F: linearity, opposition and superpositioning. Reproduced with permission from Tilley 1991.

(signifier) and its identity (signified) is arbitrary. However, if the boat were actually a sled, the structure elk:sled::land:water crumbles because sleds pertain to land, not water. Tilley admits the ambiguity and variability in boat designs, but never abandons the boat identification (p. 73). Thus, when he rejects this 'increasingly unconvincing' structuralist exercise and moves to a hermeneutic method in the hopes of a better accommodation with meaning and content (p. 114), the boat/sled problem remains. Tilley's argument that boats underscore that which is out of humanity's control because they are subject to wild and restless waters (p. 146) does not work, of course, if the boats are actually sleds. Tilley's attempt to incorporate ideology into the rock carvings is equally questionable since the interpretation of privileged contact with distant, maritime populations and their exotic goods depends on a reading of boats as symbols of such outsiders (p. 164).

In the rock carving example, problems arose from inadequate attention to the content of a specific element in a structural pattern. In the next example we illustrate problems of interpretation that arise once a structural pattern has been soundly identified. In his study of the Iron Age settlement of Sollas, in the Hebrides of Scotland, Campbell (2000) comments on an exceptional assemblage of well-preserved cattle and sheep remains in burial pits. Campbell noticed that the cattle were cremated more than any other species, while sheep were most often inhumed. Data from middens and residues of pots showed that sheep were often roasted for food, while cattle were boiled in earthen pots. Cremation and roasting both involve open-air firing, whereas boiling and inhumation both involve containment in earth and water (inhumation at Sollas involves water because of the high water table). Thus, in the realm of food, we have the relationship cattle:sheep::water:fire, because cattle are boiled and sheep roasted. However, in the realm of burial, the relations are reversed: cattle:sheep::fire:water, since cattle are cremated and sheep are inhumed. Having identified these structural patterns, Campbell interprets them as models of the Hebridean worldview (cf. Douglas 1969, pp. 41–57). Campbell thus concludes that this worldview consisted of dualisms such as death (burial) and life (food), fire and water, above and below, etc.

Campbell is cautious about these dualisms and draws attention to alternative readings, such as the possibility that a dichotomy between young and old animals might be more important than that between cattle and sheep. However, the most important interpretive problems arise not from interrogating the specifics of his structural models, but from asking simply 'of what are they a model?' As mentioned above, Campbell assumes that these patterns in animal remains have to do with worldview, but the dualities that Campbell documents could just as easily refer, for example, to social organisation in the sense of two opposed moieties. Why should anyone believe that there is a relationship between animal remains and worldview? Campbell's decision to link animals and worldview springs from two very reasonable premises: first, a frustration with narrow archaeozoological approaches that reduce animal remains to the realm of subsistence; and second, a conviction that 'transformations' such as animal inhumation and cremation are heavily influenced by cosmological beliefs. We sympathise with these premises, but believe that the assumption of a connection between animals and worldview should be open for examination, not taken for granted. The possibility of a linkage between animals and worldview could have been strengthened by discussing the context of animals in other realms of the Hebridean Iron Age archaeological record or in other time periods if Sollas is truly unique in terms of its wealth of animal burials. In his conclusion, Campbell takes a step in this direction by briefly mentioning dichotomies in pottery and architecture, but such dichotomies must be explored more thoroughly to determine whether or not they relate to the dichotomy found in the animal remains.

The problem of relating one structure to another without adequate consideration of the meaning content of the artifacts involved also appears in discussions of settlement patterns and human burial. For example, Fritz (1978) identifies symmetrical relationships in the organization of settlement in Chaco Canyon. The balanced and unbalanced symmetries (arranged W–E, N–S) occur at both regional and within settlement scales. The structural arrangements are then said to be adaptive, relating to hierarchical social structure on the one hand and symmetrical social relationships on the other. While there is some concern to give cultural meanings (e.g. sacred/profane) to the spatial oppositions, the plausibility of the argument would be increased if more attention were paid to the content of the settlement space in the Chaco Canyon context. We must await more evidence about what the various sites and parts of sites in the settlement pattern were used for.

Parker Pearson (1999) generalises that burials communicate attitudes to the body, and that the way a corpse is treated reveals the social relationships between and among the living. For instance, in Iron Age Britain the different positions in which offerings are placed in burials of men and women reflect normative gender relations in which women serve and men are served. Animal bones (pig for elites, sheep for commoners) mark the social status of the deceased and restate for the living the distinction between ruler and ruled. Burials which deviate from these cosmological rules are explained away as a response to the need to overcome the pollution of the corpse in those cases where the mode of death threatened the community at large. We applaud Parker Pearson's attention to animal symbolism, spatial orientation of burials and other overlooked structural details, but note that this approach still succumbs to the unquestioned, systems logic of the direct relation between burial and social organisation. There is a potential for fuller consideration of the sensuality of death (Kus 1992) or the alternative meanings that burial may carry, such as commemoration, memorialisation and bereavement (Chesson 2001; Hutson 2002a; Joyce 2001; Tarlow 1999).

Without some notion of the meaning content of decorative or spatial elements, it is difficult to see how the structures of signification can be interpreted in relation to other aspects of life. But how are the meanings to be assigned? Here we can return to the pioneering work of Leroi-Gourhan. He attempted to bracket off the content of the images in Upper Palaeolithic caves and thus avoid attributing them any superficial meaning. The meaning was to come from the deep structures that generate the patterns and pairs in which the images appear, like the co-presence of male and female figures. However, before turning from the specific content to the structural relations, Leroi-Gourhan had to make meaningful interpretations of the content, such as his decision to regard 'full' geometric motifs as female, and 'thin' motifs as male (Conkey 1989). In our view, the inadequacies of his work derive not from the attempt to interpret meaning, since, as we have seen, we cannot avoid attributing meaning to material culture. Rather the inadequacies derive from the general limitations of the structuralist approach (see below) and the limited information he had about the Palaeolithic. It can be argued that Leroi-Gourhan did not devote enough attention to other sets of Upper Palaeolithic visual imagery (statuettes, bone cutouts of animal heads, 'spearthrowers'). Nevertheless, Leroi-Gourhan had little information available to him regarding the signs used in the parietal art.

There is a limited degree to which the designs can be followed through into other cultural domains (burial, artifacts, settlement space) in order to identify their associations. Without more research on the social geography and the historical contexts in which the cave painters and their art was embedded (Conkey 1984; 1989; 1997; 2001), one cannot easily identify the particular meanings of these design motifs in the south-west French Palaeolithic.

To interpret meaning contents one has to be willing to make abstractions from associations and contrasts in the archaeological record. This can be done with greater care and rigour where – unlike the Upper Palaeolithic – there is more associational information in different types of data. An example of associational, contextual analysis, in which meanings are assigned and links are made between structures occurring in different activities, is provided by McGhee's (1977) consideration of prehistoric archaeological remains from the

Thule culture of arctic Canada. The initial observation was that ivory and sea mammal bone are associated with harpoon heads, while arrowheads are made of antler. In trying to understand this dichotomy, McGhee looked at the other associations of ivory and antler in Thule culture. Ivory was used for items associated with sea mammal hunting: snow goggles, kayak mountings, dog trace buckles and so on. Other items made from ivory are those connected with women and with winter activities: needle cases, thimble holders, female ornaments, small bird-woman figures. Antler, on the other hand, is linked to land mammals, particularly the caribou, men and summer life on land. The following structure thus emerges, based on the contextual associations of antler and ivory:

land:sea::summer:winter::man:woman::antler:ivory

This structured set of differences is supported further by showing that there is no functional reason why antler and ivory need to be used for different hunting tools and weapons. In addition, ethnographic and historic evidence indicates that the Inuit concept of their environment was centred around the dichotomy between land and sea. The meat of caribou and sea mammals could not be cooked in the same pot. Caribou skins could not be sewn on the sea ice. Associations between women and sea mammals and between land, men and summer life are also found in historic Inuit mythology. Such evidence is not of a radically different nature to the archaeological data; it simply supplies more contextual information concerning the hypothesized structure and its meaning.

McGhee's analysis provides a clear example of the way in which structuralist analysis has the potential for rigour, when combined with an analysis of context and content (i.e. that ivory is associated with sea mammals and women in the Thule culture). It seems reasonable to expect that, as the 'hard' nature of archaeological science becomes demystified, some types of structuralist analysis involving the assigning of meaning will become more common and acceptable. There is an enormous potential, scarcely tapped at the moment, for careful analysis. For example, it is possible to identify differences in the use of left/right, front/back, centre/periphery parts of houses, settlements, cemeteries, graves, ritual sites and so on. Other dichotomies between ritual and mundane, life and death can also be sought. All such structuralist analysis includes some imposition of meaning content.

A further example of potential interest is domestic/wild in relation to inside/outside settlement. For example, Richards and Thomas (1984) have noted that the 'inside' areas of Bronze Age ritual henge monuments in England do not contain bones of the wild equivalents of domesticated animals even though all types of wild animal bone occur on the edge of these sites. Thomas (1988) and Thorpe (1984) have noted regularities in the placing of pig and cattle bones in British Neolithic tombs and enclosures. Such 'structured deposition' does not only occur in ritual contexts. In the central European Neolithic there is a shift through time from the deposition of refuse in pits along the sides of houses to discard away from houses towards the edges of the settlements (Hodder 1990a). The deposition of 'dirt' marks salient social and cultural boundaries between clean and dirty, culture and nature, us and them. The change in discard behaviour in the European Neolithic is associated with the increased definition of group boundaries beyond the household level. It seems that as larger groups were increasingly well demarcated, so refuse 'dirt', initially used to mark the boundaries around the house, was used to help define larger entities. (For other work on the symbolism of settlement boundaries see Hall 1976.)

Critique

Although the concern of this book is to seek an adequate account of the relationship between the material and ideal, the contribution of Levi-Strauss is primarily towards a theory of the superstructure. The relationships with the infrastructure are not the prime focus of study.

Following the semiological approach to linguistics in the work of Saussure, which had a major influence on structuralism, the concern is to examine the organization of signs so that they have meaning. Thus, the word 'pot' is an arbitrary *signifier* of the concept *signified*.

'pot'

signifier   *signified*   *object*

One studies the relationships between signifiers and between signifier and signified, but there is little interest in the thing itself – in this case the real material pot. For a number of reasons, such approaches do not help us in our search for the relationships between the ideal and the material (Hodder 1989a).

To begin with, the abstract analysis of signs and meanings that we find in the Saussurean approach is problematic for archaeology because Saussure was concerned exclusively with language, whereas archaeologists must also contend with material culture. Objects of material culture are not arranged in a linear, narrative sequence in the sense of words arranged in a sentence. Also, an object can be seen both as an object, the result of processes of production and action, and as a sign, since the object (pot) can itself be the signifier for other concepts. However, when objects are used as signs, the relationship between the object and that which it signifies is often not arbitrary. For example, when a restaurant uses a pot symbolically to advertise the traditional or 'home-cooked' nature of their meals, the connection between the pot and a certain culinary style is not arbitrary. But, because objects are physical objects as well as signs, the use of objects as signs may be not be fully conscious. In contrast, words are nothing but signs, and therefore cannot avoid drawing attention. The unconscious or semi-conscious nature of objects as signs introduces ambiguity: in so far as their symbolic nature is not consciously commented upon, such ambiguity may go unnoticed. Finally, objects, unlike words, contain a materiality that can be fixed in ways that words cannot. Objects, and perhaps their meanings, are thus more susceptible to control by certain factions of society (Herzfeld 1992; Joyce 1998, p. 148).

This last point is crucial. In seeking the relationships between structure and action, structuralism plays a necessary but insufficient role. Since objects (not just words) can be signifiers, people can affect the signified, the *meaning*, of a pot by manipulating those objects. Thus structures are the media for action in the world, but actions such as the control and manipulation of objects can effectively change those structures by altering meaning.

We therefore arrive at the possibility of agency: we see how people can change structures. Saussure's semiology and, later, Lévi-Strauss' structuralism leave no room for agency, even when we overlook the problems of adapting their linguistic approach to material objects. Despite granting a speaker the capacity to use linguistic structures to generate an infinite number of sentences, the Saussurean model pays no attention to the actual uses that speakers make of language nor to the social structures of power that authorise what can and cannot be said (Bourdieu 1977, p. 25; 1991). In other words, we must move from the abstract, structured 'linguistic' code to discourse or 'situated communication' (Ricouer 1971; Barrett 1987; Hodder 1989a).

In structuralism and in post-structuralism (Bapty and Yates 1990) there is little room for agency. The individual is passive. Rather than being determined by adaptive regulatory laws, the agent is now determined by structures and/or universals of the human mind. Indeed, Lévi-Strauss was more interested in the general question of how the 'savage mind' works, than he was in the rich, contested saga of social relations in any particular 'savage' society (Geertz 1973, pp. 345–59). The inadequacy of this view can be seen by asking the question 'what is good style?' in relation to design or any structured domain of activity. To be 'stylish' is not simply a matter of doggedly following the rules. O'Neale (1932) found that North Coast Californian Indian basket weavers said that designs were 'good' if they were pleasing and well arranged, while badly structured designs were thought 'bad'. But such verbal evidence simply supports the notion that a structured style exists – within the structure, or even transgressing it, it is still possible to be 'stylish'. A 'pop star' such as Boy George or Marilyn Manson can create a new style and be thought highly stylish even though no design grammar could ever have generated their selection of clothes, ornaments and sexual innuendos. Rather, Boy George and Marilyn Manson create style by using, playing on and transforming structural rules concerning clothing. They use structure socially to create new structure and new society. Of course, neither Boy George nor Marilyn Manson is independent of the structure of society. Both are products of (1) late capitalism, which enables the creation of unique personae through the consumption of commodities (Jameson 1984), and (2) subcultural tradition in which outrage is the norm: Boy George and Marilyn Manson stand in a long line of icons who exploit and depend upon a calculatedly scandalous style for their success and promotion (Hebdige 1979).

Our theories about structure must allow the role of agency. In much structuralist archaeology the rules appear to make up a set of shared norms: everyone in society is assumed to have the same structures, to see them from the same angle and to give them the same meaning. This is a strongly normative view which, despite attempts at repair (Bekaert 1998), this book seeks to question.

Another aspect of the critique is that structuralism is ahistorical in three senses, despite Lévi-Strauss' open concern for the study of history (1963, pp. 1–30). First, Saussure emphasized the arbitrariness of the sign. Any word could have been used to signify the concept of a pot, and any object or space could have been used to signify boundedness, sexuality, tribal group, summer and winter. Such an approach is clearly lacking in a discipline which can follow the way in which signs come to have non-arbitrary meanings through long-term historical sequences. Second, specific signs are often taken out of their historic and geographic contexts and arranged abstractly to reveal deeper structures of opposition. The signs juggled in Leroi-Gourhan's study of Upper Palaeolithic cave paintings, for example, are drawn from 20,000 years of images and many different caves. Third, it is unclear how structural changes occur. Certainly one can always say that change involves structural transformation and this notion is an important one; but within the structuralist analyses themselves there is little need for change, and it is difficult to see why the transformations occur, why they do so in a certain direction, and why or how the structures themselves might change radically. This problem again results from the inadequate linkage between structure and process and from the minimal role given to the active individual in the creation of structures.

When pressed to explain differences in structures of neighbouring societies in South America, Lévi-Strauss (1963, p. 107) offers a murky account of common foundations that undergo historical migrations, diffusions and syncretisms. But he quickly rejects this culture-historical account of change and difference because it does not 'correspond to reality, which presents us with a global picture'. In archaeology, Nash (1997) locates the source of deep structures of meaning in Jung's concept of the collective unconscious. Here, meaning occurs when archetypes – *a priori* forms that are hereditary and grounded in the nervous system – imprint themselves as images on the world, such as the hero, the trickster and the mother goddess. This account of structure is unsatisfactory because it essentially denies the existence of difference: meaning is universal in the strongest sense – a part of human biology unmediated by time or place. Our actual experience in the social and physical world counts for nothing.

It can be argued that some of the problems discussed above – trouble with material culture, lack of agency, ahistoric tendencies – are caused not by semiotics itself, but by the particular form of semiotics developed by Saussure. The semiotics of Charles Peirce, on the other hand, represents a fruitful approach in archaeology because of its ability to incorporate material culture and agency (Bouissac 1994; Capone and Preucel 2002; Gottdeiner 1993; Maquet 1995; Preucel and Bauer 2001; Tilley 1991, p. 44; Yentsch and Beaudry 2001). Whereas in Saussure's approach, signs are arbitrary, in Peirce's approach, signs can be both arbitrary (symbols) and

non-arbitrary (icons and indexes). Icons show a formal relation to that which is being signified, in the sense of a drawing
of a pot referring to an actual pot. Indexes have an existential
relation to their referent: for example, a crust of grime on the
wall of an empty bathtub is an index of the level of the bath-
water. Preucel and Bauer (2001; see also Capone and Preucel
2002) illustrate the archaeological applicability of these three
types of signs (index, icon, symbol) in a hypothetical discussion of a jade axe in a burial. The axe would be an index of
trade across the area between the site of the axe's deposition
and the source of the jade. The axe also indexes its particular spatio-temporal context and therefore references the body
of the burial and other offerings. Indexicality therefore introduces a specific, historic, situated context for material objects.
Owing to formal resemblance, the jade axe is also an icon of
utilitarian axes of the same area. Lastly, the jade axe can be a
symbol of a moiety, in which case the relation between the
signifier (axe) and the signified (moiety) may be arbitrary.
One sign may thus have many kinds of meaning (see Maquet
1995 for additional meanings).

Whereas Saussurean semiotics is dyadic, stressing only the
signifier and the signified, the Peircean approach is triadic, allowing interaction between sign, object and the 'interpretant',
which we might define simplistically as the actor, speaker or
interpreter who mediates the relation between the object and
the sign (Fig. 5). Semiotics thus contains a theory of how
signs are related to material objects and the experience and
behaviour of sign users. Semiotics is pragmatic in the sense
that it stresses the connectedness of people and contexts, needs
and results (Preucel and Bauer 2001, pp. 88–9). In this manner,
semiotics contains space for agency and situated communication. This is important because semiotics has a tendency to
reduce communication to encoding and decoding meanings as
opposed to treating it as an ongoing performance (Joyce 2002,
p. 15). A potential shortcoming includes the issue that not all
material culture behaves as a sign. Rather than pointing or referring elsewhere, objects may have their own life or may be
inseparable from a subject's sense of self (see chapter 6). Also,

Structuralist, post-structuralist and semiotic archaeologies

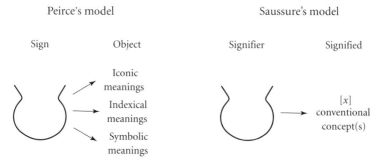

Fig. 5. Meanings of material signs in schemes of Peirce and Saussure.

at certain everyday levels of experience, meaning and object (or event) simply coincide; there is no semiotic explanation: things just are as they are (Bekaert 1998, p. 17). Furthermore, Peirce's triad supports a problematic dichotomy between object on the one hand and sign/interpretation on the other (Thomas 1998).

Post-structuralism

A very different type of critique is that associated with post-structuralism (e.g. Tilley 1990a and b; Bapty and Yates 1990; Derrida 1976). In structuralism signifiers have meaning through their difference from other signifiers. But these other signifiers themselves only have meaning by being opposed to yet other signifiers in an endless chain of signification. Also, the meaning of a signifier shifts based on the context in which it is found (Moore 1996, pp. 120–7). It is thus always possible to deconstruct any structuralist analysis which proposes a neat closed system of oppositions. Indeed it is possible to deconstruct any analysis which claims a totality, a whole or an original meaning, a truth, because these 'origins' of meaning must always depend on other signifiers. But the meaning of the message is open-ended in a second important sense: the way in which it is received. Roland Barthes (1975) insisted that the author does not have authority over the meaning of a text. Instead, the reader introduces other voices and other backgrounds, and as time passes between the act of author-ship and the act of reading, the reader 'translates into the text the intervening history of theoretical and sociocultural de-velopment' (Olsen 1990). In a similar though subtly different vein, Foucault (1979) argued that the author is dead. Foucault meant that the author is not a creative source of ideas because ideas and the language in which they are conveyed precede the author. Ideas and language have lives of their own: the au-thor merely functions as a place holder. An author's writing is just one of the many loci at which ideas are reproduced.

Like Barthes and Foucault, Ricoeur (1971, p. 78) also appre-ciates how 'the text's career escapes the finite horizon lived by its author' but suggests that some aspects of the author's original meaning may be fixed. In other words, Ricoeur ar-gues that the author does have some control over how people interpret what he or she writes. With Austin (1962) and Searle (1970), Ricouer recognises that a statement has many effects. When a statement is transferred to text and distanced from the author, the author cannot control the mood of the state-ment (the illocutionary effect) nor the reaction of the reader (perlocutionary effect). Nevertheless, the act of writing – of inscribing the words in some durable medium – ensures that what is said (alternately referred to as the propositional con-tent or the locutionary effect) cannot be erased. Thus, part of the meaning of speech is inscribed in the text; meaning does not escape the authors' intentions entirely. Ricoeur's work benefits archaeologists because he shows that material culture fixes part of the meaning of action in much the same way that text fixes part of the meaning of speech (see also Hutson 2002a; Tilley 1991, pp. 118–21).

Paul Connerton, Michael Herzfeld and Rosemary Joyce discuss another way in which meaning can be stabilised: materialisation (see also Demarrais *et al.* 1996). Conner-ton begins with the distinction between 'embodied prac-tices' and 'inscribed pratices'. Embodied practices are singular performances and experiences that are inherently short-lived, such as a dance. On the other hand, inscribed practices, such as sculpture, leave material traces that transcend the spatial and temporal context of their original performance (Joyce 2000, p. 9). Meaning thus has two temporalities: it is fleeting when embodied and long-lasting when inscribed. Materialisation, the inscription of meaning in durable media, is an inscribed practice that can leave imperishable traces. Materialisation can be a political strategy because when a particular meaning is materialised in durable, long-lasting form, that meaning comes across as permanent. Things that are permanent may seem natural, and therefore beyond question; uncontestable. Thus, through materialisation, certain actors can render self-serving values or opinions as natural, unchanging and good for everyone. As we will discuss in the next two chapters, such attempts are always resisted. Since the above authors emphasise the perseverance of alternative readings, their observations on fixation remain consistent with the post-structural tendency towards untamability. Yet, unlike a post-structuralism which radically decentres the individual agent, the recognition that meaning is embedded in political strategies – that meaning is not always wild – reconciles our goal of searching for meaning and the role of agency in its constitution in the past.

In sum, the meaning of structures in the past is unstable in two senses: (1) meaning is dispersed along an endless chain of signification; (2) actions are subject to multiple interpretations. Post-structuralism focuses not only on the instability of structures in the past, but also on the systems of power that order archaeology as a discipline in the present. In other words, whereas a traditional archaeologist would say that archaeology is simply about the past, and that the archaeological record has the final word on what counts as good archaeology, a post-structuralist would open the enterprise and claim that the criteria for evaluating work extends to a shifting and emergent chain of present considerations. In defining its boundaries as a discipline, archaeology carves a space in which only certain things can be said (others are unthinkable and, naturally, inadmissible) and only some people (those with proper qualifications) can speak. Thus, the production of statements about the past 'is at once controlled, selected, organized and redistributed by a certain number of procedures whose role it is to ward off its powers and dangers, to gain mastery over its chance events, to evade its ponderous, formidable materiality' (Foucault 1981, p. 52). Archaeology is 'the locus of a struggle to determine the conditions and the criteria of legitimate membership and legitimate hierarchy' (Bourdieu 1988, p. 11). Post-structural approaches to archaeology attempt to identify and decentre the structure of archaeological practice and to create less absolute, less totalised ways of interacting with the past. The former includes documentation of rhetorical strategies, hiring practices, gender inequities, citation practices and much more (Claassen *et al.* 1999; Conkey with Williams 1991; papers in Gero *et al.* 1983; Hutson 1998; 2002b; papers in Nelson *et al.* 1994; Tilley 1989; 1990). The latter includes the production of new textual strategies, ranging from self-reflexivity and dialogue to hypertext and the inclusion of semi-fictional vignettes 'from' the past (Edmonds 1999; Hodder 1992; Joyce 1994; 2002; Moran and Hides 1990; Tringham 1991; 1994). Such approaches have great power in allowing the critique of absolutes claimed in archaeological writings and the tracing of the real world effects which discourses produce (Eagleton 1983).

Verification

Perhaps the major critique of structuralism centres around the notion of verification. How does one do structuralist archaeology with rigour? Structuralism is notoriously linked to unverifiable flights of fancy, ungrounded arguments, since all the data can, with imagination, be seen as transformations of each other and of underlying structures. Many structuralist analyses *do* appear rigorous and have been widely accepted. The perception that one can judge structuralist analyses and decide that some are better than others implies that procedures for making plausible arguments can be discerned (Wylie 1982).

The most widespread validation procedure adopted in structuralist archaeology appears to be to demonstrate that the same structures lie behind many different types of data in the same historical context. The more data that can be slotted into the same organizing principles, the more plausibility is gained by the organizing principles themselves. As with systems analysis, structuralist analysis is convincing if it can draw together, or make sense of, previously unconnected data. As we have seen, simply looking for pattern (horizontal and vertical zoning, symmetry and so on) is inadequate – we also need to make some abstraction about the meaning of the pattern. Thus, in Deetz's (1977) convincing analysis of refuse discard, burial, and pottery styles on historic American sites, a temporal contrast between abstractions which he calls communal and individualizing ethics can be seen to run through the study, and to explain a wide variety of different types of data.

More recently, Parker Pearson (1999) has strengthened his idea that the orientations of doors in British Iron Age roundhouses relate to symbolic concerns with the passage of the sun by demonstrating that the same structuring principle accounts for other realms of the archaeological record, such as the patterned spatial organisation of activities in the roundhouse interiors.

David Clarke (1972), in his study of structural relationships in the Iron Age, Glastonbury site, supported his case by showing the repetition of the same male:female structure in different living compounds and in different time periods. Fritz (1978) sought to find the same structure at local and regional levels. Tilley (1984) shows how an abstraction termed 'boundedness' can be observed to change at the same time in both pottery decoration and burial ritual. In an analysis of the Orkney Neolithic, Hodder (1982a) attempted to show that structures in settlement, burial and ritual uses of space could be correlated, although the data were scarcely adequate.

The question of verification of structure – does the structure relate to the data? – is a conventional one. All archaeological analysis involves interpreting the real world in the process of observation, and then fitting one's theories to these observations in order to make a plausible, accommodative argument – claims to do anything else are illusory. Structuralist analysis proceeds by the same principles. For example, in the analysis of the Nuba art (see above, p. 48), the more art, and the more varied the art, that the generative grammar can generate, the more plausible is the grammar. We can ask whether any designs occur which do not fit the rules. For example, are the 'words' ever joined at the sides rather than at the angles? In fact ⟶ rarely, if ever, occurs in the art. The same applies to ◆. These motifs are not allowed by the grammar, and that they do not occur in the art supports the grammar itself.

It is important to recognize that the structures need not be universal, and their proposed universality should not be a major part of the validation procedure. The structures themselves may be quite specific (as in the Nuba use of the cross design). But it is the meaning content especially that may have particular historical significance. Thus the Nuba cross is not just a design structure – it is a highly emotive symbol, with a strong but particular historical significance which affects its social use in Nuba art (Hodder 1982a). Part of the validation of structuralist analyses in archaeology must therefore concern the abstraction of particular meanings related to the structures.

In some cases, where there is historical continuity with the present, meanings assigned to the past appear convincing. Thus, Glassie's (1975) identification of certain types of building, façades, and room spaces, as 'public' or 'private', or his association of asymmetry with 'nature' and 'the organic', is convincing because eighteenth-century America is close to us. We would personally be much less convinced if asymmetry were related to 'the organic' in Kenya or in prehistoric Hungary. It is when meanings are applied cross-culturally, without reference to context, that the dangers emerge. Thus, Leroi-Gourhan (1982) was much more cautious about identifying 'male' or 'female' designs in Palaeolithic caves. But in prehistoric periods where more contextual and associational data are present, the imputation of meaning can be carefully constructed. Thus, in the Neolithic of Europe, Hodder (1984a) has argued that the tombs mean houses on the basis of eight points of similarity between them. Contextual and functional associations also allow a commonality of meaning to be inferred. Clearly we cannot assume with confidence that if an object is found in a male grave it has 'male' qualities, or that an artifact found in a ceremonial site has 'ritual' meanings, but such assumptions are routinely made by archaeologists. By careful and critical consideration of context, the meanings can be made plausible.

It might be thought that a dichotomy ought to be presented between structural and functional explanation, suggesting that an important way of supporting a theory about the one is to show that the data are not adequately explained by the other. Certainly, McGhee supports his case by suggesting that there is no functional need for ivory and antler to be used for different categories of tool and weapon. This type of argument is dangerous in that it often assumes a primacy of the material, functional side: the functions are explained first, and anything left over is 'mind'. But the argument also fallaciously assumes that there is a dichotomy between function and symbolic meaning. As McGhee's example shows, an item may be part of a tool-kit, but at the same time it may be part of a structured set of categories. As archaeologists, we may take depositional and post-depositional factors into account and still find functional associations between objects on our sites. Such functional linkages play a part in the meanings assigned to objects – part of the symbolic and cognitive significance of objects derives from their use. In chapter 2 we saw that the assignment of function depends on imputing symbolic meaning. Once again we return here to the notions of material culture as both object and sign, of two-way influences, of a necessary unity.

A purely hypothetical example may clarify the point (for a comparable real-world example see Parker Pearson 1999). Imagine that some prehistoric long houses have been found in a region. They are all aligned NW–SE, with the entrances at the SE ends. Two 'conflicting' hypotheses are suggested: either the alignment is because the prevailing wind is from the NW, or the NW–SE axis has symbolic significance. Both hypotheses can be supported in their varying ways, the one by showing that the prevailing wind was indeed from the NW, the other by identifying the same structure in other domains. For example, the same NW–SE axis might be found in burial and ritual sites, and in other aspects of the use of space in settlements. But in fact the two hypotheses are not contradictory. In giving meaning to the world around us we commonly make use of the positions of the sun, moon, rivers, hills, and wind; equally, the symbolic significance attached to wind and its prevailing axis will affect decisions about how to arrange houses and settlements. Thus functional use and environmental features are parts of the process of giving meaning to the world, and validation of meaning structures should not depend on ironing out such factors.

We have seen that plausible structuralist arguments can be made by showing that the structures account for much, and many different categories of, data. It is also necessary to ground the structures in their meaning content and in their context of use. In these various ways one can show, in the data, that certain arguments just do not hold water. Thus an item that is supposed to be 'male' is found in a female grave, or a phase of 'communal' activities has many 'individualing' characteristics, or too many arrowheads are made of ivory. Of course one could argue that a 'transformation' of the structure has occurred in the cases that do not 'fit', but at some stage one's intellectual ingenuity becomes implausible, at least to others, and different structures are sought to account for the data.

Conclusion: the importance of structuralist archaeology

In this chapter the emphasis has moved to symbolic codes and structures of the mind. In the next chapter other types of structure, technological and social, will be described. The major importance of all such work in archaeology is that it takes us to another level of analysis. We are no longer bound to the quantification of presences, but we are also drawn to the interpretation of absences. The system is no longer all that there is – there are also structures through which it takes its form. Because the continuous shades of variation in life overwhelm our capacity to make sense of the world, we impose these structures to help simplify difference and organize it into categories we can grasp. We still have not adequately found the agent in a cultural and historical context, as the critique above makes clear, but we have come some way along our road, particularly in the understanding of culture as meaningfully constituted.

Structuralism provides a method and a theory for the analysis of material culture meanings. Processual archaeologists have been largely concerned with the functions of symbols. As we have seen, function is an important aspect of meaning: the use and association of a pot with its contents, with the fire on which the pot's contents are cooked, with tribal identity and with the social hierarchy, are all important in, although not determinant of, the pot's symbolic meanings. But processual archaeologists have not been concerned with the organization of these functional associations into meaning structures. Whatever the limitations of structuralism, it provides a first step towards a broader approach.

Moreover, structuralism, in whatever guise, contributes to archaeology, of whatever character, the notion of transformation. Schiffer (1976), of course, has noted the importance of cultural transforms, but structuralism supplies a method and a deeper level of analysis. As Faris (1983) points out, material culture does not represent social relations – rather it represents a way of viewing social relations. From work on artifact discard showing that notions of 'dirt' intervene between residues and societies (Okely 1979; Moore 1982), to work showing that burial is a conceptual transformation of society (Parker Pearson 1982), the structuralist contribution is clear. The rules of transformation can be approached, it is claimed, through systematic analysis.

A related and equally important contribution is that different spheres of material culture and of human activity (burial, settlement, art, exchange) may be transformations of the same underlying schemes, or may be transformations of each other. Rather than seeing each domain as a separate sub-system, each can be related to the other as different outward manifestations of the same practices. The importance of the notion that culture is meaningfully constituted is clear in this drawing together of the various strands of archaeological data and analysis.

Thus far, we have given scant attention to one of the most fertile encounters between structuralism and archaeology: historical studies of American material culture (Deetz 1967, pp. 86–93; 1977; Glassie 1975; Leone 1988; Leone and Potter 1988; Palkovich 1988; Yentsch 1991). We close this chapter with some of these authors because they provide case studies (see also Tilley 1991) that retain the structuralist contribution yet situate it within lived and contested contexts. For example, Yentsch's study of how hierarchical meanings in pottery relate to hierarchical structures in the division of space (public vs. private, male vs. female) in 17th- and 18th-century American homes goes beyond the simple detection of these opposed spheres to a consideration of the people (slaves, women, children, lesser and greater men) who animate these spaces. Yentsch considers how occupying certain spaces, such as rooms of a house, and using the pottery types appropriate to each space produces and reproduces inequality among members of the same society and same family. Essays by Palkovich (1988) and Leone (1988) highlight the ways in which people may have challenged these same meaningful structures (the 'Georgian Worldview' after Deetz 1977) and the hierarchical system of values they entail. These examples from American historical archaeology reveal how cosmological structures serve the interests of only some sections of society and how those structures become a medium for conflict between different sections. We discuss this concern with sectional interests and social conflict in the next two chapters.

4 Marxism and ideology

The main concern in this chapter is to examine the contribution of Marxist archaeology to the understanding of social and ideological relations. In considering social structures in this context, the contrast with processual approaches again needs to be identified. In this chapter the term social structure does not mean the pattern of roles and relationships; rather it refers to the scheme of productive interactions which lies behind that pattern. However, our concern here is not to debate the full width of Marxist archaeology, which has been adequately covered elsewhere (Spriggs 1984; Trigger 1984; McGuire 1992; Kristiansen and Rowlands 1998). Rather, we wish briefly to outline the types of social structure that have been identified in Marxist archaeology, before considering Marxist archaeological discussions of ideology.

Marxist archaeology

Here we return to materialism, although some Marxist archaeologists would now claim to avoid the materialist/idealist split (Spriggs 1984). We shall see below that such claims can rarely be substantiated in archaeology, and the similarity with processual archaeology is clear in this respect. Rather, it is in the Marxist incorporation of the notion of structure that the major break with processual archaeology occurs. This is not to argue that Marxist archaeology avoids functional arguments, because we shall see below that it does not. What is new is an additional component, that all social practices involve dialectical relationships: the development of society occurs through the unity of opposites. Underlying the visible social system are relationships which embody incompatibilities, which are made compatible and which generate change. It is thus to the realm of contradiction and conflict that we must turn in order to assess the essence of Marxist archaeology.

Within the structural Marxism of Althusser and those writers in archaeology influenced by him, the two main types of contradiction are those between the interests of social groups (as in the class struggle) and those between the forces and relations of production (to be defined below). In the first type of contradiction, an important emphasis in Marxism is on class divisions, in which a dominant class controls the means of production and appropriates surplus. The interests of the two classes are contradictory since the expansion of one class is at the expense of the other. This general notion has been applied in pre-capitalist societies, to social divisions based on age, sex, lineage and so on. Thus Faris (1983) suggests that in the Upper Palaeolithic in Europe men appropriated the products of the labour of women and maintained a position of dominance at the expense of women. The notion of 'structure' in such studies, although weakly developed, concerns the relations of production and appropriation that lie behind the apparent social relations (between men and women, chief and commoner etc.).

The second type of contradiction, clearly linked to and often underlying the first type, is structural incompatibility. Here the forces of production are in conflict with the relations of production. One view of these terms and their relationships is provided by Friedman (1974; see diagram below). The forces of production include the means of production (technology, the ecosystem: the means by which an environment is transformed into a product for man) and the organization of production (the organization of the labour force). The relations of production, on the other hand, are the social relations which correspond with the forces of production. These social relations will vary from society to society: for example, in some societies kinship orders the forces of production, whereas in the contemporary West it rarely does. The social relations of production organize the way in which the environment is to be used within the available technology; they also determine who works and how the product of labour

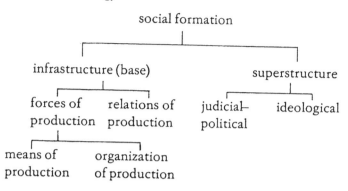

is appropriated. In archaeology, as in other areas of Marxist analyses, major variation occurs in the relative importance given to the forces and relations of production. In some writings the forces of production appear to develop on their own, internally generated, leading to contradictions between the forces and relations of production. An example of this position is provided by Gilman's (1984) account of the Upper Palaeolithic Revolution. He argues that the Domestic Mode of Production (Sahlins 1972) characteristic of this period has internal contradictions: on the one hand local groups need external alliances in order to survive, but on the other hand they wish to maintain control of their own resources. More self-sufficient groups want to move out of the alliance network. As technology improves, each group becomes more self-sufficient and the contradiction between the alliance network and local production leads to bounded local alliances, which establish closed circles of mutual aid and limit obligations to assist others. Although Gilman claims (*ibid.*, p. 123) that technology does not specifically determine the social changes, and that the materialist determination is in the last, not the first, instance, the technological changes do appear primary (Fig. 6). They are generated as the result of the Darwinian selection of primary adaptive improvements in stone-tools (*ibid.*).

In such analyses contradictions between the forces and relations of production are generated by changes in the forces of production, and, as we shall see below, these contradictions

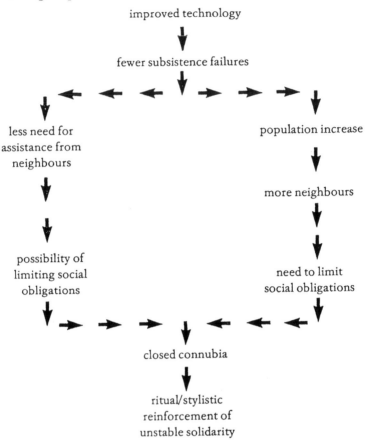

Fig. 6. The relation between technological improvements and social change over the course of the Upper Palaeolithic, as suggested by Gilman (1984).

lead to changes in the arena of style and ideology. Such viewpoints appear inadequate, particularly if one is interested in the reasons for technological change and the reasons for the precise form of the social relations. Thus many Marxists would now argue that, at least in pre-capitalist social formations, it is the social relations of production which either dominate or are in a dialectical two-way relationship with the forces of production.

An interesting example of the view that the social relations dominate is provided by Bender's (1978) account of the adoption of agriculture. She suggests that prior to the adoption of farming local groups were competing for domination through rituals, feasting and exchange. It is these strategies of social dominance which lead to the need for increased local subsistence production and hence to more intensive production and the adoption of agriculture. Here changes in people's relationship with the environment, the forces of production, are dependent on social relations.

Such notions of the growth of dominance and ranking in initially egalitarian groups are outlined with clarity by Friedman (1975) and are developed and applied to the appearance of state societies by Friedman and Rowlands (1978). One aspect of Friedman's model, the prestige goods system, has now been widely applied in European prehistory (see for example Bradley 1984; Kristiansen 1979; Frankenstein and Rowlands 1978; Kristiansen and Rowlands 1998) and parts of the American southwest and midwest (Bender 1985; McGuire and Howard 1987; Gledhill 1978). In all such studies the social relations of production dominate, and ideology in particular plays a secondary role. There is little discussion of material culture as meaningfully constituted.

So far we have seen something of the concept of 'structure' in Marxist archaeology – that it concerns relations of production and appropriation. One of the reasons this structure is 'underlying', hidden from view, is that it is masked by ideology. We can now return to the main theme of this chapter: what is the role of ideology in relation to the social structure in Marxist archaeology?

Ideology

Archaeologists often make use of Marx's statement, made in 1859, that the superstructure, incorporating ideology, is founded on and arises from the infrastructure. Ideology then functions by masking the contradictions and conflicts within and between the forces and relations of production. The difference between the analysis of structured systems of ideas and Marxist analyses of ideology can be seen by comparing Deetz's (1988) account of change in eighteenth- and nineteenth-century North America with the accounts of the rise of capitalism by Leone (1988) and Paynter (1988). For Deetz, ideology was a general worldview, whereas for Leone and Paynter, ideology is connected to a specific means of production. Most Marxist archaeology has provided explanations in which ideology is determined by and functions in relation to the economy. While a reflexive relationship between base and superstructure is sometimes claimed, in practice applications have been largely materialist and functionalist (see below).

While, in the Marxist approach, ideology is often explained by reference to its functions, there is a sense in which material culture is 'active'. As in the Wobst view (p. 24), material culture acts so that the system can work. However, on the whole this 'activity' is the fairly passive end-product of functional needs, even though these needs are rather different from those found in processual archaeology. The distinction is made clearly by Gilman (1984) in his Marxist reading of the Upper Palaeolithic transition, in contrast to that made by Wobst (1976). Rather than seeing Upper Palaeolithic style as functioning to facilitate cooperation within social groupings and to identify differences between them, Gilman argues that style and ritual develop because that cooperation incorporates inherent contradictions. The desire to break out of alliance networks and concentrate on retaining production within local groups leads to unstable closed connubia. Thus style and ritual help to create social groupings which would otherwise be continually breaking down. Material culture here functions by providing a masking ideology, hiding or misrepresenting the internal contradictions.

Another important Upper Palaeolithic analysis which incorporates a symbolic structure which ideologically 'hides' social conflict is carried out by Faris (1983). Faris notes a contrast between western European Palaeolithic wall painting and mobiliary art. The parietal art mainly depicts big game animals which require a lot of skill in hunting. The art itself is skilled and must have involved considerable effort, including the construction of scaffolding in some places. In contrast, plants and small animals, although these are known from archaeological deposits to be an important part of the diet, are not depicted. Female figurines, on the other hand, misrepresent reality in another way. In this mobiliary art, it is the mid-body sexual and reproductive parts that are emphasized at the expense of arms and facial features – the image is not of a working body. In the art as a whole, then, it is male hunting activities that are emphasized, even though such activities probably only produced a portion of the resources consumed. Small animals and plants and female production are not represented; the woman appears only as reproductive.

Faris is careful to identify his own perception biases in this reconstruction. But here both symbolic form and content are examined. The structure of signs misrepresents the role played by women in society – in other words the symbolism acts ideologically to transform the relations of production. Male dominance is based on the appropriation of female labour, and the cave wall art mystifies the contradiction and prevents conflict. Material culture has to be understood both as part of an aesthetic tradition, and as part of an ideology within social strategies of domination.

In both of the above studies of the Upper Palaeolithic, ideology is interpreted functionally in relation to the economic base (the forces and the social relations of production). A further example is provided by Kristiansen (1984) in his study of the role of ideology in the construction of megalithic burial in Neolithic Europe. His aim is to determine how ideological and cultural norms correspond to their material functions of reproduction (*ibid.*, p. 77). The megalithic monuments are seen as representing a ritualized extension of production organized through the communal lineage structure. Surplus production for lineage leaders is transformed into ritual feasting and ancestor worship.

In Kristiansen's study, the materialism is clear, but it should also be noted that the social reality against which the ideology is compared can only be accessed archaeologically through the ideology itself – that is, through the interpretations of the burial monuments. Thus, as with the processual studies discussed in chapter 2, the materialism is more apparent than real. It is certainly not possible to determine the ideology from the material base since the material base is only known through the ideology.

A further characteristic of Kristiansen's study is that the ideology is the conscious world of ritual. Other studies, such as that of Leone (1984), have concentrated more on the ideological aspects of the unconscious taken-for-granteds that are inherent in all aspects of life (Althusser 1977). For Leone, these 'givens' – ideas about nature, cause, time, person – serve to naturalize and mask inequalities in the social order. Ideology disguises the arbitrariness of social relations of production, making them appear resident in nature or the past and thus inevitable. Leone focusses in particular on the layout of an eighteenth-century garden, recovered by historical archaeologists, in Annapolis, Maryland. In the eighteenth century, social control by plantation owners was being weakened in a number of ways, and wealthy members of the planter-gentry, such as William Paca, the owner of the Annapolis garden, held contradictory beliefs, on the one hand basing their substantial inherited wealth in part on slavery and on the other hand passionately defending liberty. To mask this contradiction, Leone suggests that Paca's position of power was placed within nature. The ideal of Georgian order in the house and the carefully laid out garden conform to rules of bilateral symmetry and perspective. In this way the arbitrariness of the social order is naturalized, and the gentry is isolated and distanced from attack on the established order. The balance and organization of the garden appear convincingly natural and ordered, thus making the elite the natural centre of social control.

In this example, once again, the materialist conception of ideology is clear – the ideology functions in relation to growing contradictions within eighteenth-century society. But the important contribution of such studies to the concerns in this volume, as outlined in chapter 1, is that an attempt is made to examine the way in which structures of symbolic meaning may relate to social structures and systems. In Leone's example we are back with symbolic structures, but now these are linked to social structures via ideological and social processes. As we saw in chapter 3, in structuralist archaeology such linkages are not the central focus of concern.

We wish to use Leone's convincing account of the role of material culture in ideology (for further examples see Miller and Tilley 1984) in order to begin a four-point critique of ideology as discussed in Marxist archaeology.

First criticism

It often appears in the Marxist analyses of the 1980s that ideology is shared by all in society – thus, once again, aspects of a normative view are retained (see p. 9). In Leone's Annapolis study, for example, there is no indication that the same material culture may have different meanings and different ideological effects for different social groups. The extent to which people are said to be duped by the ideas of the dominant class is remarkable. The ordering of architecture, street plans, rows of trees, the training of gardens, disguise the arbitrariness of the social order. It may be true that the ruling classes themselves believe their own ideology, but no evidence is provided that all members of society make these linkages between garden layout and social order or that they in any way value or respect the garden. In the late 1980s, however, Marxists successfully responded to this critique by embracing theories of practice. Armed with a more sophisticated understanding of power relations, newer studies shift from domination to class struggle. They replace dupes with active social agents who challenge the ideologies and institutions that oppress them (see McGuire 1992). We postpone our commentary on these studies of resistance until the next chapter, which discusses those ideas of practice, power and agency upon which any discussion of resistance depends.

Second criticism

A second, closely related point concerns the tendency in all Marxist archaeology to oppose ideology and the social reality, the 'real' conditions of existence, the 'real' contradictions. As we have seen, ideologies are described as naturalizing or masking inequalities in the social order; but 'inequality' is itself a value-laden term and can be described as ideological. The Marxist notion of false-consciousness implies that people cannot see the reality of their existence because that reality is hidden from them by ideologies. But what *is* the social reality?

For many Marxist archaeologists the social reality is defined as the forces and relations of production. But Marxism then has to face its own critique, that the Marxist definition of the social reality is itself ideological. Since reality has to be perceived and created by the observer, it is itself ideology. To take the position that Marxism offers the one true science that can identify objective reality is simply to state a belief. There is no end to ideology (Giddens 1979, p. 197).

As we have seen in discussing Kristiansen's study, the problem of the definition of social reality is particularly acute in archaeology since material culture serves as both social reality and ideology. Thus the lineage mode of appropriation of surplus may be identified from burial, but the same burial monuments are interpreted as ideologies masking social reality. Where, then, is the social reality?

For different social actors, the social inequalities and contradictions may have different 'realities'. For Althusser (1977), whose work has been discussed in archaeology most fully by Shanks and Tilley (1982), ideology is not distorted communication, but is functionally necessary in all societies. Rather than opposing ideology and reality, Althusser seeks to express ideology as the practical unconscious organization of the day-to-day. But it is particularly Foucault's discussion of power as ever-present, a constituent of all social action, that has come to the fore in archaeological debate (Miller and Tilley 1984). In *Surveillir et punir* Foucault (1977) shows that power is not simply repressive, negative; it is also positive, productive of knowledge. It does not just mask, conceal, repress – it also produces reality. Power is not a general system of domination exerted by one group over another. Rather, power is everywhere, produced at every moment in every action. It is present in the ideal as much as in the material. One can argue that there is an unceasing struggle in which power relations are transformed, strengthened and sometimes reversed by the manipulation of symbolic and material capital, the two being fully interdependent and difficult to distinguish.

Following the direction of Foucault, Miller and Tilley (*ibid.*) define power as the capacity to transform, and they make a distinction between *power to* and *power over*. *Power to* is the capacity to act in the world and is an integral component of all social practice. *Power over* refers to social control and domination. Ideology is essential for both types of power and relates to the interests inherent in power. Though groups have no interests, actors have interests by being members of groups in the sense that culture is public and needs and wants are socially constructed (Giddens 1979, p. 189; Geertz 1973). To examine ideology is to see how symbolic meanings are mobilized to legitimate the sectional interests of those groups. Following Giddens (1979; 1981), there are three ways in which ideologies function: (1) the representation of sectional interests as universal, (2) the denial or transmutation of contradictions, and (3) the naturalization of the present, or reification. These ideas have immediate implications for archaeologists (Hodder 1982c; Miller and Tilley 1984). For example, if burial remains are seen as ideological naturalizations of the social order, then burial variability within cemeteries (how the bones are laid out, the contents of the graves, and so on) will correlate directly with the structure of the society, but if burial remains in a particular society deny contradictions, then the archaeological burial data cannot be used to 'read off' the social organization. Material culture, then, is a type of social reality, but it is not the only type. Systems of value and prestige are integrally related to systems of material resources in the definition of power.

Reading the past

Different sectional interests in society develop their own ideologies in relation to other ideologies and interests. Social interests and power relations can be seen from many different points of view within the same society. Interest and power can be defined in terms other than the control over labour and material resources. Different ideologies coexist in relation to each other and the dominant ideology is continually being subverted from other points of view. Any arena of material culture use (domestic, ritual, exchange, burial) frequently involves the negotiation of these different meanings/powers in relation to each other. What may be seen by one group as an inequality on one dimension may be seen as an equality on another. William Paca's garden may have worked well for William Paca, legitimating his own social interests, but whether anyone else was taken in by it is less clear. It could be argued that a material culture statement of this type was socially divisive. Indeed all ideologies that appear to 'mask', in the process 'reveal'.

Third criticism

The third criticism of archaeological uses of Marxist approaches to ideology is that the cross-cultural method applied usually pays insufficient regard to the specific historical context. It is easy to apply Giddens' three types of ideology in a wide range of circumstances. In the examples discussed in this chapter, notions of prestige, naturalization, masking and so on are applied with little attempt to see if the cross-cultural model is appropriate. In Leone's example, how do we know the garden acts ideologically in the way described? We are told little of the context of use: how is the garden used, do subordinate groups ever visit or even see the garden, do subordinate groups use such ordering in their own homes and gardens on a smaller scale or are their gardens very different, and so on?

Equally, the cross-cultural emphasis leads to an inability to account for the specificity of ideological forms. Thus in Gilman's analysis, the general interpretation of style and ritual as ideology does nothing to explain why cave art is found as opposed to other ritual. In relation to Faris' study, it is informative to ask, why does cave wall art not occur in central Europe in the Upper Palaeolithic, despite the existence of appropriate caves? The generalized references to ideological functions do little to account for such differences. Equally, there are many ways in which William Paca could have projected a sense of order.

Fourth criticism

A final limitation of Marxist approaches to ideology concerns the generation and generative role of ideology. The inability to explain the specificity of ideology (third criticism) is associated with an inability to explain its 'becoming'. To be fair, this is more a shortcoming of Marxist archaeologists than of Marxism itself because Marx, as an historical materialist, was concerned with the interaction between subject (people in society) and object (the material world), which slowly and constantly transforms and generates new human needs and purposes over time, thus giving a history to ideology. In archaeology, Marxist case studies have related ideology to function, but can it really be claimed that the ideological need to mask appropriation by lineage heads leads to megalithic burial monuments, or that a need to legitimate social control in Annapolis leads to an organized garden? The poverty of stimulus argument is here at work, throwing doubt on the ability of Marxist analysis to explain both the specificity of ideology (third criticism) and its generation (fourth criticism). These criticisms are very similar to those made in chapters 2 and 3. As in all the other approaches described so far in this book, one is left with the question, where does the particular ideology (structure, ideational sub-system or whatever) come from?

Since the specificity and 'becoming' of ideology have not been approached in Marxist archaeological analyses, so too there has been little attempt to show how the ideology itself determines and creates society (see, however, McGuire 1988 and Miller 1985a). Since the emphasis has been on the functioning of ideologies, and because of the materialist bent of such analyses, the reflexive role of ideology has been little discussed. For example, the Georgian order manifest in Paca's house and garden is seen by Leone as appropriate for the needed social functions, but ideals concerning the organization of space and time, which Leone identifies in the garden, are themselves part of a long historical tradition which harks back to the Classical civilizations of the Mediterranean world. It would be possible to argue that this Classical ideal of order has itself played a part in generating Western society and in determining the social interests to which Paca aspired – in other words, we could give a move creative and active role to ideology, and to material culture as ideological.

Ideology and power: conclusions

Ideology, then, is an aspect of symbol-systems. It refers to that component of symbol-systems most closely involved in the negotiation of power from varying points of interest within society. Cultural meanings and symbols are used within strategies of power and in the negotiation of control, but they also partly form those strategies. Ideology cannot be opposed to social relations of production. It cannot be explained as functioning in relation to some social reality, because that reality, and the analysis of the relationship between ideology and reality, are themselves ideological. Rather, ideology is the framework within which, from a particular standpoint, resources are given value, inequalities are defined and power is legitimated. Ideas are themselves the 'real' resources used in the negotiation of power; and material resources are themselves parts of the ideological apparatus.

To study ideology thus involves two components for which archaeologists are theoretically ill-equipped. First, since ideologies cannot be measured in terms of objective conditions and functions, they must be studied 'from the inside', on their own terms. These terms of reference are historically generated. We need methods, then, for getting 'inside' the principles of meaning through which societies are generated. This problem will be addressed in chapter 7.

Second, critical analysis of Marxist archaeology leads back to the importance of social agents. As we elaborate in the next chapter, the outcome of an event is never predetermined: there is no rulebook which, when properly consulted, specifies the correct response to each and every social situation. Actors thus always have at least some space for negotiation, and in this space they consciously and unconsciously apply a considerable understanding of the struggles between sectional interests and the diverse social positions from which these interests emanate.

In the following chapters we will examine approaches which owe a considerable debt to Marxism. In chapter 5 we will explore agency and practice theories in archaeology which are heavily influenced by Giddens and Bourdieu, both of whose work can be seen as responding to Marxism. In archaeology a developed theory of agency has been discussed from within Marxism by McGuire (1992). In chapter 6 we examine theories of embodiment – how power and society are constructed through the body. Much of the early work of Marxist-influenced archaeologists such as Kristiansen and Rowlands described power in general evolutionary terms. But more recently Kristiansen and Rowlands (1998) have studied the embodiment of power. Power is not described as general but is seen as specific to a particular conception of bodies, body substances and flows. The account of power is here much more subtle, focusing on the details of body practices and beliefs. Recent developments within Marxist archaeology itself have contributed substantially to contemporary debate concerning the relationships between power, practices, agency and bodies.

5 Agency and practice

Practice and structuration

In outlining a 'theory of practice', Bourdieu (1977) notes the difference between, on the one hand, observing and analysing social events, and, on the other hand, participating in activities. Structuralism, for example, allows us to see how pattern is generated, but gives us no indication of how we make relevant use of structures in constantly changing situations. Giddens (1979; 1981) is also concerned to escape notions of change which involve the playing out of some pre-set code.

Both Bourdieu and Giddens thus develop theories of practice or social action, called by Giddens 'structuration', in which there is a recursive relationship between structure and practice. Bourdieu's account is of particular relevance to archaeologists because he develops his theory in relation to material culture and the use of space. Indeed his ideas have been applied in ethnoarchaeology by, for example, Donley (1982), Moore (1982), and Braithwaite (1982), and in archaeology by Barrett (1981) and Davis (1984).

Bourdieu situates the notion of the habitus, a term first coined by Marcel Mauss (1973 [1935]), between structure and practice. However, any attempt to *define* the habitus (singular and plural) goes against the grain of Bourdieu's project. As part of his challenge to certain types of objectivism, Bourdieu argues that a concept is understood through its use: any attempt to formalise it – to step back from the context of use and construct a rule that systematises the ways it is used – misrecognizes the ambiguity and unpredictability of the situations in which the concept is exercised. Nevertheless, we can provisionally understand the habitus as systems of durable but transposable dispositions, including, for example, a sense of honour, but also left/right, up/down and other structuring principles. The habitus are strategy generating propensities

90

enabling agents to cope with unforeseen situations. Rather than seeing habitus as abstract sets of mechanistic rules in a filing cabinet in the mind, Bourdieu emphasizes the importance of practical logic and knowledge. All the schemes of categorization and perception are included, but the habitus is unconscious, a linguistic, physical and cultural competence. In day-to-day activities, there is a practical mastery involving tact, dexterity and *savoir faire* which cannot be reduced to rules. In the same vein, Giddens suggests that the knowledgeability of lay actors, which mediates between structure and practice, includes both discursive and practical consciousness. Practical consciousness involves knowledge of 'how to go on' in society – it is skilled, an artistry in day-to-day activity, varied and strategic, dependent on context. Individuals reflexively monitor their actions and can penetrate or gain an understanding of the structures of society. Regular patterns of behaviour occur as a result of practices generated through habitus, not through norms or rules. When asked to explain our actions we may indeed declare that we are following rules. But, rather than clarifying action, our native explanations add to or mystify it. Native references to rules confuse the logic of practice because they are produced after the action took place. There is always a distance between theoretical reconstructions of the native world and the native experience of that world (Bourdieu 1977, pp. 18–19). Rationalising and strategising intervene in the gap between action and explanation, between experience and reconstruction. The explanation becomes an after-the-fact intellectualisation and justification whose logic disguises and often exceeds the logic of practice itself. In those cases where agents do follow rules, we must remember that they follow them not simply because rules are rules, but because they may gain from following them, from being seen to conform to socially sanctioned values: 'the rule's last trick is to cause it to be forgotten that agents have in interest in obeying [it]' (p. 22).

Nevertheless a commonality of behaviour does occur within social groups. Many things contribute to the regularity of behaviour, though none determines it. As mentioned above, owing to 'the trick of the rule', there is often much to be gained by following those behaviours that are sanctioned. 'The more the working of the system serves the agent's interests, the more they are inclined to support the working of the system' (p. 65). These conscious, reflexive, self-regulating devices reinforce practice, but, according to Bourdieu, do not produce it.

Bourdieu assigns only a secondary importance to conscious, intentional action as a contributor to the commonality of behaviour (p. 73). Bourdieu also considers how the habitus is passed from generation to generation without going through discourse or consciousness. The central position of processes of enculturation in Bourdieu's theory is of importance for history because it links social practices with the 'culture history' of society. As the habitus is passed down through time it plays an active role in social action and is transformed in those actions. This recursiveness, Giddens' 'duality of structure', is possible because the habitus is a *practical* logic.

The schemes of the habitus – the sense of what is reasonable and what is unreasonable – are passed down from practice to practice, but this does not mean that learning is a mechanistic remembering of appropriate actions. In the daily pattern of life, in proverbs, songs, riddles, games, watching adults and interacting with them, a child has no difficulty in grasping the rationale behind the series of events. The child adjusts and accommodates subjective and objective patterns, patterns 'in here' and 'out there', giving rise to systematic dispositions. The habitus which results is based on the child's own social position as he/she sees how others react to him/her.

The physical setting of action, built or otherwise, also plays a role in the implicit pedagogy in so far as places may be pegs on which stories and meanings are hung, or may simply keep certain people separate from other people and things (Bourdieu 1977, pp. 87–94; Basso 1983). In this way, inculcation is not extraordinarily far from the forms of discipline produced by institutions (Foucault 1977). In particular, the house, and the use of space and objects in a house, lead a child to understanding of the habitus. The ' "book" from which the children learn their vision of the world is read with the body' (Bourdieu, p. 90), in moving through space, from 'male' to 'female' parts of the house, from 'light' to 'dark' and so on. A 'body' of wisdom results from these regularised learning processes. They inscribe a manner of being; a corporal scheme of perception and appreciation. The same home then comes to be perceived differently by different social groups, through their different habitus. Donley (1990) provides an elegant example of how in Kenyan Swahili houses, men and women learn their place in the world through the use of space and objects in the house. It is the practices, in the process of enculturation, that act back on the habitus, so that Bourdieu can talk of 'the mind born of the world of objects' (*ibid.*, p. 91).

Bourdieu admits that the habitus is not the exclusive principle of all practice. The regularity that we observe in behaviour is also produced by norms, symbols, emblems, rites and objective material considerations, such as the location of actors in socio-economic hierarchies and other fields of distinction (Bourdieu 1977, p. 20; 1984, p. 55). Nevertheless, in much of Bourdieu's writing, we feel that the habitus and other structures, such as class, exert too much influence on the outcome of practice. The diagram below, which shows a unidirectional relation between habitus and practice, illustrates the way in which structures constrain practice.

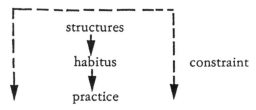

Bourdieu's theory of practice presents an implicit invitation to archaeologists to come to an understanding of the principles lying behind other cultural practices through an examination of and involvement in objects arranged in space and in contexts of use. In the same way that the child absorbs the principles of actions, so the archaeologist can 'read' the surviving 'book', without necessary reference to abstract or spoken meanings. We shall return later to the implications of this realization for archaeological 'theory' and for the public presentation of archaeology.

The potential offered by Bourdieu's insight is considerable. It is exciting to realize that mundane items in the material world, of the type excavated by archaeologists – pots, bones, pins and door-frames – can all play a part in the process of enculturation, in forming the social world. Through practical enculturation it is possible to instil 'a whole cosmology, an ethic, a metaphysic, a political philosophy, through injunctions as insignificant as "stand up straight" or "don't hold your knife in your left hand"' (Bourdieu, *ibid.*, p. 94). 'Stand up straight', for example, may relate, in the particular cultural associations of straightness (such as straight male spears), to valued notions of 'talking straight', 'being straight', as opposed to being bent over, submissive. A whole philosophy of male dominance is thus taken for granted. Every mundane pot and scratched decoration, every pig and cow skull, is in this way the node of a network of associations and oppositions which tell us about the way the world is put together.

Both Bourdieu and Giddens link structuralism and Marxism, and outline a theory of practice of considerable importance in archaeology. Bourdieu's concern is to combine both objectivism (the idea that social life must be explained through the structural relations of inequality of which actors are ignorant) and subjectivism (the idea that social life must be explained by the agents' own accounts of the meaning of their world), therefore avoiding the extravagances caused by embracing one to the exclusion of the other (Bourdieu 1990). For Giddens, there is a duality of structure: the structure is both the medium and outcome of action. The individual plays a central role as self-monitoring, creative and with degrees of competence. Material culture in particular plays a highly active role, creating society and creating continual change.

Shanks and Tilley (1982) concentrate on an area of practical knowledge that Bourdieu inherits from Merleau-Ponty (1962, pp. 303–4) – the use of the body as a map or framework by which people 'live through' their habitus. The world is known through the body, unconsciously. Within the body there is a variety of possible whole/part relations. Disarticulated human bone remains from Neolithic tombs in Britain and Sweden were found to have been grouped into piles showing body/limb, upper limb/lower limb, right/left distinctions. The body symmetry is then seen as naturalizing contradictions in society, for example between social control by lineage heads and socialized production. The symmetry between body parts is a denial of asymmetrical relations in life.

Although in this example a sophisticated account is given of the relationship between structure and practice, with the role of the individual considered, some of the limitations that have been encountered in other studies remain, particularly in relation to contextual meanings and history. As in other studies influenced by the work of Bourdieu and Giddens (see the articles in Hodder 1982c) particular historical meanings are not taken into account; the approach remains largely cross-cultural and 'from the outside'. Thus Shanks and Tilley do not examine whether there are other realms of evidence in Neolithic society in Britain and Sweden which show left/right symmetries, nor what these symmetries might represent there. Childe argued for Neolithic Orkney (Hodder 1982a) that a right/left division of huts might relate to male/female on the basis of artifacts and bed sizes. Hodder (1984a) has also argued that the Neolithic tombs 'mean' houses found elsewhere in central Europe where they played an important part in male/female relationships. If further work could establish the relevance of such contexts, the bone organization in the tombs might be shown to have had specific meanings in the male/female negotiation of power and authority, rather than being related to the types of power relations described by Shanks and Tilley.

Without consideration of the content of meaning in a culture-historical context (what do left/right, burial tombs etc. mean in Neolithic Britain and Sweden?) it becomes impossible to explain the ideological functions of symbol-systems. Equally it is impossible to explain why any *particular* symbol-system was employed, how it came about. For example, the ideological analysis of the Neolithic tombs cannot explain why the same monuments are not commonly found in central Europe, where similar structural contradictions can be presumed. Shanks and Tilley's elegant and innovative analysis of one type of habitus needs to be tied to careful consideration of historical and contextual meanings.

Resistance

An important aspect of Giddens' theory of structuration is his modification of the concept of power. Power is not a resource and the exercise of power is not an act. Rather, power involves the reproduction of relations of autonomy and dependence. These relations are always two-way: the capability of an actor to secure an outcome always depends on the agency of others. 'Even the most autonomous agent is in some degree dependent, and the most dependent actor or party in a relationship retains some autonomy' (p. 93). In other words, every actor always has the ability to do otherwise – the ability to foil the wishes of someone else – even if doing otherwise is self-destructive (p. 149). 'Where there is power, there is resistance' (Foucault 1981a, p. 95). There is thus a 'power to' in addition to Weber's classic notion of 'power over'. In so far as every actor is powerful in the sense of 'power to', every actor has some degree of agency. In the next section, we will scrutinise the concept of agency more carefully; the key point here is that domination can no longer be taken for granted because the compliance of the dominated is never a given.

Various writers agree that Marx's 'dominant ideology thesis' – that 'the ideas of the ruling class are in every epoch the ruling ideas' (Marx and Engels 1965) – must be rejected (Abercrombie *et al.* 1980; de Certeau 1984; Giddens 1979, p. 72; Scott 1985, p. 317; 1990; Willis 1977). One must not overestimate the degree of conviction with which all members of society (subordinate and even dominant) accept symbol-systems. Subordinate groups within society understand to some degree how existing ideologies and institutions attempt to oppress them and can formulate skilled tactics of resistance. However, acts of resistance elude researchers because authorities control the dominant modes of discourse. Peasants, proletarians and other 'dominated' people often live on the margins of subsistence, where even small favours can make a significant difference. In such a context of insecurity, it is in the best interests of the weak to act with obedience (Abercrombie *et al.* 1980, p. 50; Scott 1985, p. 278). Thus, the 'public transcript' is saturated with acts of submission performed in bad faith. The weapons of the weak breed in private and the tactics are petty, anonymous, but multiple and multi-sited.

Stoked by new theories of power, agency and ideology, and perhaps the chic currency of 'resistance' in other disciplines, archaeologists began documenting resistance to authority in a number of contexts (Beaudry *et al.* 1991; Braithwaite 1984; Brumfiel 1996; Ferguson 1991; Hutson 2002a; Joyce 1993; Joyce *et al.* 2001; Little 1997; McCafferty and McCafferty 1988; 1991; McGuire and Paynter 1991; Miller and Tilley 1984; Miller *et al.* 1989; Orser 1991; Paynter 1989; Pyburn *et al.* 1998; Shackel 2000). Archaeologists would seem to have an advantage over other disciplines in detecting resistance when it takes the form of everyday, often material practices that do not appear in public representations/symbol systems and do not enter the historical transcript. In his excavations of the 19th-century brewery at Harper's Ferry, West Virginia, Shackel (2000) detected hundreds of hidden beer bottles. Because the bottles were hidden, Shackel concludes that the workers covertly consumed the products of their labour, thus drinking the owner's profits (see also Beaudry *et al.* 1991). Shackel also noticed the curious trend of workers' wives buying pottery styles that were out of fashion. Shackel argues that the preference for older styles reflects a nostalgia for previous generations when access to markets and a more favourable division of labour gave women more control over their everyday lives. The preference for outdated styles may also reflect a rejection or lack of commitment to the current industrial era and ideology which reduced their power and control. Shackel's study encourages us in that he finds the voice of groups who are partially muted because they must express themselves through goods whose production was controlled by the dominant group (Little 1997).

Shackel's study also illustrates the irony of resistance (see also Pauketat 2000). Because subordinates do not know everything about the system that oppresses them, their actions have unintended and unwelcome effects (Willis 1977). The stealing and drinking of beer on the job contributed to a higher incidence of work-place injuries. Through a subtle jujitsu, the 'system' uses the resistors' momentum to bring them down (Kearney 1996, p. 155).

Though historical archaeologists like Shackel have produced many notable studies of resistance, archaeologists without written texts have also contributed important case studies. In ancient Mesoamerica, space has been a key element in methods used for documenting the recursivity of domination and resistance. For example, Joyce *et al.* (2001) note that common folk at the regional centre of Rio Viejo, on the Pacific coast of Oaxaca, Mexico, inhabited the monumental platforms of the site's civic-ceremonial centre after the collapse of centralised institutions at the end of the Classic period. According to Joyce *et al.* (2001), these commoners rejected the dominant ideology of the previous era by dismantling and denigrating the architecture and carved stones that once valorised and materialised that ideology. Likewise, Brumfiel (1996) argues that powerful Aztec ideologies of male dominance expressed in official carvings at the capital city are contested in the countryside by popular images that assert the high status of women in reproductive roles.

We applaud the studies profiled above for developing robust approaches to power relations in the past. Nevertheless, we fear that domination and resistance can be 'bad subjects' (Hutson 2002a; Meskell 1996) if they come at the expense of the balance and rigour of a more nuanced approach (Brown 1996). Politics are often multidimensional: an approach that views them through the binary lens of domination and resistance unjustly simplifies and sanitises their coarse texture

Agency and practice

(Ortner 1995). As Shackel admits, 19th-century domestic consumption is complex and not easily reduced to statements of power. The assumption that differences in consumption or foodways relate directly to power struggles (see, for example, Ferguson 1991) disregards the cultural complexity of the context under examination. By not attending to the meaning of such differences, we threaten to dissolve the subjectivity, intentionality and identity of the dominated. Joyce prudently negates the top-down approach to power. The people reoccupying the Rio Viejo acropolis lived rich and meaningful lives: to study them only as resistors flattens this richness and presumes that they existed only as a foil to the intentions of the elite few.

Agency

The theme of agency has attracted much interest in recent debates in archaeology (Arnold 2001; Silliman 2001; Smith 2001; papers in Dobres and Robb 2000a), but it remains apparent that agency means different things to different researchers. We focus on three broad, internally diverse and sometimes overlapping categories. In the first category, we find an antihumanism, which maintains that agency works through individuals, rather than being wielded or exerted by them (Dobres and Robb 2000b). In fact, the individual human agent we know today is merely a product (and a recent, post-medieval one at that!) of various disciplinary technologies which gain a life of their own (Foucault 1977). Disciplinary norms create a body politic – an orthodoxy of bodily practices, such as posture, gait and gesture, and a schedule for their appropriate display – and it is through the disciplinary norms that actions become intelligible.

Thus, in the writing of Foucault (prior to his final work on the history of sexuality) and other post-structuralists, particularly Lacan, 'discourse', language, and symbols precede the agent and produce the conditions for the possibility of agency. The agent is merely a precipitate of pre-existing 'texts'.

Though we agree with the need to deconstruct the modern enlightenment conception of humanity and to expose it as a construct of various processes, we note that such approaches lack a mechanism of change and minimise the space for intentionality. Working within the Foucaultian model, however, Judith Butler (1993, pp. 12–15; 1998, p. 157) finds room for agency in her idea of citationality, derived from Derrida's notion of iterations. Each action, Butler argues, is only an imperfect citation of the norm. This discrepancy between practice and norm, as well as the time that intervenes between one practice and the next – the open-endedness of citationality – assures the generation of new meanings and the reformulation of norms. Butler cautiously circumscribes the scope of this form of agency. Norms do not simply specify models to which acts conform; the norms mobilise action, and no act stands alone – every act is a reiteration in the tracks of previous iterations. Agency in this first sense is thus not some kind of voluntaristic operation in opposition to structures or norms: 'the subject who resists such norms is enabled, if not produced, by the norms' (Butler 1993, p. 15). In archaeology, recent work by Rosemary Joyce, discussed in the next chapter, deploys this notion of agency.

The second group of approaches to agency focuses more closely on the impact of action on others and on the material world. These consequences can be intended or unintended (see below) and they can be short, medium or long term. They can be local or 'global'. Perhaps the main way that this impact-view of agency has been used in archaeology is in terms of 'power over' (see pp. 85 and 96). Dominant groups are described constructing a monument, controlling exchange, or holding a ritual that persuades others or manipulates them ideologically. Or elites may control the labour of others through the use of force. In these cases, there is almost no attempt to infer the intention of the actors: it is simply assumed that the outcome – domination – and the intention were the same. Since the specific intention or meaning behind the action is of little concern, analysis focuses narrowly on the effects of actions (see Earle 1990; Barrett 1994, p. 1).

Impact is certainly a component of agency, but the third use of the term (the use favoured here) is that agency has something to do with intentional action. Let us take an extreme example which highlights the need to consider intentionality. A passer-by crosses the road and catches a bullet that was meant for a president. The unintended consequence of this happenstance may be considerable. So there was much 'agency' according to our second definition. But the only intentionality involved on the side of the passer-by was to cross the road. To focus on the third definition of 'agency' creates a very different picture of history.

The original aim of discussing agency in the earlier editions of this book was to focus attention on meaning. This was in response to the behaviourist dimension of much processual archaeology in which people played little role. The emphasis was on the systems behind action and on the resources needed for action. In our view, some recent discussions of agency (e.g. Barrett 1994) focus too much on the conditions needed for action and not enough on a people-centred approach in which intentionality is important.

The third sense of agency can be discussed further by considering the rather provocative views held by Latour (1996; 1999), Gell (1998) and Weiner (1992) that objects can have agency. What is meant by such a claim? Let us consider the example of the speed bump. The object may cause motorists to slow down and therefore it has agency in the second sense above – it has an impact on people's lives. In the case of the speed bump, the object has an impact on us because of its physicality as an impediment that blocks us and can damage our vehicle. On the other hand, the speed bump was placed there by someone in authority. There is an intention lying behind it and a sanctioning that derives from the speed bump's association with the project and goals of law enforcement.

But in considering the relationship between agency and intentionality, we need to discuss different aspects of intentionality. We can again be assisted here by considering the agency of objects. Let us observe some actual anthropological examples of objects having agency through their connections to people. Many objects in different societies are media through which spirits or supernatural powers can act, as in Gell's (1998) discussion of art that is seen as apotropaic in that it protects members of society from illness or evil spirits, etc. Weiner (1992) argues that objects are embedded in social relations, in the sense that a valuable in the Kula gift exchange in the Trobriand islands carries a history of associations with past possessors. Objects have a life span and acquire personal histories. Thomas (1996, pp. 80, 153) points out that such objects do not merely symbolise, they embody a force which calls to mind social relationships and which makes visible the richness of intangible history. In some societies, these objects are significant neither as embodiments of historical relations and networks between other people, nor as the media for non-corporeal essences – spirits and supernaturals – residing elsewhere, but as real, animate people who have the power to act in the world as humans do (Appadurai 1986, p. 4; Monaghan 1998). In all such cases the objects (appear to) have intentionality because they bring to mind associations that are meaningful to the person affected by the object.

Indeed much intentional action only has effects because it is perceived to be agentful. Thus we 'give' powers to others and to objects such that they can act on us. Much ideology works in this way. So in exploring agency as intentional action we need to recognise two phases – the intentionality of an actor before or within an act, and the ascription of intentionality to an act by participants or observers.

In fact it may be useful to try and break down agency into some of its component parts, arranged temporally. While this can only be a brief and partial exercise here, the attempt points to the complexity of the processes summarised by the term 'agency'. It becomes quickly clear that even the simplest acts involve many complex stages. Archaeological discussion of agency has often been at cross-purposes because the different stages and dimensions of agency have not been distinguished.

As examples we can consider an individual joining a group of potters to make a pot, or a person working in a group by contributing earth to a ritual monument, or someone adding an item to a grave. Minimally such actions involve the following stages.

1 Positioning and assessment. This involves (a) having general knowledge about how to make pots and being positioned in society to be able to get access to such knowledge and the material resources needed to make a pot. There is thus a need for power/knowledge. To focus on such issues is to focus on the conditions for action (Barrett 1994): the conditioning allows 'correct' evaluations and situates the actor in a position to act. (b) However much general power/knowledge is available, there is a need to assess each particular situation to see which class of situations it fits. What is the purpose of the group of potters one is about to join, or what is the aim of this particular monument, building or burial? The evaluation thus involves a personal judgment of the intentions of others.

2 There is development of an intention to act, although this may happen prior to (1) and form as a part of (1) and it may influence (1). The intention may be socially derived or it may be highly idiosyncratic; it may be unconsciously or non-discursively formulated.

3 Then there is a doing or saying on the basis of (1) and in relation to some intention (2).

4 The impact of the action is evaluated and responded to both at the social level (the effect on others and on one's own social experience) and at the individual level (in terms of particular aims and intentions). Again, power is involved – for example, the ability to collect information which enables monitoring to take place depends on access to resources.

Looking through this exercise, we can make a number of points. First, throughout all stages, power, knowledge and meanings seem to be involved. Second, agency has unacknowledged conditions and unintended consequences. An agent may be situated so as to have only partial knowledge of a situation. Owing to incomplete knowledge, action may have unintended outcomes. As McCall (cited in Dobres and Robb 2000b, p. 10) notes, unintended outcomes occur not simply when an actor's plan goes awry, but 'in the unwitting reproduction of all the social contexts within which the actor's intentions and strategies make sense' (see also Bourdieu 1977, pp. 52, 65).

Third, throughout the stages, there is an interplay between agent and society. As discussed earlier, we are not presuming that the agent is an individual in a Western sense. Indeed, following the first view of agency, the degree of self-hood ascribed to an agent is one of the frameworks of meaning within which agency has effects. These considerations highlight the cultural and historical malleability of what we call 'the person'. Different cultures and ages not only attribute personhood to different things (and not all biological humans are guaranteed personhood), but construct different criteria for where a person begins and where a person ends. In other words, as we discuss in the next chapter, the boundary around the self is not isomorphic with the biological body, which is itself culturally and historically mutable.

Fourth, it has been possible to describe the components of agency without any reference to 'free will'. The notion of free will is undoubtedly influenced by notions of the individual as able to act 'outside society'. In our view, there can be no 'free will' in this sense. One's thoughts, words, perceptions and intentions are inseparable from, though they cannot be reduced to, society.

Fifth, agency is a characteristic of individuals, not groups. Clearly many individual acts derive their force from being situated within the actions of larger groups. But to say that groups have agency is to take the argument back close to the view of individuals as passively determined by larger forces. Individuals often act in groups, and their actions are always social. But the actions of groups are built from the reflexive agency of individuals. Group action is thus a form of individual agency. The group is a resource for the individual agent.

Finally, we must reiterate the complexity of social action. We are not prescribing a fixed definition of agency: each of the points above are heuristic devices that contain a degree of uncertainty. Agency is created within history and must be understood on a case by case basis (Barrett 2000). Acknowledging the uncertainty and historically situated nature of agency is necessary if we wish to avoid the careless association of agency with androcentrism, individualism, neo-liberalism, etc. (Gero 2000; Dobres and Robb 2000b).

6 Embodied archaeology

Many of the approaches considered thus far – processual-ism, structuralism, Marxism – lack adequate consideration of the agent. This lacuna was filled in part by the discussion of agency in the concluding section of the previous chapter. Nevertheless, a close reading of that section shows that in our presentation of different forms of agency, we never paid close attention to the nature of the agent that exercises (or is exercised by) agency. We were careful not to presume that the agent is always an individual in a Western sense and we argued for the cultural and historical malleability of 'the person', but we have yet to consider what might be dangerous about the term 'individual' or what justification we might have in claiming that the 'person' and its close relatives the 'self' and the 'subject' are so malleable.

To explore the nature of the agent, however, is not simply to add the finishing touches to an account of agency or structuration. In archaeology, theories of practice contain flaws that no amount of tinkering or refinement will eliminate. In other words, practice does not make perfect. Both Giddens and Bourdieu have increasingly come under attack in the social sciences (e.g. Turner 1994), the main criticism being that they do not in the end provide an adequate theory of the subject and of agency. Though we find in Bourdieu the elements of a rather sophisticated theory of the subject, we agree that both his and Giddens' notions of structure leave little room for transformative action. In search of alternative theories of the subject, various archaeologists have turned to phenomenology. Many phenomenologists believe that we relate to the world not through detached, pensive reflection – not by creating internal representations of things outside of us – but by a more basic, bodily understanding gained through years of dwelling. This 'dwelling' is often referred to as 'being-in-the-world'. Though we do think abstractly, perhaps when reading this book, our prior existence and orientation with the world gives us the footing necessary for reflection. The phenomenological turn has had the salutary effect of challenging dichotomies between subject/object and nature/culture, but, as we hope to demonstrate, archaeological uses of phenomenology have in some cases re-installed some of these Cartesian dualisms, created a very one-sided subject, or have failed to address the transformative capacities of the agent.

Regardless of these shortcomings, which we will discuss in greater detail below, phenomenology as well as feminist critiques sensitise us to the importance of the body, since lived experience derives from the body being in the world. Themes concerning bodies and embodiment have been popular for some time in many other fields, such as philosophy, literature, cultural studies, queer theory and anthropology, and are a welcome addition to archaeology. In this chapter, we demonstrate the importance of the body and we present exemplary archaeological case studies concerned with embodiment. Of course, too much has been said about bodies to summarise here (see Hamilakis *et al.* 2002; Meskell 1996; 1999 for extended treatment of the body and archaeology). To use an idiom familiar to and in accord with phenomenology, our goal is not to map the entire terrain of scholarship on the body, but to take a specific, partial path through the theories of the body afforded by this terrain. Our destination will be slightly different from and hopefully preferable to those reached thus far.

Materiality and malleability

In the study of gender, there was once a consensus that sex was biological, natural and therefore fixed, whereas gender was fluid: a socially contingent, reversible reading of the 'facts' of the body. Gender could change as often as one's clothes, but sex was unalterable because bodily facts were said to be physical – natural. Beginning in the 1980s, various writers (Butler 1990; Fausto-Sterling 1985; Keller 1985; Wittig 1985) argued that sex was not natural, forcing a destabilisation of the sex/gender dichotomy. We will soon return to this 'denaturalisation' of sex; what interests us now is the place of the body in such schemes. The body was seen as given in nature, physically immutable. The body snugly occupied the 'nature' side of the nature:culture dichotomy and thus served as a stable foundation for a variety of similar dichotomies, such as sex:gender, matter:mind, object:subject. Classic works by Marcel Mauss and Norbert Elias start us off in denaturalising the body.

In *The History of Manners*, Elias (1994 [1936]) documents a pattern of 'decisive changes in human beings' in 16th-, 17th- and 18th-century Europe. Among other things, it became bad manners to urinate and defecate openly in front of others, to blow one's nose in one's hand, to eat from a communal plate without a fork. Up until the sixteenth century, 'the sight of nakedness was an everyday rule' (p. 135). Such shifts do not merely reflect changes in attitudes to the body: Elias argues that changes in eating, sleeping, spitting and toilet indicate the growth of barriers and boundaries between one body and the next: a growing consciousness of the body itself.

In archaeology, Treherne's (1995) study of the practices of the body and the self in the European Bronze Age complements Elias' work. Treherne asks why toilet articles such as tweezers and razors appear at a particular moment in prehistory and shows that such items are connected to a changing aesthetics of the body. Part of the rise and transformation of a male warrior status group, the new aesthetics focuses on the 'warrior's beauty and his beautiful death'. This aesthetic, along with the intensification of additional activities such as warfare, the hunt and bodily ornamentation, created a distinctive form of self-identity.

In his essay 'Techniques of the Body', Mauss (1973 [1935]) argued that bodily functions (walking, swimming, sleeping, giving birth) must be learned, and because they are learned, there is no natural adult body. The techniques of the body differ by sex, age, culture and more. Some of Mauss' conclusions may seem obvious but his discussion of the hold that these techniques have on our bodies – 'In my days, swimmers thought of themselves as a kind of steamboat. It was stupid, but in fact I still do this: I cannot get rid of my technique' (p. 71) – is precocious. In describing this hold, he coined the term 'habitus' and alluded to physiological, psychological, and social factors that determine which techniques will be imitated.

Elias and Mauss show that the body has a history and a geography; it is different across time and space. Poststructural writers have reiterated the same point, whether it be Foucault's insistence that the body is produced by the politics of the age or Lacan's insistence that the body is constituted by language, not given at birth (Moore 1994, p. 143). We will review both of these positions in more detail below, but for now the major point is that 'neither our personal bodies nor our social bodies may be seen as natural, in the sense of existing outside the self-creating process called human labor' (Haraway 1991, p. 10).

If the body is no longer natural, a number of dichotomies disappear. Let us return to the dichotomy between sex and gender. Judith Butler and Thomas Laqueur both provide cogent challenges to this dichotomy by questioning whether biological sex is truly natural. If sex is said to be given in nature, how is it given? Butler (1990, p. 7) responds that sex is in fact 'given' by gender. For Butler, gender is akin to cultural ideas about sex. In her own words, gender is 'the discursive/cultural means by which sexed nature or "a natural sex" is produced and established as prediscursive, prior to culture, a politically neutral surface on which culture acts'. Sex is given by gender because gender – our ideas about sex – motivates studies that naturalise sex, or causes us to think that differences between the two sexes are biologically fixed in nature. For example, in biological research, gendered assumptions about sex skew laboratory investigations into the factors that determine whether a person is male or female. A 1987 study declared that sex was determined by a DNA sequence that governs the development of testes. The presence of this sequence results in males; the absence in females. When it was determined, however, that this sequence was found in both X and Y chromosomes, the researcher speculated that what mattered was that the sequence was active in men, but passive in females. Clearly a gender ideology which sees males as present and active and females as absent and passive guided both the research design and the formulation of the results. Why does research on sex determination always focus on the testes when we know that ovaries are just as actively produced in the process of development (Fausto-Sterling 1989)?

Thomas Laqueur notes that ovaries were only given a name of their own relatively recently: two thousand years ago, anatomists such as Galen used the word for testes to refer to the ovaries (1990, pp. 4–5). The same word was appropriate for both men and women because, prior to the Enlightenment, women's genitals were understood to be the same as men's: the only difference was that women, lacking heat, held their genitalia inside the body. For two millennia there was only one sex, the male sex, and women were considered less perfect, less vital versions of men. What we would call biological sex was flexible, dependent upon sociological matters that we would call gender. For instance, if men spent too much time with women 'they would lose the hardness and definition of their more perfect bodies' (1990, p. 7). One might object, however, that all this is irrelevant. Thanks to scientific anatomy, which exposed these quaint musings as nonsense, our current understandings of sexual difference directly reflect biological reality. But Laqueur shows that the Enlightenment switch from a one-sex to a two-sex world preceded any anatomical discoveries or advances in our understanding of biological reality. New ways of interpreting the body were not the consequence of increased scientific knowledge: they are the results of epistemological and political developments (p. 10). In fact, theories of sexual difference – what we might call 'gender' – greatly influenced the course of scientific progress (p. 16). This is not to deny the biological reality of difference and sameness between bodies. It does mean, however, that things outside of empirical investigation determine which differences and similarities count and which ones are ignored.

Nature, then, is not natural. It is produced, and its production is always strategic because particular definitions of nature benefit particular interests and actors in society. In this sense, Butler and Laqueur work from some of Foucault's central lessons. Bodies only gain sex through professional (i.e. scholarly) discourses on sexuality, and are therefore only intelligible within systems of meaning. Though 'women' certainly existed in Ancient Greece, the notion of a second sex was simply unthinkable and therefore abject: outside of the prevailing discourse and the subjects it produced.

These approaches have the potential to challenge conventional prehistories and allow the past to be truly different, rather than a different version of ourselves (Joyce 2000, p. 1). The two quite different case studies that follow illustrate the breadth of work possible within this paradigm. Timothy Yates (1990; 1993) notes that in rock carvings from Bronze Age Sweden, *c.* 1000 B.C., sexual identities 'are not regulated in the way that we, in our society, would recognize as natural'. Previous interpretations of heterosexual 'marriage scenes' – in which figures identified as a man and a woman embrace – fail at both empirical and theoretical levels. At the empirical level, Yates notes that in some scenes, both figures have penises. Furthermore, all proposed schemes for identifying females, when applied systematically, run into the problem of identifying phallic figures as women. On the theoretical level, these problems are created by the assumption that sex is naturally heterosexual and limited to male or female. Yates argues that we should instead treat the body not as a natural category, but as an historical one formed through discourse. In other words, masculine identity in the carvings, for example, can only be achieved by applying signs to the surface of the body, and these signs can be detached, as seen in the free-floating calf muscles in a rock carving at Hogdal. If we treat sexuality and the body not as fixed, but as fluid and in the process of becoming, odd scenes such as men copulating with deer and humans becoming animals cease to appear unnatural or unorthodox. Rather, they are in conformity to radically different logics that question our modern conceptions of humanity, further exposing it not as natural but as a discursive construct.

Rosemary Joyce (1998; 1999; 2000) also notices past practices that force a radical reformulation of the sex/gender distinction. However, she calls attention to materiality as a strategy through which discourse can naturalise and normalise particular views of the body. Joyce (1998, p. 148) argues that human images from Prehispanic Central America actively constituted theories of the body and its limits and subdivisions. Citing Herzfeld and Laqueur, Joyce notes that because the representations were of the body, which is a 'natural' as opposed to an 'abstract' object, they lend themselves an aura of objectivity, which makes them more easy to accept as appropriate models of and for beauty. As in all discourses, some representations of the body were materialised, others excluded. Thus only a small fraction of the fleeting postures, practices and bodily actions of everyday life were re-enacted in durable media. Since these representations were executed in permanent material such as fired-clay figurines, inscribed stone and painted pottery, they would have been a lasting subject of commentary. The permanence of these particular readings of the body reinforces and naturalises the status quo.

From an archaeology of the body to embodiment

As we noted above and as Joyce's work demonstrates, discourse does not simply produce the body: it also provides a set of representations that make the body intelligible and make the order established by these representations seem normal and natural. This study of the effectiveness of representation should not be confused, however, with studies that focus on the body itself as a representation or symbol (Douglas 1970; Scheper-Hughes and Lock 1987). In the well-trodden path of symbolic anthropology, the body may be seen as a model of (and a model for) anything from cosmology, to culture, to nature, to social relations. In archaeology, Thomas and Tilley (1993) offer an interesting example in which the body and its anatomy are taken up into the symbolic domain. They argue that certain motifs carved on the stones of passage graves in Brittany during the 4th and 5th millennia B.C. represent torsos, breasts and ribs (as opposed to the bucklers, cupmarks and crooks identified by earlier analysts). Based on the patterned distribution of these body parts and their degree of articulation and disarticulation, Thomas and Tilley (p. 261) believe that passage graves such as Mane Lud and Gavrinas contain narratives of breaking up, decay and disintegration, which parallels what happens to the buried ancestors themselves. In some cases, the pictorial narrative of disintegration ends in a conglomerate of bones that form a social body (Gavrinas) or the regeneration of an individual, articulated, fleshy torso (Les Pierres Plattes). Thomas and Tilley argue that these pictorial narratives were experienced as a part of rites of passage, and that the transformation and regeneration of the physical body is symbolic of the regeneration of society (pp. 269, 275).

Thomas and Tilley argue that the meanings of the tomb art could only be fully appreciated after seeing many tombs. This challenges systemic interpretations in which each passage grave is said to reflect an autonomous, isolated social group and in which passage graves are said to function as markers of a group's claim to the surrounding land. We applaud Thomas and Tilley's attention to meaning, but note that their interpretation of torsos objectifies the body as a thing devoid of intentionality and intersubjectivity (Csordas 1995, p. 4).

This process of objectification brings up the important distinction between the archaeology of the body and the archaeology of embodiment. An archaeology of the body sees the body as an object of culture: as a sign or tool. On the other hand, an archaeology of embodiment sees the body as the subject of culture: only through dwelling in the world do we get a feel for signs and tools and come to recognise them as objects. For example, we recognise a boulder as an object only through the intentional act of surmounting it (Csordas 1990, p. 10). To give a second example, only through using our hands are we able to recognise them as objects. To 'use' is thus not to interact with an object, but to bring about both self and object through engagement in a task (Ingold 2000, p. 352). Thus, objectification is the end result of intentionally guided projects that we engage in as part of being and surviving in the world (Heidegger 1996). The body is not simply a tool whose varied techniques enable us to live, as per Mauss, but the 'original substance out of which the human world is shaped' (Csordas 1995, p. 6). We can objectify the body but seldom are we disengaged enough to do so, and never prior to inhabiting the world – being caught up in intentional actions and practices. In other words, we can treat the body as an object only because it is always already a subject. A dichotomy between subject and object is thus impossible to maintain.

If culture is grounded in the human body, then any account of past cultural meaning must attempt to reconstruct sensual experience and the body as lived (Kus 1992). Before commenting on archaeological studies of embodiment, however, we will use literature from psychology, psychoanalytic theory and philosophy to explain what it means to live through the body and why bodily experience is important.

James Gibson (1966), a pioneer of ecological psychology, proposed many decades ago that the media through which we perceive and gain information about ourselves ('propriospecific' information) are the same media that we use to perceive the environment 'exterior' to the self. In fact, Gibson argued that vision, once thought to be of most importance in perceiving things 'exterior' to the body, is also the most important faculty in learning the body itself (Bermudez 1995, p. 154). Furthermore, things that are not part of our body help us develop a sense of our body. In other words, our understanding of our physical existence in space is not simply 'given internally by a kinesthetic sense mediated by muscle and joint receptors' (Butterworth 1995, p. 88): we also become aware of our movements and positioning through visual, auditory and tactile cues 'outside' of the body. Gibson's proposal has since been strengthened by various studies of developing embryos, infants and children (Bermudez 1995; Butterworth 1995; Russell 1995). Since we come to know ourselves by using the same tools that we use to gain experience of other things, and since experience of other things helps us experience ourselves, the development of a sense of self is a product of experience in the world. Our sense of self is not formed prior to an 'encounter' with the world, because there is no 'encounter' as such. We are always already in relation with the world and our awareness of our body is built as part of this relation.

Object relations theorists have made similar points. In the intellectual history of psychoanalysis, object relations theory arose in opposition to Freud's idea that the quality of mental life depends upon the satisfaction of internal drives, such as the death drive and the libido. Object relations theorists such as D. W. Winnicott and Erik Erikson suggested instead that relations with other things and other people, particularly the mother, were most important for mental and social development. We will return to the relational notion of the self in the next section, but at this point we emphasise the fundamental linkage between self formation and the environment (Elliott 1994, p. 64). Even if successful mothering enables an infant to build a stable sense of self, the infant 'is not yet capable of forming fully fledged social relationships. Caught in an imaginary realm of illusory omnipotence, the small infant is unable to recognize that it does not create and control the world' (Elliott 1994, p. 69). According to Winnicott, the infant orients itself to outer reality through transitional objects such as blankets or toys. These objects are transitional because the infant feels that it creates them, but also comes to realise that they are separate from the self, and therefore belonging to and representing a world outside the self. In the transitional space, objects are not 'encountered' but learned and made.

In the paragraphs above, we have put quotations around the words 'outside' and 'exterior' because of a series of findings summarised by Lakoff and Johnson in their book *Philosophy in the Flesh* (1999). We have known, at least since John Locke, that things like colour have no independent 'exterior' or 'outside' reality. Colour is a product not only of lighting conditions, the reflective properties of an object's surface, and wavelengths of electromagnetic radiation: it is also a product of our neural circuitry. Colour is therefore an interaction between our brain and other qualities; a product of our embodiment. But Locke argued that colour was a special case, different from a world of concrete objects said to exist 'independent of any perceiver' (p. 26). Lakoff and Johnson show, however, that all phenomena – even the most concrete of objects – are interactional. 'The qualities of things as we can experience and comprehend them depend crucially on our neural makeup, our bodily interactions with them and our purposes and interests' (p. 26). To give an example, spatial relations such as 'in front of' are not objectively there in the world. The teacher is in front of the class only relative to our ability to project a front to a classroom. Perceiving a teacher as being in front of the class is a fictive projection resulting from our embodied nature (p. 35).

These points have archaeological counterparts. In his interpretation of Avebury, Barrett (1994, p. 18) stresses that the physical form of the monument itself does not create an orientation: the way humans position themselves in relation to the monument does. Tilley's analysis of Swedish megaliths (1994, p. 73) also stresses embodied positionings; though monuments create axes of vision, some monuments do so only when people interact with them. Commenting on the interactional construction of objects, Thomas (1996) notes that Neolithic exchange goods such as maceheads, carved stone balls and chalk drums became powerful and desirable not because of essential qualities in the artifacts themselves but because of their engagement with the people who gave and received them. 'Artifacts are never abstracted things, but always a part of a mobile set of social relationships maintained between persons and things' (p. 159).

Having questioned the boundary between things and people and the distinction between interior and exterior, we must now reconsider the dichotomy between perception and conceptualisation (Lakoff and Johnson 1999, p. 38). In much of the Western philosophical tradition, the bodily senses are said to guide perception, but concepts, though informed by perception, are said to be guided by reason. However, studies in neuroscience show that reason is embodied, thus erasing the dichotomy. It appears that the same nerve systems that allow perception also allow conceptualisation. This may explain why embodied, sensorimotor domains shape the way we think about even our most abstract, 'mental' concepts and experiences, such as morality, intimacy and importance. For example, the abstract concept of 'understanding' is often conceptualised in terms of sensorimotor actions, such as grasping. The point is not simply that subjective experience is understood through bodily metaphors, but that these metaphors are 'acquired automatically and unconsciously simply by functioning in ordinary ways in the everyday world from our earliest years' (pp. 46–7). For infants, the subjective experience of affection is associated (and later conflated metaphorically) with the bodily sensation of warmth, from a hug.

Many of the findings above effectively license the well-rehearsed tenets of phenomenology. Maurice Merleau-Ponty (1962) famously argued that the body is known only through our interactions with the things around us. Heidegger, influenced by pragmatists, felt that pure consciousness, detached from things, did not exist (Dreyfus 1991, p. 6). Our body and these things are co-produced through being in the world. For example, a river guides our intentions to build a bridge, but our intention to cross gathers the opposed shorelines into being as a connected pair: it unites two river banks that would not otherwise be associated (Heidegger 1971, p. 152).

Though Heidegger (1996) felt that most of the skills and practices that enable us to cope in the world remain in a background of which we are not discursively conscious (see also Taylor 1999), he felt that this background could be successfully analysed and he coined many new words to help conceptualise it. However, critics believe that phenomenological introspection will not uncover the nature of experience. Much of our experience and perception is automatic, beyond conscious control. Neuroscientists agree that only 2 per cent of what the brain does enters our conscious awareness (Gazzaniga 1998, p. 21). Furthermore, phenomenological knowledge misperceives the objective conditions that make experience possible. Though feminist critiques of science have rightly noted that our ways of seeing cannot be entirely cut loose from our situated positions in the world, we must escape the narrow focus of seeing things only through the body if we hope to build a more robust account of social life (Bourdieu 1977, p. 3; Latour 1999, p. 9). Given these refinements, we find the term 'embodied' preferable to 'phenomenological'.

Our brief tour of psychological and neurological literature shows a convergence with that of embodied philosophies (see also Ingold 2000, p. 173). Given the support of these other fields, philosophies of embodiment are in some sense no longer 'just philosophies'.

Archaeologists often approach embodiment through the study of landscape, assuming that practical engagement with the surroundings creates our visions of the world (Ingold 1995). Mark Edmonds (1999) makes impressive use of a landscape perspective in his book *Ancestral Geographies of the Neolithic*. Unlike other landscape studies which focus on sacred or monumental places (Barrett 1994; Tilley 1994), Edmonds also considers the quotidian and explores routine activities occurring in everyday contexts. Felling trees to create a track, clearing space for a camp, or tending and reworking land all leave long-term marks on the landscape; living and learning among these meaningful marks shapes the inhabitants' sense of self. Yet these marks are not symbols understood through purely cognitive operations (Ingold 2000, p. 148). They are meaningful because attention has been trained to notice them by *inhabiting* the same land: by engaging in activities that require some of the same environmental sensitivities. Places and people mutually construct biographies, yet just as no two biographies are alike, the same place is experienced differently by different people. The memories we forge through inhabiting a landscape vary from person to person because each person dwells in that landscape differently:

at different times of the year, with different people, while doing different things, and through different subject positions with regard to gender, age, class, etc. (pp. 111–13; see also Thomas 1996, p. 180).

Despite its advances, Edmonds' account shares with other phenomenological case studies in British prehistory a folksy complacence about the creation of a sense of place (Hodder 1999b). His poetic accounts of being on the land and its familiarly named landmarks cultivate a rural nostalgia. The past is like taking a walk in the country or chopping wood in the forest. This kind of familiarity with the past is even more clear in Tilley's account of the Neolithic Dorset cursus, in which we indeed follow Tilley on a walk. We regard Tilley's book *A Phenomenology of Landscape* as a pathbreaking and highly praiseworthy attempt to introduce phenomenology into archaeology. Yet as with any incipient approach, there are many issues in need of refinement. Tilley's book (1994) builds his interpretations on the basis of his own bodily interaction with the features along the route of the cursus: 'walking down into the boggy depths of the valley provides a sensation of the entire world being removed' (p. 181). Our own personal sensations are assumed to be isomorphic with the bodily sensations of subjects who lived thousands of years ago. A universal body responding to stimuli in universal ways substitutes for the thorny specificities of lived bodies (Hodder 1999a, p. 136). The promotion of an uncritical, self-evident connection with the past sits uneasily with contemporary politics in which multiple stakeholders lay claim to prehistory.

Often, archaeological studies of the body emphasise purely physical, embodied actions without considering the meaning that such actions may have had. In his treatment of Cranborne Chase in the Neolithic and Bronze Age, for instance, Gosden (1994) speculates that monuments such as the Dorset cursus added a sense of regularity to the timing of activities since the charting of astronomical bodies with the cursus involved repeated visits, accompanied, presumably, by repeated ceremonies. Gosden argues that this sense of regularity stood in stark contrast to Neolithic subsistence activities, which were sporadic and scattered in time and space. As the rhythm of habitual practices at the cursus regimented the bodies of Neolithic actors, the learned sense of regularity began to shape the timing and location of other activities, thus leading to a more settled, predictable life in the Bronze Age. Gosden has given an excellent account of embodiment. In his account, the body is the subject of culture: the existential grounds through which order is reproduced. Yet the 'actors' in this account seem rather machinelike: there is no intentionality or meaning behind action. Despite trying to eliminate the mind–body dichotomy, this study risks reinstating it by stressing only mechanical, physical activities in space and time (Hodder 1999b, p. 137).

Another prominent feature of the phenomenological approach in archaeology is the way in which landscapes and monuments create power relations (Barrett 1994, p. 29; Smith 1999). According to Tilley (1994, p. 11), 'because space is differentially understood and experienced, it forms a contradictory and conflict-ridden medium through which individuals act and are acted upon'. Despite this well-grounded declaration of the multiplicity of lived experience, Tilley concludes that Neolithic monuments 'are about establishing control over topographic perspective and the individual's possibilities for interpreting the world' (p. 204). According to Brück (2001, p. 652), the idea that the layout of architecture constrains action and interpretation – that 'human bodies were ordered, regulated, and categorized through the segmentation of space and construction of bodily movement' – presumes a modern Western account of the body and personhood as a bounded, individuated, manipulable entity. If we get away from the idea of the person as a stable entity with a unified, essential core, and move towards a vision of the self as embedded in spatially and temporally dispersed relations with other people and things, then we see how each person will have complex and divergent understandings of the world, which ensure interpretations of monuments that diverge from the controlling interpretation (pp. 654–5). Following Edmonds (1999) and Bender (1993, p. 275), Brück (2001, p. 660) interprets the variability of deposits in the ditches at Mount Pleasant, Dorset, as a 'cacophony of voices', each telling a different tale, not necessarily orchestrated by a dominant power.

The limits of the body

Brück's account of Mount Pleasant depends on the capability of distinguishing the individual activities that contribute to the formation of each deposit. Discerning individual actions and lives located in particular times and places is of utmost importance because individual negotiations are central to understanding how actors draw upon long-term structures in the practices of daily life (Hodder 1999, pp. 136–7; Meskell 1998a). However, the same individual subject can take on different identities (Thomas 1996, p. 180) and an individual is itself a larger whole constructed from individual events. We cannot assume that the multiple acts and identities of a subject will always amount to 'an individual' in the sense of a distinctive pattern of behaviour associated with a single body (Hodder 2000, p. 25). Finally if places, things and people mutually bring each other into being, how can we detach the individual from these places and things?

Thus, we come across a paradox in the definition of individual. In previous editions of this book, the word 'individual' was used abundantly and uncritically as a synonym for agency. We now recognise the complexity of the individual and the unhappy sense of atomisation that the word implies. In an attempt to clarify our stance on the individual, we include in this chapter a closer look at the silhouette of the self.

Are there boundaries to the body, and if so, where are they? Piaget and Lacan both thought that when born, humans have no sense of limits: the self incorporates the whole world. Piaget presumed that infants could only see in two dimensions because the retina is two-dimensional. Three-dimensional vision would have to be learned. Until infants learn this (which, according to Piaget, happens at about 18 months when children locomote independently), they have no depth perception, which means that there is no distance between the self and the world (Butterworth 1995, p. 90). This situation is called 'adualism'. Lacan argues that before children learn language – before they come under the sway of symbols – their bodies are without zones, subdivisions or differentiations. The body and the universe are integrated into a smooth, seamless surface. When the body is socialised, the symbolic order cuts this surface, separating the body from the other, and localising pleasures into specific zones (Fink 1995, p. 25). In that they are subject to direct empirical refutation, Piaget's ideas have been most roundly dismissed. A variety of observations show that even at birth, and perhaps before, infants are able to differentiate themselves from the surrounding environment (Butterworth 1995; Russell 1995). For example, newborns distinguish their own cries from those of others.

Despite their critique of adualism, ecological psychologists still stress that the body is formed in dialogue with other things. Infants need a parent to be able to sit upright, and the floor to stand erect. 'The dialogical self exists from the outset in the inherently relational information available to perception' (Butterworth 1995, p. 102). Dialogical notions of self and body receive support from a variety of positions. Within psychoanalytic theory, object relational theorists assert that 'it is only through an intimate relationship with primary caretakers . . . that a sense of difference between self and others is at all possible' (Elliott 1994, p. 64). From a very different stance, Bourdieu (1977, p. 11) uses dialogical metaphors to describe social action: 'In dog fights, as in the fighting of children or boxers, each move triggers off a countermove, every stance of the body becomes a sign pregnant with a meaning that the opponent has to grasp while it is still incipient.' In encounters with other people, we semi-consciously read the way in which the other person carries herself. We communicate our own sense of footing in relation to the other through postures (of deference, authority, etc.). To converse successfully with a person we must coordinate ourselves through continuous though non-reflexive adjustments: the listener periodically nods the head, mumbles things like 'hum', or 'uh huh', and senses the appropriate moment to interject. Charles Taylor (1999) calls these sorts of dialogical interactions 'harmonising'. These examples show how we harmonise bodily with our surroundings and with other people. They also question the subject–object dichotomy, in which the reasoning mind is said to be completely detached from its surroundings.

In ethnography, the relational or sociocentric view sees the self as decentred; as stretched along various interpersonal relationships. Maurice Leenhart (1979 [1947]) produced a classic statement of the relational self in *Do Kamo*, his ethnography of the Canaque of New Caledonia. Amongst the Canaques, the *kamo* or 'personage' is poorly delineated: 'He is unaware of his body which is his only support. He knows himself only by the relationships he maintains with others. He exists only insofar as he acts his role in the course of his relationships. He is situated only with respect to them. If we try to draw this, we cannot use a dot marked "self" ' (p. 153; cf. Strathern 1996, p. 89).

Conclusion

In this chapter, we have presented a paradigm of embodiment (Csordas 1990) that overcomes the traditional understanding of agents as individualised actors disconnected from the worldly contexts and lived experiences that bring them into being. In doing so we have challenged dichotomies between self and other and mind and body. Where does this take us in archaeology? Brück (2001, p. 654) has emphasised the sociocentric nature of the self while Thomas (1996, p. 86) has emphasised the shifting boundaries of the physical body: a hammerstone can be seen as an extension of the arm. Mithen's (1998b, pp. 181–4) discussions of material culture come peculiarly close to what Haraway (1991) would call the cyborgic nature of modern humans. In the Upper Palaeolithic, for example, humans use material culture to extend the mind, expanding the possibilities of information storage. An embodied archaeology, however, would not treat material culture merely as a tool wielded by a module of the mind, as Mithen does. Rather, it would emphasise that the self is continually forged and reforged through its relations to material culture. This recalls the discussion in the previous chapter of how objects gain agency through their relation to human actors.

Because of the dependence of self and embodiment on the physical world, archaeologists are well situated to explore changing embodiment through time – to write histories and prehistories of the body. Where this has been most successful, as in the account of private lives in ancient Egypt (Meskell 2002), there is a full linking of general theories about embodiment, and a detailed reconstruction of the diverse daily practices in which different individuals participated. There is a recognition of the need to discuss unconscious practical engagement with the world. But in Meskell's account there is also a careful attempt to explore conscious and unconscious understandings of people and objects. We have noted at a number of points in this chapter that embodiment does not simply come about through bodies interacting with objects and persons. How we interact with people (such as mothers) or objects (such as the landscape, the house) depends on historical circumstances and the values given to mothers and landscapes. Our embodiment is orientated – we engage with the world in a particular way, which endures or changes historically. It is the particular historical orientation that contributes to the way the world, and ourselves, have meaning.

We have already come a long way in our search for adequate theories of agency and meaning, and accounts of embodiment are clearly central. But we have paid less attention so far to the way in which we as historians and prehistorians interpret and make sense of past meanings in the present. This will be the task of the following chapters.

7 Archaeology and history

In this chapter it will be argued that archaeology should re-capture its traditional links with history (Deetz 1988; Young 1988; Bintliff 1991; Hodder 1987; 1990a; Knapp 1992; Morris 1999). Unfortunately the term 'history' is used with a variety of different meanings by different people, and it is first nec-essary to establish what we do and do not mean by the word here. We do not mean the explanation of change by reference to antecedent events; simply to describe a series of events leading up to a particular moment in time is a travesty of the historical method. Neither do we mean that phase n is depen-dent on phase n-1. Many types of archaeology involve such a dimension. Thus many social evolutionary theories expect some dependence in the moves between bands, tribes, chief-doms or states, or in the adoption of agriculture (Woodburn 1980). In the application of Darwinian-type arguments, the selection of a new social form is constrained by the existing 'gene-pool'. In systems theory the 'trajectory' of a system is dependent on prior conditions and system states. Each trajec-tory may be historically unique and specific in content, but general laws of system functioning can be applied. Within Marxism the resolution of conflict and contradiction is emer-gent in the pre-existing system, as part of the dialectical pro-cess of history.

History, in all such work, involves a particularist dimen-sion, but it also involves explaining the move from phase n-1 to n according to a set of universal rules. As such, the his-torian remains on the *outside* of events, as a natural scientist records experimental data. But history in the sense intended here involves also getting at the *inside* of events, at the inten-tions and concepts through which the subjectivities of actors are constituted. The historian talks of 'actions' as well as be-haviour, movements and events. Collingwood (1946, p. 213) provides an example. Historians do not just record that Caesar crossed a river called the Rubicon on a certain date – they talk of Caesar's defiance of Republican law.

This book began with the question, how do we get at past cultural meanings? We have gone to and from materialism and back again. Throughout, the core of the reconstructions attempted within any 'ism' has been seen to be based on weakly developed arguments about cultural meaning. Within the materialist systemic-processual approach, it was assumed that, for example, burial is for social display, so that in conditions of challenged norms of succession burials will reflect status rivalry (p. 28–9). To interpret the function of burials in this way we must make assumptions about what they meant to the people at the time. Equally, a head-dress can only mark social affiliation (p. 28–9) if it is perceived by those involved to have had meaning in these terms. It might be counter-argued that, whatever the artifacts meant, they still had the suggested functions. Yet it is difficult to see how an artifact can have a social function (such as burial for social display) if the meaning is not appropriate to the function (as when death or material accumulation comes to be seen as 'dirty', 'uncultured').

As a result of this inadequate approach to meaning we turned in chapter 3 to structuralism, but here it was found that meaning content was often imposed without care. Units of analysis were defined *a priori*, symbols were given meanings (male or female, for example), the symbols were assumed to function very simplistically according to Saussure's semiology (cf. semiotics, chapter 3), and assymetries were interpreted (as 'organic', for example). The structuralist method was non-historical in the sense that symbolic structures were assumed to be timeless: little attention was paid to how such structures maintained their stability, what could cause them to change, and what generated them in the first place. Furthermore, this method provided few guidelines as to how one might reconstruct the subjective meanings in which the structures are built.

So we returned to materialism. In chapter 4 it was shown that in most Marxist analyses of material culture it is again the functions that are examined (to mask social reality etc.)

rather than the meaning content. In other words, meaning content is subsumed under ideology, and too often the function of the ideology (as an instrument of domination) is given more attention than the content of the ideology. A second problem with traditional Marxist approaches in archaeology is that individual actors are too often presumed to be duped by dominant ideologies. In chapter 5 we showed how the development of practice theory and the incorporation of notions of resistance and agency into archaeological theory and practice have remedied this shortcoming. Nevertheless, better accounts of social strategy, intentionality and the logic of practice provide a necessary but not sufficient account of meaning. As we explain in this chapter, meaning often resides in structures of the long term, what we might call 'mentalités'. In this case, where the vitality of meaning exceeds the time scale of an individual life, we require an account of the reproduction of meaning over longer historical periods.

Chapter 6 addressed the agent as a subject: subject *of* the world and subject *to* the world through the body. The consideration of embodiment provided models of how meaning can be experienced, thus filling in one of the key gaps in structuralism. Yet, like practice theories, theories of subjectivity and embodiment must be supplemented by an approach that can account for the fact that the formation and re-formation of meaning occurs on a time scale that exceeds the life of any one body.

Even within approaches not discussed in this book, subjective meanings are assumed in the minds of people long dead. For example, the economy of a prehistoric site is often reconstructed on the basis of bone residues (chapter 1, p. 15). But to assume that bones discarded on a settlement bear any relation to the economy is to make assumptions about how people perceived animals, bones, discard etc. In many societies complex social meanings are attached to domestic animals, bones and dirt. To assume that the bones are not transformed culturally is to assume that 'they' had attitudes not so dissimilar to 'ours'. As a further example, if we say that the population at a certain site was probably about 'x', there is hidden in this statement a reconstruction of meanings in the minds of people long dead. Since we cannot directly 'see' the population in the past, we have to infer it from, for example, settlement space. Of course we can bolster our argument with cross-cultural evidence. But even if we could show that all societies today have a predictable relationship between population size and settlement area (which we cannot – see Hodder 1982d), to use such information to interpret the past is still to make assumptions about peoples' attitudes to space in that particular historical context. How much space individuals or groups need or think they need for certain activities is, at least partly, a question of symbolism, meaning and intention. As Collingwood (1939, p. 133) and Taylor (1948) noted, it is almost impossible even to describe archaeological data without some interpretative terms implying purpose, like 'wall', 'pottery', 'implement', 'hearth'. While Neolithic polished stone axes were thought to be thunderbolts their utilitarian functions (to cut down Neolithic trees) could not be elucidated by mere analysis. It is only when we make assumptions about the subjective meanings in the minds of people long dead that we can begin to do archaeology.

Throughout the approaches described in this book there has been a refusal to face this unhappy situation directly. Archaeologists have preferred to avoid the problem, and have grasped the comfort of empirical science, a cracked and broken façade. We must now face the subjectivity of meaning directly.

We take it to be the role of history to grasp the meaning of human action (see also Morris 1999, p. 13). Our stance builds from positions taken by a series of prominent 20th-century historians. In 1929, Marc Bloch stated that 'One could not pretend to explain an institution if one did not link it to the great intellectual, emotional, mystical currents of the contemporaneous *mentalités*... This interpretation of the facets of social organization from the inside will be the principle of my teaching, just as it is of my own work' (cited in Burgière 1982, p. 430). In the same year, Bloch and Lucian Febvre founded the journal *Annales d'Histoire Economique et Sociale*, from which the renowned French *Annales* school of history takes its name. Subsequent generations of *Annales* historians shared Bloch's concern for documenting *mentalités*, which can be defined as contextual belief systems expressed in collective representations (myths, symbols), whose history is one of subconscious growth (Bintliff 1991, p. 11), or perhaps simply as ideology and symbolism within a cultural context (Knapp 1992b, p. 8). Like Bloch, Collingwood was also interested in 'the inside' of events. In talking about *mentalités* and the inside of events, we do not mean to imply that we can approach the subjective meanings which might have been expressed if we could talk to people in the past. Like the habitus, the subjective meanings that concern us are not necessarily conscious and would not necessarily come out in conversation. Furthermore a barrage of authors, from Bourdieu to Foucault, have taught us that conscious representations (what people say) are only part of the story. Our aim is to interpret the subjective meanings in the sense of the structuring concepts and ideas that were used to organise the recurrent material practices of groups. These social and public ideas were used to constitute subjectivities and they can be examined to see how they were transformed historically through material and social practices and through individual action and interpretation.

Today, a concern for the inside of events continues in the field of cultural history (Morris 1999). Here, 'historians move ... from being "fact grubbers" to being "mind readers" ' (p. 13). *Mentalités* and mind reading would appear to link history with idealism. By idealism, we do not mean a view that the material world does not exist: rather, the term as defined earlier (p. 20) suggests that the material world is *as it is perceived*. It has to be perceived before it can be acted on. Though mind reading implies getting inside the heads of past actors, we believe that meaning is public and social (Geertz 1973). Therefore to get at a *mentalité* or the inside of events does not mean getting inside someone's head or some other form of radical empathy.

Cultural historians like R. Chartier and Gareth Stedman Jones (cited in Morris 1999, p. 12) maintain that all history is at least partly idealist. Earlier historians believed that it was possible to use documents to distinguish how people in the past saw their world from how that world really was, and, in a silently Marxist fashion, to use the 'real' order of things as a basis for explaining subjective understandings of them. More recently, cultural historians maintain that we cannot move from documents that present the world to how the world really was because the documents themselves are re-presentations. On the other hand, cultural historians recognise that re-presentations of the economy, for example, do not determine the economy. Though a historian learns about the economy only through language and discourse, economic processes are not prescribed by discourse alone. For this and other reasons, historical idealism, like its close kin subjectivism, cannot stand alone (see also Bourdieu 1990).

There are two aspects of history that we want to discuss in this chapter. First, we wish to look at ways in which subjective meanings are regenerated over the long term in relation to practice. Second, Collingwood's historical method will be critically examined.

History of the long term

The usual way in which archaeologists discuss developments over long spans of time is to divide up their data into phases and to discuss the reasons for change between the phases. History is thus a discontinuous process, whether the approach being followed is culture-historical (when the discontinuities are invasions and so on), processual (systemic, adaptive change) or Marxist (change from contradiction and crisis). As we have seen (p. 62), structuralism does not cope well with change.

While attempts have been made within these approaches to blur the edges between phases (see for example Higgs and Jarman 1969), there is little notion of history as a continuous process, and few archaeologists have attempted to reconstruct the way in which contextual meanings are related to practice over the long term. If we want to understand the contextual belief systems of people at one moment in time, in order to understand their society (or ours), how far back do we have to go? Do the meanings change, but always in relation to what went before, as a continuous process?

Almost by definition, those who are interested in the continuity of cultural meanings over the long term tend to be interested in the particular. If each phase is to be explained separately, in comparison with other societies, the unique historical development is played down. But for those interested in cultural meanings, cross-cultural generalities have to be proved, not assumed, so emphasis is placed on understanding the particular in its own terms. We have already seen that all archaeology is concerned with the particular historical context to some degree, and Trigger (1978) has shown that, on the other hand, history involves generalization. But in both archaeological and non-archaeological studies it is particularist studies combined with a concern for the 'inside' of events which have led to the most profound and far-reaching statements on the nature of the relationships between meaning and practice.

An important study of such relationships over the long term is Max Weber's (1976; first published in 1904–5) analysis of the relationship between the Protestant ethic and the spirit of capitalism. Although this is not an archaeological example, we intend to discuss it at some length for reasons which will become clear below. Weber begins with a particular problem to which he gives a particular answer. His question is 'why does capitalism emerge in western Europe and not in other parts of the world?' Some form of capitalism existed, he suggests, in China, India, Babylon, but the particular ethos or spirit found in Europe, which laid the basis for the modern capitalist ethic, was lacking. Weber identifies this ethic as 'one's duty in a calling', whatever that profession might be. Rational conduct on the basis of the idea of the calling could be linked to other specific and peculiar forms of rationalism found in Western culture, as seen in music, law and administration as well as in the economic system.

Weber suggests that the distinctive character of Western capitalism is linked to (though not in any direct sense caused by) the rise of various forms of ascetic Protestantism, especially Calvinism. Data are quoted which show that business leaders, owners of capital and skilled and technical grades of labour are overwhelmingly Protestant in western European countries of mixed religious composition. Catholic traditionalism was authoritarian and did not sanction the pursuit of gain at the expense of others; its greater 'other-worldliness' inhibited capitalist enterprise. Calvinism, however, sanctioned 'this-worldly' asceticism. Individuals were born into an apparently unalterable order of things, and predestination led a person to 'do the works of him who sent him, as long as it is yet day' (Weber 1976, p. 156).

In his analysis Weber is specifically arguing against Marxist historical materialism in which the forces and relations of production are primary. Not that he ignores such factors or even thinks they are unimportant, but he wishes to give equal weight to an idealist notion, that an historically specific set of ideas influences the way people organize their society and economy. His concern is to examine the subjective meaning-complex of action and to emphasize that 'rationality' is subjective, in relation to particular 'ends' or 'givens'. He suggests that every artifact can be understood only in terms of the meaning which its production and use have had or will have for human action.

The Protestant asceticism is seen as developing over long stretches of time, and as being regenerated through enculturation so that it becomes taken for granted. Ultimately the formation of rational jurisprudence inherited from Roman law played a role in the development of a specific Western type of rationalism. The origins of the capitalist spirit can be traced back to a time previous to the advent of capitalism (p. 54), and the Puritan emphasis on continuous bodily or mental labour is partly derived from the fact that 'labour is...an approved ascetic technique, as it always has been in the Western Church, in sharp contrast not only to the Orient but to almost all monastic rules the world over' (p. 163).

But Weber does not see this set of ideas developing on its own. Rather, the material and the ideal are integrated, so that to explain each action or social product it is necessary to consider both the historical context of subjective meanings and the practice of daily life. The religious ideas change partly through debate amongst religious leaders, but also in relation to, but not dominated by, the totality of social conditions, especially economic ones (p. 183). Richard Baxter, a writer on Puritan ethics, 'continually adjusted to the practical experiences of his own ministerial activity' so that his dogma changed in relation to practical activity (p. 156). Weber continually notes the difference between philosophers and religious ideals versus 'the layman', 'the practical', and 'the average'. Under Calvinism 'The moral conduct of the average man was thus deprived of its planless and unsystematic character [that it had in Catholicism] and subected to a consistent method for conduct as a whole' (p. 117).

The spirit of capitalism was born from the spirit of Christian asceticism. The dogma went into everyday life, began to dominate wordly morality, and played its part in building the modern economic order. However, the practical consequences may be unintended. Thus the religious reformers of Calvinism and other Puritan sects were concerned to save souls; the pursuit of worldly goods was not an end in itself. The purely religious motives had cultural and social consequences which were unforeseen and even unwished for (pp. 89–90). The results were often far-removed from and even in contradiction to all that the religious reformers were trying to attain.

We see, then, in Weber's account, the dialectical relationships between theory and practice, between idea and material, and the same emphases on social action (purposeful behaviour), unintended consequences and contradictions that were identified in preceding chapters. Here however, because a *long* historical context is provided, the equal contribution of ideals and values is identified. In the short term, in the instant of action, Bourdieu's habitus appears dominated by the conditions of existence, but over the long term, and in contrast with other historical sequences, the social and economic conditions are themselves seen to be generated within sets of cultural meanings.

Through time, Weber records, the relative dominance of religious ideas and the social economy varies. Initially, the ascetic tendency of Puritanism led to social action and allowed the further development of an economic system, forms of which already had been in existence. Certain aspects of capitalist business organization are considerably older than the Reformation (p. 91), but it was the religious changes which allowed the new economic order to develop. In addition, Puritanism was 'anti-authoritarian', leading to fanatical opposition of the Puritans to the ordinances of the British monarch (p. 167).

So, at first, 'the Puritan wanted to work in a calling', and religion directed the capitalist enterprise, but now 'we are forced to do so' (p. 181). Through time the rational order became bound to the technical and economic conditions of machine production. Today these material conditions 'determine the lives of all the individuals who are born into the mechanism' (p. 181), and the religious basis has been lost.

We have discussed Weber's account at some length because his work contains many of the aspects of historical interpretation for which this book searches. There is a full consideration of contextual meanings, an account of how these meanings develop and can be understood in their own historical terms, and the location of the individual in society. Weber argues against functionally deterministic relationships, and sees individual action as the building block of social totalities. The social whole is full of tensions, divisions, and contradictions, and individuals variously interpret the world(s) in which they live.

Despite the emphases on the contextual and specific, Weber does not lapse into sceptical relativism and particularism – he thinks that it is possible to understand other people's subjectivity. One need not have been Caesar in order to understand Caesar. The mind can grasp other contexts and other meanings, as long as it pieces together the 'spirit' of other times from individual segments of historical reality rather than imposing the formula from outside (p. 47). Equally, having carried out such detailed interpretation, generalization is possible both within historical contexts and between them.

As Giddens (1976) points out, much of Weber's data and interpretation have since been questioned. It has not been our concern here to demonstrate the validity of Weber's account, but to use the example to show how consideration of historical meanings, over the long term and in contrast to historical developments in other parts of the world, points to the inadequacy of materialist and objectivist accounts and emphasizes the importance of the subjective and particular.

While Weber's account already provides some indication of the relationship between idea and practice, it is perhaps Sahlins (1981) who provides the clearest example of the way in which the types of approaches outlined by Bourdieu and Giddens (see chapter 5) can be applied to the long term. In Hawaii, Sahlins recognizes sets of preconceptions and ideas which are part of action. For example, *mana* is a creative force that renders visible the invisible, that gives meaning to goodness and godliness. The divine *mana* of chiefs is manifest in their brilliance, their shining, like the sun. On the daily level, such notions orientate actions, as habitus, but they are changed in practice, in 'structures of the conjuncture'. No-one can ever know exactly how a particular event or meeting will be played out in practice. The intended and unintended consequences of action lead to reformulation of the habitus and of the social structure.

More clearly, at moments of culture contact, as when Cook came to Hawaii, two opposing habitus come into conflict in practice and radical change may ensue. Sahlins shows how, on their arrival in Hawaii, Cook and the Europeans were perceived within traditional frameworks, were seen to have *mana*. But in the playing out of practical scenes from different viewpoints (Hawaiian and European), unintended consequences rebounded back on these perceptions, causing contradictions and conflict. Ultimately Cook was killed as part of these processes, and *mana* became transferred to all things British, leading to social reordering within Hawaii.

There is much in this example which relates to Weber's accounts, but the more detailed work and greater awareness of the problem of the relationship between structure and practice leads to a fuller understanding of how society and economy are embedded within subjective meanings but are yet able to act back and change those meanings.

The variation between the work of Weber and Sahlins can be paralleled in the *Annales* school, which has now had a direct impact on archaeology (see Iannone 2002; Kirch 1992; Last 1995; and articles in Bintliff 1991, Hodder 1987b, and Knapp 1992a). Fernand Braudel, the successor of Bloch and Febvre, categorised historical processes as occurring on three different time scales: long, medium and short. The *Annales* approach is quite relevant to archaeology because archaeology can document change in all three scales and note dynamic interactions between them.

Braudel's first scale of process occurs over the *longue durée* and encompasses slowly changing structures, such as *mentalités*, and long-term continuities, such as geography. Many archaeologists have been successful in documenting and tracing persistent, peculiar cultural values. Lechtman's study of Andean metallurgy provides an excellent example. Lechtman (1984) notes that the lack of a 'Bronze Age' and an 'Iron Age' in New World prehistory may have resulted from the importance of metals in warfare, transport and agriculture in Europe, whereas in the Andes, for example, metals had a more symbolic role in both secular and religious spheres of life.

Lechtman is thus interested in the specificity of a cultural sequence in the New World, and she is drawn to a particular set of cultural values which centre around the ritual and political significance of the colours gold and silver. Bronze was a late development in the Andes – other metals were used to produce the desired colours. However, another set of cultural values prevented the Andean metallurgists from adding the gold and silver colours to the surface of metal items. A technically highly complex method was developed so that what was visible as colour on the outside of an object derived from the inside. 'The basis of Andean enrichment systems is the incorporation of the essential ingredient – the gold or the silver – into the very body of the object. The essence of the object, that which appears superficially to be true of it, must also be inside it' (*ibid.*, p. 30).

Lechtman supports this argument by reference to cloth production, which has the same 'structure' as the metal working (the design is incorporated into the cloth), and she shows the way in which the cultural values had ideological functions in legitimating domination within the Inca state. But the particular form of that ideology, and of the clothworking, and the particular technical process of electrochemical replacement and depletion, can only be understood in their own terms, related to practice but not reducible to it. Ultimately we will only be able to 'explain' the system of cultural values by going back in time, in an infinite regress.

Others (for example Coe 1978) have also been concerned to explore the particularity of New World culture as opposed to the Old World. Flannery and Marcus (1983) have argued, linking archaeological and linguistic studies, that Meso-American cultures over thousands of years have adapted to local conditions and undergone radical social change via a structured set of meanings, including the division of the world into four, colour-coded quarters and a 'spirit' termed *pe*. Although there is little attempt in their study to examine *how* structure, meaning and event are integrated, it is important that the ideational realm is shown in this example to have long-term influence. Furthermore, the ideational does not cause, or obstruct, or become reduced to the effect of, practical action; rather it is seen as the medium for action.

Within Old World archaeology, the vista has at times opened up, of working backwards over the long term to find the common cultural core from which European societies and cultures developed – this has been the concern of linguists and archaeologists involved with the Indo-European problem. Childe, for example, envisioned his purpose in writing *The Dawn of European Civilization* (first edition 1925) to be the understanding of the particular nature of European culture and the identification of the origin of that spirit

of independence and inventiveness that led to the industrial revolution. But we can also incorporate a more detailed
scale of analysis, trying to see how the different regions of
Europe have been formed, divided and diffused. Christopher
Hawkes, for example, has on a number of occasions noted
the 'Western inhibition of furnished burial – or of burial altogether' (Hawkes 1972, p. 110) which leads to lack of status
differentiation being expressed in indigenous burial customs
in England (see also 1972, p. 113; 1976, p. 4). Such attitudes,
or at least descriptions of behaviour, in relation to burial,
are seen as continuing over the long term, and yet Hawkes
allows for cumulative change, as in his discussion of 'cumulative Celticity' (1976) in which the Celtic style is traced back
to its origins in the Bronze Age. It was in 1954 that Hawkes
suggested a regional approach in which archaeologists used
an historical method of working backwards through cultural
sequences to find 'things common to all men as a species, inherent in their culture-capacity from the start' (1954, p. 167).
'It works as one peels onions; and so it reaches the final question, has the onion in fact got a central nucleus at all or is it
just all peel?' (*ibid.*, p. 168).

Hawkes' question about the onion touches on profound
issues of time and politics. With regard to time, we are inclined to answer that the onion is all peel. By searching for
origins and common beginnings, Childe and Hawkes imply
that the onion of prehistory has a core; that there are places
where time starts and from which beginnings emerge. If we
think about time 'from the inside' – in other words, from
the perspective of a living, embodied actor – we soon realise
that the temporal experience of life is continuous. Certainly
biographies contain critical events, and certainly people sometimes conceive of their lives as narratives with distinct stages
or phases, but acknowledging the unevenness of lived time
does not justify the use of a temporal scheme in which time
is separate from life and can therefore be measured in equivalent units and divided any which way. Time is not an empty
container, existing independent of life; it is created by people.
Thus, for 'Europeanness' to have an origin, the origin must

occur in a peopled time, which would seem absurd: can we imagine a point in time when a nondescript person becomes a European? The basic idea is that time is not so easily split into stages, and without clean breaks in time, we cannot hope to find clean origins. For this reason it may be preferable to conceive of time not as a series of stages or steps but as a flow – a stream (Hodder 1987b, p. 2).

With regard to politics, origins research has multiple present-day consequences. One consequence is seen in the practice of archaeology itself. Archaeologists who research origins – of the state, for example – can give their work the broadest scope of relevance and the most opportunities for citation. Authors who write on later developments of the state, regardless of geographic region, will need to cite the origins research to help contextualise their contribution (Wobst and Keene 1983). Thus, writers who 'get in early' by affixing their name to the origin of a topic can colonise the topic as a whole, and, much like a tax, collect citations from the widest possible network. More importantly, the search for origins presumes essentialism (Conkey with Williams 1991), as if there were an essence of Europe waiting to be exposed in all Europeans once the superficial layers of difference have been peeled away. When applied to humans, the notion of essence justifies a Platonic scheme of ideal types, which has motivated and continues to motivate genocidal episodes of racism, nationalism and ethnic cleansing.

Few archaeologists have attempted to use the great advantage of their data – that it covers long time spans – to contribute to questions about the flows of time over the long term. Detailed historical studies of regional sequences which involve interpretation of subjective meaning are few and far between. We have already discussed (p. 29) the interesting work of Flannery and Marcus (1976; 1983), while Isbell (1976) has identified a 3000-year continuity in settlement structure in the South American Andes, despite major discontinuities in social and economic systems. Other important work of this type includes W. Davis' (1982) account of the principles or 'canon' of art identifiable throughout

Egyptian history, Hall's (1977) identification of principles of meaning lying behind Hopewellian processes of economic and political change and interaction, Bradley's (1990) account of long-term and widespread continuities in hoards and votive deposits in North and North-West Europe. In Europe, many archaeologists are aware of remarkable patterns of continuity which link the distant past to the present, particularly in Scandinavia, but few have made such questions the focus of research.

Equally, diffusion is now little studied as a component of cultural development. With diffusion decried as descriptive, processual archaeologists placed the emphasis on local adaptive sequences. Yet within the framework of the questions being asked in this volume, diffusion does have explanatory power. It can help to explain the particular cultural matrix. Objects or styles derived from other groups are given meaning in their new context, but these new meanings may be based on, and may bring with them, meanings from the old. The new traits are selected and are placed within the existing system, changing it. The aim should be less to classify different types of diffusion (Clarke 1968), than to see, for example, stimulus diffusion as an active social process working on and within systems of meanings which develop over the long term (cf. Kehoe 1979).

There is a danger that archaeologists will be content with vague continuities in cultural ethics, falling back on the excuse of their fragmentary data without adequate consideration of how structured internal meanings are actively involved in society and in social change, and how they come to be changed themselves. Braudel's second and third time scales help the historian focus on change. The second scale – the medium term or *moyenne durée* – encompasses economic cycles, demographic trend and changes in socio-political structures. Change in such cycles and trends, called conjunctural history, can be observed within decades or over many centuries. The third scale is the shortest, dealing with individual events in the lives of men and women. Braudel notoriously undervalued the contribution of short-term events and therefore failed to grasp the way in which human action can initiate change in longer-term cycles. However, Braudel's intellectual successors have given closer attention to the interplay between long-term structures, social strategies and individual events (e.g. Ladurie 1980; Le Goff 1985). These writers focus on smaller geographical areas and on shorter time periods, an approach exemplified by Ladurie, who writes about one particular event: the 1579–80 carnival/uprising in Romans. Recent *Annales* work also moves closer to a humanistic approach, rejecting various forms of determinism and embracing a 'principle of indeterminacy' (Knapp 1992b, p. 8) that resembles ideas about complexity now gaining popularity in the human and biological sciences (Colwell 1998).

Writers in the field of cultural history (see Morris 1999) have also focused on smaller slices of the past while at the same time bringing an extraordinary breadth of material to bear upon them. Darnton's (1984, pp. 75–106) account of a cat massacre in an 18th-century Parisian printing shop provides an excellent example of the active individual, the historical context, and culture as meaningfully constituted. As told by an apprentice in the shop, the shopmaster's wife's command to get rid of cats provoked a delirious hunt, mock trial and cat massacre in which not even the wife's cat was spared. Darnton frames his essay around the question of why this seemingly inhumane event was so funny to the shop workers. Darnton's explanation takes him through a thick description of cat folklore, of popular carnivals, ceremonies and mock trials, of customs and rites of passage within guilds, of the sexuality of women and cuckolding of men, of the exploitative economy of the supposedly idyllic, pre-industrial, artisanal mode of production, etc. Darnton moves back and forth between the account of the cat massacre and its various historical contexts, eventually attending to every peculiarity of the event (Why cats? Why a print shop?). In the end, there are many explanations for why the cat massacre was so funny and we realise that the reward of such deep inquiry is not 'explanation' but arriving at an understanding of how 'workers made their experience meaningful by playing with themes of their culture' (p. 99).

In the work of Weber, Sahlins and Darnton, we begin to see how archaeologists might include both structure and process in their interpretations of the past. Duke's study of the Blackfoot Indians and their prehistoric ancestors on the Northern Plains of North America provides an interesting example. Duke (1992) begins by identifying two *mentalités* that span multiple millennia: procurement (centred around hunting) and processing (centred around cooking). The tools for hunting change rapidly over time and show high investment in details, whereas the tools for food processing show little change over time. Based on the innovations in procurement technology and the conservatism in processing technology, Duke believes the procurement *mentalité* is characterised by competition between men over prestige and status, whereas the processing *mentalité* stresses conformity to traditional notions of behaviour. European contact altered both *mentalités*. Before contact, these heavily gendered *mentalités* helped establish and maintain male dominance. The European trade in fur and hides transformed Indian men from independent warriors and hunters to territorially restricted, subordinate trade partners. At the same time, some women gained high-status social positions normally reserved for men. Duke argues that to compensate for their loss of control, the men attempted to exert greater control over women by shifting to polygyny: more wives meant more wealth in trading. In sum, an historical event – European contact – destabilised traditional gender relationships yet aboriginals actively contributed to the shaping of new gender relationships using a model informed and naturalised by the traditional, gendered *mentalités*.

In Duke's example, like Sahlins' account of 18th-century Hawaii, events from outside (arrival of Europeans) initiate social transformations. A more recent paper (Hamann 2002) shows that viewing change as coming from either the inside or the outside does not appropriately characterise most events. Though Hamann's example is not archaeological, we include it because it foregrounds more clearly the issue of interaction between long-term structures and short-term events. With exceptional erudition, Hamann identifies a structure of the long term in the pan-Mesoamerican, centuries-spanning recurrence of indigenous accounts of a previous age and its vanished inhabitants. Hamann then presents three case studies in which Mesoamericans draw on these structures of the long term to create and legitimate inequalities. The third case – the affairs of Chan Kom, an early 20th-century Maya village located 13 kilometres from the ruins of Chichen Itza, Mexico – is especially informative. The villagers of Chan Kom had multiple ties to the ruins (they went there for sacrifices, hunting and medicines, they evoked it in prayers and adages, they used Chichen motifs to decorate their houses, they built a tower to observe it and a majestic road to get to it), and powerful beliefs about their meaning (the original architects of Chichen, though they had vanished, still survived beneath the surface of the earth and could return to assist the modern villagers). Unsurprisingly, when an ambitious actor by the name of Don Eustacio made a bid to gain political, social and economic power, Chichen figured prominently in his strategy. With partial success, Don Eustacio mobilised labour using the rhetoric of the ruins at Chichen, insisting that, with hard work, they could initiate an age of prosperity not unlike that of the magical era in which the impressive ruins were originally built. In fact, Don Eustacio believed that his millenarian revival had already begun: he likened the archaeologists working at Chichen in the 1920s and 1930s to the vanished builders, now returned. Thus, it was both 'inside' and 'outside' factors that motivated Don Eustacio's actions.

The example of Don Eustacio says a great deal about the relation between structures of the long term and events in the short term. *Annales* co-founder Lucian Febvre thought that individuals were free to act, yet the actor could only do what the social environment allowed. This paradox resonates with Marx's famous observation that 'Men make their own history, but they do not make it under circumstances chosen by themselves, but under circumstances directly encountered, given, and transmitted from the past' (1977 [1852], p. 300). Certainly Don Eustacio was a manipulative opportunist, but he did not invent his rhetoric about the past and could not glibly 'choose' whether or not to 'deploy' it.

Bintliff (1991, pp. 12–13) interprets Febvre's paradox to mean that the impact of a short-term event is random and will only gain wider importance if it reflects significant medium- and long-term trends. The motivation behind the event can be ignored because it is the long-term structures that determine an event's significance. Indeed, Hamann's example shows that Don Eustacio's actions were effective precisely because they drew upon common understandings of Chichen. Yet Don Eustacio was only partially successful – many villagers de- serted him, others opposed him directly. Thus, the structure of the long term cannot be said to determine the impact of the event, most likely because the structure has multiple mean- ings and can be used in many different ways. The success of a particular usage will in part depend on precisely those factors that Bintliff dismisses: the intentions and motivations of the actors involved (see the section on resistance in chapter 5).

Everyone, Bintliff included, would agree that 'large scale processes cannot be invoked to explain small scale processes' (Knapp 1992b, p. 13). At stake is the determinacy of the im- pact of actions at the scale of the event. We favour indetermi- nacy among the scales and processes of history (Fletcher 1992; Morris 1999, p. 9). We argue that short-term events cannot be reduced to the 'material end results of tensions between the long term structures and medium term cycles of social interaction' (Iannone 2002, p. 75). For this reason, we argue that archaeologists must view the archaeological record as a series of events and attempt to distinguish one individual ac- tion from another (Hodder 2000). This idea also entails an approach to variability in the archaeological record that does not dismiss deviant cases – an idiosyncratic arrowhead, a rare architectural floor plan – as events that simply fail to initiate or affect longer-term trends (cf. Bintliff 1991, p. 13).

Giving more attention to internal meanings, the 'inside' of events, will thus not be easy for archaeologists. How do we reconstruct *mana*, Celtic spirit, Protestant ethic, European inventiveness, attitudes to left and right, from archaeological evidence? The problem develops like this: if we deny materialism, we can no longer predict the 'ideas' from the material base. Thus cross-cultural, predictive forms of inference are ruled out. If each historical context is unique and particular, how can we interpret it? In the conclusion to this chapter we will evaluate these issues and in the following chapter (chapter 8) we will introduce a more adequate contemporary response termed critical hermeneutics.

Historical theory and method: Collingwood

The emphasis on archaeology as a form of history is widely found in the period up to the 1960s in America and Britain, and it is probably true to say that it remains the dominant viewpoint in much of Europe. Taylor (1948), while drawing a distinction between archaeology and history, emphasized in his conjunctive approach the 'inside' of cultural units, the particular internal relationships and meanings. Archaeologists in Britain, many of them influenced by Collingwood, often emphasized the historical dimension of archaeological inference (Clark 1939; Daniel 1962; Hawkes 1954). Piggott (1959) suggested that archaeology is history except that the evidence is not intentionally left or recorded as history; it is 'unconscious'. For Hawkes (1942, p. 125) cultures have both an *ex*tension in space and time, and *in*tention in the social and economic field. All viewed culture as involving norms and purposes which were historically produced, but which could change over time.

While overarching norms and rules of behaviour are often stressed, there is also much lip-service paid to the individual as an important component in social theory. Collingwood, in particular, has a well-defined theory of social action. 'What is miscalled an "event" is really an action, and expresses some thought (intention, purpose) of its agent' (1939, pp. 127–8). He does not see action as a response to a stimulus, or as the mere effect of the agent's nature or disposition (*ibid.*, p. 102). So Collingwood says that action is neither behavioural response, nor is it norm. Rather it is situation specific, the 'event' being played out and manipulated according to bounded knowledge of the situation. Because situations of standardized types arise, action appears to be rule-bound, but in fact in many aspects of life there are no rigid unchanging rules. Each specific situation is so context dependent, with different combinations of factors involved, that it would be impossible to have a full rule-book of behaviour. Rather, it is a matter of 'improvising, as best you can, a method of handling the situation in which you find yourself' (*ibid.*, p. 105).

As a result of this emphasis on action rather than event, a recursive relationship between theory and practice is produced. Culture is therefore a cause and an effect, a stimulus as well as a residuum, it is creative as well as created. Because each creation is context-dependent, generalisations are seen as losing their value.

For Collingwood, as for Daniel (1962) and Taylor (1948), the use of cross-cultural generalisation in interpreting historical data is denied. Collingwood pointed out (1946, p. 243) that, properly speaking, the data do not exist because they are perceived or 'given' within a theory. Historical knowledge is not the passive 'reception' of facts – it is the discerning of the thought which is the inner side of the event (*ibid.*, p. 222). How then, asks the positivist-trained archaeologist, do we validate our hypotheses? Well, certainly not through the application of universal measuring devices, Middle Range Theory. These would be, in Collingwood's terms, superficial, descriptive universal theories. How then do we proceed to validate?

Well, one answer is to say that we don't. Collingwood and many other early writers imagined no security, no robustness, no proof. There can only be continual debate and approximation, and this is the view embraced in this book. But such an answer would be altogether too glib. As Collingwood was at pains to demonstrate, we can be rigorous in our reconstructions of the past and we can derive criteria for judging between theories.

The procedure to be followed is first to immerse oneself in the contextual data, re-enacting past thought through your own knowledge. But, as emphasized by Bourdieu (see p. 91), this is a practical living through, not an abstract spectacle to be watched. 'Historical knowledge is the knowledge of what mind has done in the past, and at the same time it is the redoing of this, the perpetration of past acts in the present' (Collingwood 1946, p. 218). The past is an experience to be lived through in the mind.

What does Collingwood mean by this? Much damage has been done to the archaeological acceptance of Collingwood's position by the way he expressed this point. Collingwood did not mean that we should simply sit and 'empathize with', or 'commune with', the past; rather he is, in our view, simply stating the point made throughout this book, that all statements about the past (ranging, as we have seen, from notions like 'this is a hunter–gatherer camp', to 'this tomb functioned to legitimate access to resources') involve making assumptions about meaning content in the past. In this sense we do, whether we like it or not, 'think ourselves into' the past, and Collingwood is simply pointing this out. But he goes on to say that we need to be aware that we are doing it, and that we need to do it critically.

The 'reliving' of the past is achieved by the method of question and answer. One cannot sit back and observe the data; they must be brought into action by asking questions – why should anyone want to erect a building like that, what was the purpose of the shape of this ditch, why is this wall made of turf and that of stone? And the question must not be vague ('let us see what there is here') but definite ('are these loose stones a ruined wall?'). Recall the specificity of Darnton's question about the great cat massacre: why cats?

The response to such questions is dependent on all the data available (see below), but also on historical imagination, something which is very much affected by our knowledge

and understanding of the present. Collingwood rarely discusses analogy, but it is our reading of him that he would not
have been averse to its use. Analogy with the present clearly is
important in broadening and exciting the historical imagination. However, this does not mean that one's interpretation
of the past is trapped within the present – for Collingwood,
it is possible to have insight which leads to understanding
of a cultural context different from one's own. The mind is
able to imagine and criticize other subjectivities, the 'inside'
of other historical events (1946, p. 297). Although each context is unique, in that it derives from a particular historical
circumstance, we can have an identity or common feeling
with it; each event, though unique, has a universality in that
it possesses a significance which can be comprehended by all
people at all times (*ibid.*, p. 303).

The insight is then supported or 'validated' in a number of
ways. For those working on material from the same cultural
context of which they are members, continuity between the
past and present allows us to work back, peeling off Hawkes'
onion skins (above, p. 138), to see how thoughts have been
modified and transformed. Alternatively, Collingwood emphasizes *coherence*. Since, 'properly speaking', the data do not
exist, all one can do is identify a reconstruction that makes
sense, in terms of the archaeologist's picture of the world
(*ibid.*, p. 243), and in terms of the internal coherence of the
argument. This strategy allows 'other' subjectivities to be hypothesized and it allows us to differentiate between the theories. But the coherence also concerns *correspondence* to the
evidence. Although the evidence does not exist with any objectivity, it does nevertheless exist in the real world – it is tangible and it is there, like it or not. Whatever our perceptions or
world view, we are constrained by the evidence, and brought
up against its concreteness. It is for this reason that we would
find it hard to entertain the hypothesis that 'iron-using arrived
in Britain before the advent of farming', or 'formal burial did
not begin in Britain until after the adoption of iron': too much
special pleading would be needed to make the evidence fit such
statements. So, even within our own subjective perspectives,

we often find it difficult to make our coherent arguments correspond to the evidence. At some point too much special pleading is recognized and the theory becomes implausible.

Thus our reconstructions of historical meanings are based on arguments of coherence and correspondence in relation to the data as perceived. Archaeology uses accommodative arguments; it has no other viable options. Clearly no certainty can ever be achieved in this way, but as will be seen in the examples presented below, knowledge of the past can be accumulated through critical application of the method.

Many people have been offended by Collingwood's views or at least by his way of presenting them, although in the intellectual climate of post-positivist philosophy several of his arguments seem scarcely radical. Childe was thus wrong to claim (1949, p. 24) that it is impossible for historians to re-enact in their own minds the thoughts and motives of the agent, since Childe himself continually imputed purpose and ideas to past minds as a routine part of archaeological work. And he was wrong to claim that 'Collingwood tells me in effect to empty my mind of all ideas, categories, and values derived from my society in order to fill it with those of an extinct society' (*ibid.*). Rather Collingwood argued that, standing within our own society, we can come to an understanding of other societies which it is unreasonable to claim has no relationship whatsoever with the nature of those societies. He suggested that we could critically evaluate our own and another society in terms of each other.

This is not to claim that our reconstructions of the past are independent of our own social context, and this aspect of inference will be discussed further in chapter 8. Rather, we have reached the position so far, that within the subjectivity of the data, there are still mechanisms for distinguishing between alternative theories. There is enough concrete contextual information in the evidence to restrict what we can say of it; it is the process of historical imagination which draws the evidence together into a coherence. Historical science is about criticizing and increasing these insights. Otherwise the data are used fraudulently within cross-cultural generalizations which overlook the problematic relationship between subject and object.

Some examples

It may be useful to provide some examples, taken from Collingwood's own work and from other more recent studies, of self-conscious attempts at reconstructing past motives, purposes and meanings. All the attempts are characterized by an immersing in the contextual data, asking questions of it, and reaching plausible insights about unique circumstances.

Collingwood (Collingwood and Myres 1936, p. 140), from his thorough knowledge of Hadrian's Wall and the later Antonine Wall in the north of Britain, asks 'Why was the Antonine Wall so different from Hadrian's? Why were there no milecastles and turrets, and why were the forts along the wall smaller and much closer together than on the earlier wall?'

The forts indicate that a smaller force was placed on the Antonine Wall. The construction of the wall also indicates an effort to be economical, especially in comparison with Hadrian's Wall.

> The ditch that lies in front of the ramparts is even larger than Hadrian's but the rampart itself, instead of stone, is made of turf in the western and central part, of clay in the eastern. Hadrian himself had laid it down that turfwork was very much easier to construct than masonry. And the measurements increase the contrast. The turf part of Hadrian's Wall is twenty feet wide at the base; the Antonine Wall is only fourteen, which implies that, if the height of the turfwork was the same in the two cases, the Antonine rampart required, for any given length, only two-thirds of the turf that would be required by Hadrian's. The forts, again, instead of being massively walled in stone, with monumental gateways, were surrounded for the most part with turf or earthen ramparts whose timber gateways were commonly of the simplest

design; where stone was used, the construction was simple and inexpensive. Even the official central buildings in the forts were not uniformly of stone, and the barracks were of the cheapest, wooden hutments which in some cases had thatched roofs.

From this evidence, Collingwood moves to an interpretation of purpose. 'Both in construction and in organization, then, the Antonine Wall bears the marks of a deliberate effort after cheapness, at the cost of a serious decrease in efficiency' (*ibid.*, p. 142). This hypothesis is further supported by showing that the wall is not well-sited strategically, and by contrasting the Antonine Wall with a new frontier-line built in Germany. 'These various features of the Antonine Wall, when considered together, seem less like a series of oversights than parts of a deliberate policy, based on the assumption that a powerful frontier-work on that line was not needed' (*ibid.*, p. 143).

Collingwood goes on in this study to suggest why a wall of this type might have been built in this place at this particular time, relating his argument to further evidence about the tribes and settlements in northern Britain. But for our purposes, enough has been described to show the way in which, by asking and trying to answer a series of questions in relation to detailed contextual information, a particular, one-off, interpretation of subjective intent can be provided which is plausible and which can be argued through in relation to the evidence.

Collingwood's reconstruction relies to some extent on written records about the nature of the Roman army, and so it may be useful to turn to a wholly prehistoric wall, that constructed around the early Iron Age settlement in Germany, the Heuneberg. Merriman (1987) has shown how this wall can be seen to have been built in order to gain prestige. In answer to the question, 'why was this wall built?', archaeologists have noted the use of mud-bricks equivalent in style to mud-bricks used in the Mediterranean. They also note that in the north European cultural context such walls do not exist historically, and that climatically the conditions are unsuitable. Other contextual information includes the exchange of prestige items between the Mediterranean and this part of Europe, the internal complexity of the Heuneberg centre and the associated rich burial tumuli. All in all, the insight that this particular wall was intended more for prestige, to provide local standing, than for defence, seems plausible.

In their analysis of the Zapotec Cosmos in Formative Oaxaca, Flannery and Marcus (1976) demonstrate that highly symbolic representations on pottery can be traced to naturalistic versions, and can thus be given meaning as fire serpents and were-jaguars. Similarly, it has been argued (Hodder 1984a) that many of the Neolithic tombs of western Europe mean houses. The argument is supported by noting eight points of formal similarity between the long tombs and contemporary long houses in central Europe. The meaning of the tombs as houses is then set within an appropriate social context. In an analysis of Neolithic axe exchange in Britain (Hodder and Lane 1982), it was argued that the axes had a subjective significance beyond their utilitarian value because they were the only artifact type depicted in tombs; they were often placed in ritual contexts, as were symbolic chalk replicas.

None of the above examples is in any way remarkable – they are simply routine archaeology – but that this is archaeology is important. In the above examples analogy with ethnographic data may have influenced the choice of questions, the historical imagination and the theories espoused, but in all cases the main aim has been to grasp the subjectivity of past contexts, and to understand the data themselves, in their own terms.

Conclusion and critique

So archaeology needs to go back to go forward. In the course of this chapter it has been found necessary to return to the pre-New Archaeology, to recover culture-history and to recover a coherent philosophical approach. We suspect that if one were to carry out an analysis of references or citations covering the period 1950 to 1980, one would find a sharp break around 1965. The New Archaeology dubbed all previous archaeology normative, descriptive, speculative, inadequate – it was time to make a break and start anew. Both the culture-historical aims and the interpretative methods were decried.

Of course there was much uninspiring culture-history, and much bad archaeology. But the same was to be true of New Archaeology, and will be true of all future archaeology. By examining various 'new' approaches that have been tried in archaeology over the past 40 years, we have shown that their limitations derive precisely from the rejection of cultural meanings, agency and history. By attempting to rewrite history as a natural science, knowledge accumulated in previous years (except in some cases chronological schemes and basic data descriptions) was set up as a straw man and knocked down.

In attempting to reconnect archaeology to history and to reintegrate old and new, many will feel that we have gone too far towards the contextual and speculative. A common reaction to claims that we must interpret subjective meanings in the past is to point to problems of validation, to inadequate, mute data. In fact, however, it can be argued that all cultural reconstruction depends on imputing subjective meanings to particular historical contexts. In this chapter, procedures as outlined by the *Annales* school, cultural history and historical anthropologists such as Sahlins and Hamann have been discussed.

These procedures are of course not flawless and we would now like to discuss some of their shortcomings. First, we will have to be critical about the unity and breadth of such things as *mentalités*. Advocates of the New History, such as Foucault, are sceptical of the possibility of connecting many events to a single principle, meaning, spirit or worldview. New Historians are instead sensitive to the divisions, limits and ruptures that disperse seemingly related events or actions into multiple, perhaps overlapping but never congruent series of meanings (Foucault 1972, pp. 7–10). Thus, principles – such as Celtic spirit, Protestant ethic and European inventiveness – which seem to give a common 'face' or flavour to a period may not be very coherent or common. At the least, this means that when Collingwood encourages us to 'think ourselves into' the past, we must recognise that at any historical place and time there will be many pasts to think into.

Second, the possibility of ruptures forces us to rethink notions of historical time. This chapter contains many perspectives on time. From a phenomenological perspective, we viewed time as a continuous stream or flow. This arises from the notion that human actors always live in a present, which is given meaning through reflection on the past and anticipation of the future. We used this view to challenge the value of origins research, in which meaning arises from abstract divisions of time demarcated by the analyst. However, seeing time as continuous has the politically dangerous effect of naturalising the present. To combat oppressive ideologies and institutions it is important to be able to pinpoint their origin: if we can show that they have a beginning, we ensure that they can have an end. On the other hand, if we accept the notion of ruptures and origins, we renounce kinship with the past and jeopardise the possibility of understanding ancient people. Of course, post-structuralists use this reasoning to argue that 'people' as we know them are a recent fabrication. We discuss this issue in the following chapter.

We have also viewed time as multiscalar. Braudel proposed three time scales. It is perhaps more accurate to suggest that there are as many time scales as there are social processes, and in each event or each process, multiple time scales may intersect. Furthermore, time scales may be either linear or cyclical. There is a tension between time in the sense of a scale – an abstract calibration device existing independent of the lives being measured – and the perspective of lived time given above (Gosden 1994; Shanks and Tilley 1987, chapter 5; Thomas 1996, pp. 31–5). This tension reminds us that no time scale is universally valid: people create their own sense of time through the specific rhythms of daily life and their particular understanding of past, present and future. Temporal existence is therefore socially structured and culturally relative (Knapp 1992, p. 14).

Another objection commonly raised is that to say a wall was built because someone intended to build a wall is hardly getting us very far. Certainly if no more than this was being claimed we would have got little further in one direction than Flannery's (1973) Mickey Mouse Laws did in another. But to discuss purpose and intention as deriving from a particular culture-historical context, linked into a framework of social action, is not simply to describe the data in a new way; additional information is provided. The interpretation goes beyond the data – if it did not the problem of validation would hardly arise. In the two 'wall' examples provided, construction took place in order to minimize cost in terms of garrisons and labour, and in order to gain social prestige. Both these interpretations add to the data.

Rather than allowing historical archaeology to become a 'new' natural science (Rahtz 1981), there would be benefits in transposing many of the methods and assumptions of historical archaeology into prehistory. In this chapter we have seen that history of the 'inside' of events, considered over the long term, provides us with the potential for a fuller understanding of social change, of the relationship between structure, idea and practice, and of the role of the individual in society. The archaeological data, with its unique access to the long term, can contribute to many contemporary debates concerning society and social change. For example, how resistant are subjective 'ways of doing things' to major social and technical upheaval? What is the relationship between gradual and sudden social change? By asking questions such as these, we can allow the particularity of the archaeological data to put its own case.

8 Contextual archaeology

Whatever questions one asks about the human past, even if they are only about technology or economy, frameworks of meaning intervene. After all, one cannot say what the economy of a site was until one has made hypotheses or assumptions about the symbolic meaning of, for example, bone discard. This book has been a search for an adequate answer to the question of how we infer past cultural meanings. In chapter 1, we framed the question of meaning in terms that called attention to two other issues: agency and history. Subsequently, we explored various approaches to meaning, agency and history.

The original task of comparing and contrasting the different approaches in terms of their contributions to these three issues has now been achieved and much of what was sought has been found. Structuralist archaeology contributes to the notion that culture is meaningfully constituted, but only a theory of practice can explain how meanings impact people's lives. New developments in Marxist-influenced archaeology and social theory have led to a more complete discussion of the role of agency in society, and a consideration of embodiment helps us understand how agents experience the world and how they are formed as subjects in the world. Finally, historical studies provide an understanding of how these meanings persist or change over time and how the actions of agents contribute to the transformation or maintenance of long-term structures of meaning.

In the previous chapter, we provided many loose glosses on the word 'meaning'. Meaning came in the form of (1) intellectual, emotional or mystical currents; (2) the 'inside of events'; (3) belief systems; (4) ideology and symbolism; (5) collective representations, and much more. We begin this chapter with a more careful consideration of what is meant by 'meaning'. Then, we move to the question of how archaeologists actually reconstruct meaning in the past. In answering this question, we wish to describe in greater detail what we have elsewhere called 'contextual archaeology'.

Meaning and understanding

Meaning can be defined in a number of ways – and is not easily translated into other languages (Bloch 1995). We start with the idea of meaning as making sense of a situation. We have chosen the word 'sense' to highlight the contribution of the physical, bodily senses. When something makes sense, we might not be able to explain why. We simply sense it, often without conscious reflection. We often become fully conscious only of the things that don't make sense (things that our body cannot make sense of) or things that make sense to us for the first time or in a new way. The 'situation' that we attempt to make sense of can be many things – an action, a conversation, a text, an object, a field of objects, etc. Since meaning is always of something, the differences between these varieties of situations are not trivial; we will try to illuminate them along the way.

Making sense of a situation implies that there is a distinction between a situation and the expression of meaning about that situation (Taylor 1985, pp. 15–16). Thus, meaning is not inherent in any situation. Meaning is relational; it is a joint product of the situation and the person or people for whom the situation is meaningful. Meaning is therefore always *for* someone (p. 22). Even though the geometric pattern of a snowflake contains astonishing coherence and sense, the snowflake has no meaning until human subjects come to experience it. In other words, meaning is agent-centred.

So far, our definition of meaning rests comfortably within a phenomenological paradigm. The situations in which we find ourselves – the items with which we come into contact – carry no meaning of their own: meaning is continually produced through the working sets of relationships we establish (Thomas 1996, p. 236). We may initially make sense of a spade, for example, from having used it to dig a hole (p. 65). Spade may thus mean digging tool. But if we plant seeds in that hole, we establish a relation between digging and planting. Meaning is fluid, flexible and multiple, as the spade comes to mean cultivation, or even regeneration, though to other subjects in other relationships with other spades, a spade may mean archaeological excavation. We make sense (we build 'structures of intelligibility') of the world through our active experience of it.

Meaning depends on unique individual experience in the world, but in addition to such individual meanings, it is possible to talk about social meanings. One such meaning is constitutive (or intersubjective) meaning (Taylor 1985, pp. 38–40). A constitutive meaning is the type of meaning that *constitutes* a situation. Unlike individual meaning, constitutive meaning does not refer to any of the specific senses of a spade (digging tool, gardening, archaeology, etc.). Rather, constitutive meaning is the type of meaning that creates the common language upon which all of these individual meanings depend, thus enabling the practice of making any kind of sense in the first place. John Searle (1970) provided the classic example of constitutive meaning. In the game of chess, the rules that define the possible movements of each piece constitute the game itself. Without those rules (constitutive meanings), there would be no game of chess as we know it. Other rules, such as the time allowed to make a move, regulate the game of chess but do not constitute it.

When we declare that culture is meaningfully constituted, we are referring to constitutive meaning. Before we attempt to explain a pattern of discarded bones, we must first make sense of the constellation of meaning that surrounds and constitutes (1) the bones that we uncritically refer to as 'discard', and (2) the practices that create such patterns. The concept of constitutive meaning deployed here is not too dissimilar from the kinds of structure discussed in chapters 3 and 5, and also brings us quite close to Foucault's idea of discursive formations. The way in which societies relate one topic to another and draw boundaries around forms of knowledge actively constitutes the kinds of meanings and voices that are possible. It is in this sense, then, that Foucault (1986) can declare that in ancient Greek society, which valued erotic relations between men and boys, homosexuality did not exist. This is because categories such as homosexuality and heterosexuality are only thinkable – only possible – if sex is constituted in such a way that its associations are with reproduction. Compared to modern Western society, in ancient Greece what we would refer to as sex was constituted as part of a very different constellation of meanings and associations which render the modern categories unintelligible. This discussion of sex is productive in an unexpected way: it flags an important question, first noted in the conclusion of the previous chapter, to which we will shortly return. If constitutive meanings of past societies are different from those of the archaeologist, do we lose all possibility of making sense of past societies?

Returning to the notion of individual meaning, we have thus far talked about meaning as making sense. Those archaeologists who work with an archaeological record that is hundreds or thousands of years old are making sense of societies and subjects that, because they are distant in time, are quite 'other'. Various writers have puzzled over this particular situation, in which one subject (usually an analyst) attempts to make sense of another subject (the interlocutor/informant). This type of interaction between two subjects is often modelled on a conversation, and within such hypothetical conversations the idea of translation is commonly used to illustrate the nuances of meaning. We are fully aware that a conversation is very different from the situations of meaning faced by archaeologists. However, we will now dwell on conversation and translation because they illustrate a number of subtleties that enrich our discussion of meaning. Later, we will show how a conversational model of meaning can be adapted for the study of other forms of action and their material residues.

We began with a distinction between meaning and the expression of meaning. This distinction tempts us to think that when we translate meaning from the first language to the second, the meaning itself is actually contained in a third, neutral language, and that the language of the informant and the language of the analyst contain only the varied (and distorted) expressions of that meaning. This is wrong (Gellner 1970). As we saw above, meaning is not outside of the language of expression: language constitutes meaning. Translating is therefore more than a mechanical act (Shanks and Hodder 1995, p. 6): it is not just matching words or sentences in one language with words or sentences in the other. In learning to speak the other language, we learn to live another form of life (Asad 1986, p. 149). The notion that speaking requires more than a mastery of vocabulary and grammar reminds us of Geertz's (1973) famous critique of ethnoscience: culture is not a set of systematic rules or ethnographic algorithms that, when followed, allow one to pass for a native.

In translating, we do not transpose meaning from one language to another. Rather, we transform our own language to accommodate the meaning. According to Walter Benjamin (1969, p. 79), 'The language of a translation can – in fact must – let itself go, so that it gives voice to the *intentio* of the original not as reproduction but as harmony.' To paraphrase Rudolf Pannwitz, whom Benjamin quotes, our translations should not turn Hindi, Greek or Maya into English, but should turn English into Hindi, Greek or Maya. In order to retain the agent-centred intentionality of meaning, we must 'transform our own language in order to translate the coherence of the original' (Asad 1986, pp. 156–7). But, as Gadamer (1981, p. 384) notes, for a meaning to be understood in a new language, that meaning must establish its validity in a new way. Thus, in translation, two transformations occur: transformation of the language of the analyst and transformation of the meaning itself.

The creation of new meaning introduces two important but vague terms – understanding and interpretation. Before using these blunted terms, we need to sharpen them: to give them specific definitions and use them only when these rather technical definitions are what we have in mind. We define understanding, or *verstehen*, as the meaning that results from the transformations of translation. These transformations create a new meaning which is different from the meaning in the original language but also different from anything native to the translator's language. The object of understanding is thus a hybridised form of meaning produced by fusing the horizons of the interpreter and the informant.

To understand what a person says, we do not simply master her language; understanding comes from translation and hybridisation. 'To understand what a person says is to come to an understanding about the subject matter, not to get inside another person and relive his experiences' (Gadamer 1981, p. 383). Emphatically, understanding is not empathy. In understanding, we do not adopt the subject's point of view. Instead, we relate the other's opinions and views to our own opinions and views (Gadamer 1981, p. 385; Taylor 1985, p. 117). We resist pure subjectivism – adopting the other's point of views – because native points of view arise from only a partial knowledge of the objective conditions of life (Bourdieu 1990) and can therefore be confused, malinformed or contradictory (Taylor 1985, p. 117). Nevertheless, coming to an understanding and, at the least, avoiding ethnocentrism oblige us to attend to these views and self-descriptions. We must master the agents' own meaningful accounts of their actions, but to make these actions clearer to them and to us, we must go beyond these self-perceptions and put them into the perspectives – historical, theoretical, etc. – of the analyst. As such, understanding is accountable to both the interpreter and the informant.

In sum, understanding is not 'simply a reawakening of the original process in the writer's mind; rather it is necessarily a re-creation of the text guided by the way the translator understands what it says' (Gadamer 1985, p. 386). *Interpretation* is coming to an understanding through precisely this sort of re-creation. This 'interpretive approach' is the foundation of hermeneutics, which we will return to later in this chapter.

We only interpret things that we do not understand (Taylor 1985, p. 15; Tilley 1993, p. 10). Interpretation therefore occurs only when something is confusing, incomplete or cloudy:

recall that the stimulus that guided Darnton's interpretive voyage was his failure to understand what was so funny about massacring cats. In the previous chapter, we demonstrated that Darnton and other historians have for a long time made use of interpretive approaches. However, they have expressed their search for understanding in terms that easily lend themselves to misreadings. For example, '*mentalité*', the 'inside of events' and 'mind reading' all imply that interpretation adopts the native point of view and nothing else; that we strive to think exactly like a native. However, a close reading of such historical approaches reveals that they are in fact congruent with the holistic idea of understanding developed here. Nevertheless, most archaeologists miss the nuance in these approaches, which causes them to launch into misdirected accusations of subjectivism whenever a name like Collingwood appears.

Meaning in archaeology

In archaeology, there is a spectrum of positions on meaning, ranging from the idea that meaning is inaccessible to the idea that meaning is accessible and multiple. As we have seen, processual archaeologists claim that their explanations of the past are free of meaning in the embodied, intentional, relational and historic senses that we have discussed in this chapter and others. These claims began perhaps with Binford's denunciation of palaeopsychology, but continue even in strands of processual archaeology that claim to engage in cognition (Renfrew 1994a). There is an obvious objection to this meaning-less stance: the function of burials, for example, cannot be understood without a consideration of the meanings surrounding death. But there is a more subtle objection: function itself is also a form of meaning, even if we are discussing nothing more than the function of a simple spade. This type of meaning, similar to the first model identified by Patrik (1985), involves the structured system of functional interrelationships. In seeking this type of meaning, we can ask about the human and physical environment, the depositional processes, the organisation of labour, the size of settlement, the exchanges of matter, energy and information. We give the object meaning by seeing how it functions in relation to these other factors and processes and in relation to economic and social structures. The great contribution of processual and Marxist archaeology has been made in this arena.

A processualist might claim, however, that observing how an object functions is to explain it, not to understand its meaning. We must therefore tease apart the difference between explanation and understanding. To explain an event is to determine its cause and to link the cause to general theories, principles or scientific laws. In this sense, to seek an explanation is to ask why an event occurs.

Understanding differs from explanation because in understanding we do not evacuate the realm of specificity in search for an abstract, causal principle. Rather, we continue to ask questions of the data, and even when we ask 'why' an event occurs, our answers build from specific inquiries about 'what' things were involved and how (Shanks and Tilley 1987a, p. 113).

But perhaps explanation and understanding are more alike than different. Despite the fact that understanding privileges context more than explanation, understanding also represents a move away from the original context in so far as the original context must be made sense of according to our own context. Also, though it may seem that a successful explanation closes down the inquiry by eliminating ambiguities and resolving doubts, processualists are committed to multiple working hypotheses and falsification. In other words, since the goal is not ultimately to confirm one explanation but to keep a number of explanations on hand and gradually falsify the bad ones, explanation is an open-ended endeavour.

Understanding is also open-ended, though for reasons that have to do with the social context of research. Since meaning is relational, new inquiries and new investigators will come to a different relationship with the object of inquiry and therefore derive different understandings of it. This should not come as a shock since it is rather well known that every new generation rewrites history in its own way (Collingwood 1946, p. 248). In sum, both explanation and understanding are ongoing activities. Both can be considered hermeneutics, which we describe in further detail at the end of this chapter.

Processualists are not the only ones to renounce meaning. John Barrett (1987) claims that we should not attempt to infer meaning from the archaeological record. Instead, 'what we should look at is how dominant forms of meaning were produced and maintained' (p. 472). According to Barrett, the production and maintenance of meaning occurs through the routine practices by which people live their lives. Barrett thus makes the argument that we should ignore the ways in which people thought of their world and focus solely on their practices. This is of course at odds with the interpretive method sketched above, but perhaps a more serious problem with Barrett's approach is that, in separating practice from meaning, it recreates a dichotomy between physical and mental and sides with the former (see also chapter 6).

We reiterate that meaning is not dichotomous. We make sense of the world through both practices and ideas, but since practices shape ideas and ideas shape practices, it is difficult to separate the two. Meaning is therefore difficult to distinguish from being. However, understanding is clearly different from being because it moves beyond the actor's experience to include the analyst's reflections on the actor's experience. In other words, the new meanings that come from understanding are a step removed from experience: they are the products of reflection on the experience of someone other than the analyst. Nevertheless, the work of interpretation creates a new experience for the analyst that is certainly part of the analyst's being.

In addition to the processual sense of meaning as a system of functional interrelationships, there is also meaning as the structured content of ideas and symbols. This form of meaning was the goal of the symbolic and structural archaeologies that proliferated in the 1980s (Hodder 1982a, 1982b). Attending to the content of ideas and symbols involves more than saying, 'this fibula functions to symbolize women' or 'this sword symbolizes men'. Rather, the question becomes, 'what is the view of womanhood represented in the link between female skeletons and fibulae in graves?' The aim is to search for Bourdieu's habitus, the *pe* described by Flannery and Marcus, and other structured and structuring ideas of the type discussed in chapter 5. Archaeologists need to make abstractions from the symbolic functions of the objects they excavate in order to identify the meaning content behind them, and this involves examining how the ideas denoted by material symbols themselves play a part in structuring society.

Beyond meaning as a system of functional interrelationships and meaning as ideas and symbols, there is a third kind of meaning: the meaning of specific actions for specific actors. We call this operational meaning. On the one hand, operational meaning of a thing or event depends first on the actor's previous experiences of those things or events. This simply restates the fact that meaning is relational. We use the word 'experience' in order to convey a sense of embodiment. It is important to remember bodily experience at this point because too much abstract discussion of meaning might lull us into the familiar mistake of equating 'meaning' not with sense but with a sort of message that is purely conceptual and consciously received. On the other hand, operational meaning also depends on the intentions that motivate the actions we interpret. In sum, operational meaning involves both the actor's experience of the past (biography) and intentions for the future (strategy).

Having identified these three meanings, we must now retrace our steps and make it clear that this kind of a threefold typology has nothing more than heuristic value. For example, it is impossible to disentangle the meaning of a particular use of symbols (an operational meaning) from the historically generated field of meanings that condition that particular use of symbols. In other words different types of meaning are not mutually exclusive. Here we revisit the inseparable relation between constitutive meaning and individual meaning (and perhaps *langue* and *parole*): individual meanings rest upon and are enabled by constitutive meanings.

Finally, we must talk about meaning for archaeologists. Meaning is not inherent in archaeological remains: it is *for* someone, and in the case of the interpreting archaeologist, it is for the interpreting archaeologist. This means that the contemporary context of interpretation – the politics of archaeological communities – is an integral part of the process of interpretation. In this chapter we will begin a discussion of contemporary archaeo-politics by exploring critical hermeneutics and the politics of relativism. But archaeo-politics is too broad a subject to be contained in one chapter (cf. Tilley 1993, pp. 8–9). We continue the discussion in the next chapter by observing specific examples of engagements between archaeology and other contemporary interest groups.

As already noted, archaeologists have long discussed ways of using their contextual data to build interpretations of functional inter-relationships. This is the domain of palaeo-economics, exchange theory, information theory, systems theory, optimal foraging theory, social action theory, and so on. All such theories can be faulted because of their inadequate consideration of the second and third types of meaning with which the first is necessarily linked. Our main concern here, then, will be with the content of meaning in particular historical contexts, since this is the main lacuna in current archaeological theory identified in previous chapters. The same point is made by Davis (1984, p. 12), Wells (1984; 1985) and Hall (1977). Although there is much overlap with the consideration of functional meanings, our main interest will be the use of contextual relationships to get at past meaning content.

Reading material culture

How do we get at past meaning content? First in importance, is it even possible to get at meaning? As we noted above, many analytical traditions are sceptical of the possibility of coming to an understanding of meaning through interpretation (hermeneutics). We can scapegoat some of Foucault's books (1972, 1994), in so far as his 'new history' emphasises nearly unbridgeable discontinuities between the present and the past and in so far as he was famously concerned with the order of things, not their individual meanings. Yet Benjamin and even Gadamer also admitted to an impossibility in this task. In translation, 'there will always be a gap between the spirit of the original words and that of their reproduction' (Gadamer 1981, p. 384). But as we saw above, the goal of interpretation is not direct translation, but understanding. Furthermore, despite the radical claims in his writing of the late 1960s, Foucault's histories stand as testimony to the possibility of understanding the past.

Previous editions of this book proposed a method for understanding meaning in the past that considered the archaeological record as a text to be read. But how are we to read such 'texts'? Clearly, if the past material culture language shared no features, words, grammar or structure in common with our contemporary verbal language, then any such reading would be difficult if not impossible, especially since the surviving text is partial and fragmentary, in addition to being simply different. Beyond this basic difference between language and material culture, there are other limits to the view that material culture should be compared with text and language.

Whereas language is an abstract representation, the primary function of much material culture may not be to represent but to help accomplish physical tasks. Material culture variation is often dependent on these functional considerations. In chapter 3 (p. 60) we discussed other differences between material culture and text: material culture as a signifier does not always have an arbitrary relation to the signified; material culture is ambiguous in different ways; the experience of material culture is often semi-conscious or unconscious.

There are many other troubles with text (Buchli 1995). Morris (1999, p. 27) claims that objects may be scarce whereas words are not (it is important to note, however, that certain words may be taboo and that in many situations not all people are authorised to speak; Bourdieu 1991). Bloch (1995) notes that when we consider material culture as text, we fall into the trap of thinking that meaning is something signified. In his example from Madagascar, wood carvings do not 'mean' anything; rather they 'honor the wood'. When we realise that the wood of the house indexes the founder of the house, the 'meaning' of the wood and the carvings is interwoven with the life of the founder. The wood carvings are texts only in the sense that they are the materials by which people create their own biographical texts (Thomas 1995).

These considerations challenge the central idea of this book: that the past can be read. However, we believe we can respond to these challenges and rescue the idea of reading the past. Our first response is that text is not the only thing we read. We read a variety of signs: text happens to be the most abstract and complex. We are on better footing when reading material culture partly because material culture is not as abstract or complex as text. Text is complex because it is designed to express complex ideas and thoughts, and has to be fairly precise and comprehensive. But there are no grammars and dictionaries of material culture language. Material culture symbols are often more ambiguous than their verbal counterparts, and what can be said with them is normally much simpler. Also the material symbols are durable, restricting flexibility. In many ways material culture is not a language at all – it is more clearly action and practice in the world, and these pragmatic concerns have a great influence on the symbolic meanings of material culture (Hodder 1989a). In so far as material culture is a language, it is a simple one when compared to spoken or written language. For these varied reasons, material culture texts are easier to decipher than those written documents for which we do not know the language. This is why archaeologists have had some success in 'reading' material culture, even though they have rarely been explicit about the 'grammar' which they are assuming.

Part of the reason why material culture is easier to decipher than text is that it works with a different model of signs. As we saw in chapter 3, Saussure's semiological model of the sign – arbitrary relation between signifier and signified – works well for text but not for material culture. We embrace Peirce's semiotic model of signs, which accounts for the materiality of objects by considering non-arbitrary relations, such as indexicality and iconicity (Preucel and Bauer 2001). Finally, despite the fact that most philosophers resort to 'conversation', 'translation' or 'text' as examples of the process of interpretation, a variety of writers have amplified Peirce's goal by developing additional details of the ways that material signs communicate meaning. Much of this work was reviewed in chapter 3 (p. 64) in the discussion of materialisation: meaningful actions leave their mark on the world of objects.

In sum, we can resurrect the idea of reading the past if, ironically, we remember that material culture is not text. Text is only a metaphor, not an analogy, for material culture. As human actors, we are always reading the contexts in which we find ourselves and we have done so since infancy. As we showed in chapter 6, much of the way we habituate ourselves to the settings around us is through a semi-conscious, bodily harmonising. As Gadamer (1975, pp. 259–61) points out, this Heideggerian form of 'being-in-the-world' – Dasein – is the original form of understanding. In other words, we come to know other people, other cultures and other times in the same way that we find our footing in our everyday world. Life itself is the foundation and sufficient condition for historical hermeneutics. We project ourselves into the past in the same way that we find our way growing up in our own culture or another culture. As we meet and get to know people, we can never be certain that we have properly understood what is in their minds, what they mean by things. All we have to go on is their grunts and actions. Gradually, as more of these physical events occur, we come to some approximation of this 'otherness': we come to see the grunts as words. However 'other' it seemed at first, an evaluated approximation to understanding is feasible. The goal of this chapter is to make these procedures more explicit, particularly in relation to archaeology and the type of data with which archaeologists deal.

Reading the past

For the remainder of this chapter, we present the details of what has been called 'contextual archaeology', beginning with a discussion of 'context'.

Context

The word 'context' is used frequently in archaeological discourse, in questions such as 'what is the context of your remark?', or 'what is the data context?' The word is used in a variety of different situations to mean sensitivity to the particular data – 'your general idea does not work in my context' – but in the previous section, we noted that context refers also to the contemporary social, political and economic conditions of research.

'Context' comes from the Latin *contexere*, meaning to weave, join together, connect. In reaction to the excessive claims about general laws made by some New Archaeologists (e.g. Watson, Leblanc and Redman 1971) one can argue that there were many movements in the contextual direction. As already noted (p. 42), Flannery (1973) reacted against too strong an emphasis on 'law-and-order', and emphasized instead 'systemness' – a more flexible approach in which particular relationships could be taken into account. This interweaving, or connecting, of things in their historical particularity has been described above (p. 125) as evident in many branches of archaeology (Marxist, evolutionary, processual). Butzer (1982) too has identified a 'contextual' method in ecological approaches to the past, and in Classical archaeology a contextual approach has been clearly outlined in relation to Greek painted pottery (Berard and Durand 1984). A book entitled *Contexts for Prehistoric Exchange* (Ericson and Early 1982) seeks to emphasize the contexts of production and consumption in which exchange occurs.

In spatial archaeology more generally, Hodder (1985) has argued that a new generation of analytical techniques seeks to be more sensitive to the archaeological data, and to be more heuristic. We shall see more of this below. A major arena in which archaeologists have emphasized the particularity of their data is the study of depositional processes. Schiffer (1976) made the important contribution of distinguishing the archaeological context from the systemic context, pointing to the dangers of an application of general theory and methods (e.g. Whallon 1974) which did not take this distinction into account.

In Renfrew's (1973a) *The Explanation of Culture Change*, Case (1973, p. 44) argued for a contextual archaeology 'which alone deserves to be considered a new archaeology', and which involved linking general theories more closely to the available data. This concern with context has perhaps increased recently, at all levels in archaeology. On the one hand Flannery (1982) appears critical of general and abstract philosophizing which strays too far from the hard data (see also Barrett and Kinnes 1988); on the other hand, the concern with context has become a major methodological issue in excavation procedures. Rather than using interpretative terms (like floor, house, pit, post-hole) at the initial stage of excavation and analysis, many data coding sheets now use less subjective words such as 'unit' or 'context'. It is felt that excavation should not involve over-subjective interpretations imposed at too early a stage, before all the data have been amassed.

In a sense, archaeology is defined by its concern with context. To be interested in artifacts without any contextual information is antiquarianism, and is perhaps found in certain types of art history or the art market. Digging objects up out of their context, as is done by some metal detector users, is the antithesis in relation to which archaeology forms its identity. To reaffirm the importance of context thus includes reaffirming the importance of archaeology as archaeology.

In sum, archaeologists use the term 'context' in a variety of ways which have in common the connecting or interweaving of objects in a particular situation or group of situations. An object as an object, alone, is mute. But archaeology is not the study of isolated objects. Objects may not be totally mute if we can read the context in which they are found (Berard and Durand 1984, p. 21). Of course all languages have to be interpreted, and so, in one sense, all utterances and material symbols are mute, but a material symbol in its context is no more or less mute than any grunt or other sound used in speech. The artifacts do speak (or perhaps faintly whisper), but they speak only a part of a dialogue in which the interpreter is an active participant.

Two points which have been made throughout this volume need to be emphasized here. The first is that the subjective internal meanings which archaeologists can infer are not 'ideas in people's heads', in the sense that they are not the conscious thoughts of individuals. Rather, they are public and social concepts which are reproduced in the practices of daily life. They are thus both made visible for archaeologists and because the institutionalized practices of social groups have a routine they lead to repetition and pattern. It is from these material patterns that archaeologists can infer the concepts which are embedded in them. The second way in which the feasibility of reading material culture is enhanced is that the context of material culture production is more concrete than that of language and speech. Material culture meanings are largely influenced by technological, physical and functional considerations. The concrete and partly non-cultural nature of such factors enables the 'text' of material culture to be read more easily than the arbitrary signs of language. The context of material culture is not only abstract and conceptual but also pragmatic and non-arbitrary.

In what follows, the term 'contextual' will refer to the placing of items 'with their texts' – 'con-text'. The general notion here is that 'context' can refer to those parts of a written document which come immediately before and after a particular passage, so closely connected in meaning with it that its sense is not clear apart from them. Later in this chapter a still more specific definition of 'context' will be provided. For the moment, the aim is to outline ways in which archaeologists move from text to symbolic meaning content.

Contextual archaeology

Similarities and differences

In beginning to systematize the methodology for interpreting past meaning content from material culture, it seems that archaeologists work by identifying various types of relevant similarities and differences, and that these are built up into various types of contextual associations. Abstractions are then made from contexts and associations and differences in order to arrive at meaning in terms of function and content (see Fig. 7).

We can start, then, with the idea of similarities and differences. In language this is simply the idea that when someone says 'black' we give that sound meaning because it sounds similar (though not identical) to other examples of the word 'black', and because it is different from other sounds like 'white' or 'back'. In archaeology it is the common idea that we put a pot in the category of 'A' pots because it looks like other pots in that category but looks different from the category of 'B' pots. Of course, the similarities and differences

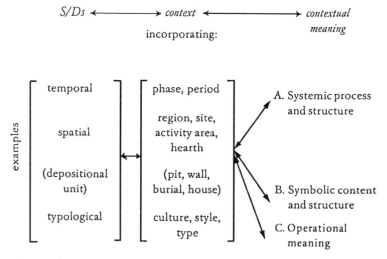

Fig. 7. The interpretation of contextual meanings from the similarities and differences between archaeological objects.

that we see as archaeologists might not be relevant. We discuss the issue of relevance in the next section, but the following example provisionally highlights the issue. In graves, we may find fibulae associated with women, and this similarity in spatial location and unit of deposition encourages us to think that fibulae 'mean' women, but only if the fibula is not found in male graves, which may be different in that brooches are found instead of fibulae. Other associations and contrasts of women, female activities and fibulae may allow an abstraction concerning the meaning content of 'womanhood'. For example the fibulae might have designs which are elsewhere found associated with a category of objects to do with reproduction rather than with productive tasks (see the Faris study, p. 64, and McGhee's analysis, p. 46).

We can formalize this process of searching for similarities and differences in the following diagram:

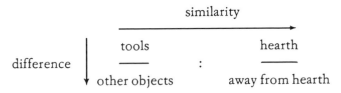

It is instructive to compare such a diagram with the following one, in which it is utilitarian functional relationships rather than symbolic functions that are being sought.

Here the archaeologist interprets the area around a hearth as an activity area because tools occur there in contrast to other parts of the site or house where tools are not found. The form of explanation is identical to the one above, in which the symbolic meaning of a fibula is sought. But, as has been claimed throughout this volume, there is no necessary disjunction between these two aims: function and symbolic meaning are not contradictory. Thus the fibula functions to keep clothes on and perhaps to symbolize women, and it can also have the meaning content of 'women as reproductive'. Equally the activity area around the hearth may indicate that certain tools have the meaning content of 'home', the 'domestic hearth' and so on. Indeed we need to assume some such meaning in order to look for the activity area around the hearth in the first place and in order to give the objects grouped there related functions. The identification of an 'activity area' is the imposition of meaning content. The forms of meaning (functional/systemic, ideational, operational) are necessarily interdependent – it is not possible to talk of the one without at least assuming the other.

The above account of meaning as being built up from simultaneous similarities and differences is influenced by the discussion in chapter 3, and it seeks to do no more than account for the way in which archaeologists work. However, a prescriptive element is also present. First, it is argued that similarities and differences can be identified at many 'levels'. Thus similarities and differences may occur in terms of underlying dimensions of variation such as structural oppositions, notions of 'orderliness', 'naturalness' and so on. Theory is always involved in the definition of similarities and differences, but at 'deeper' levels the need for imaginative theory is particularly apparent. We will return to these different levels of similarity and difference below. Second, it can be argued that archaeologists have concentrated too much on similarities and too little on differences (Van der Leeuw, personal communication to the authors). The whole cross-cultural approach has been based on identifying similarities and common causes. The tendency has been to explain, for example, pottery decoration by some universal symbolic function of all decoration or of all symbolism. Societies have been grouped into categories (states, hunter-gatherers etc.) and their common characteristics identified. Of course, any such work assumes differences as well, but the 'presence' of an absence is seldom made the focus of research. For example, we can ask why pots are decorated, but we can also ask why only pots are decorated. This is again partly a matter of identifying the particular framework within which action has meaning. If pots are the only type of container decorated in one cultural context this is of relevance in interpreting the meaning of the decoration. But on the whole archaeologists tend to remove the decorated pots from their contexts and measure the similarities between pots.

The need to consider difference can be clarified, if in a somewhat extreme fashion, with the word 'pain'. One way to interpret the unknown meaning of this word would be to search for similar words in other cultures. We would then form a category of similar-looking words, including examples found in England and France, and identify their common characteristics. But in fact the word has entirely different meanings in England and France, and one would quickly see this by concentrating on the different associations of the word in the two cultures – in England with agony and in France with bakers. This over-simplistic example reinforces the point made by Collingwood, that every term which archaeologists use has to be open to criticism to see whether it might have different meanings in different contexts. Archaeologists need, then, to be alive to difference and absence; they must always ask questions such as: is the pot type found in different situations, why are other pot types not decorated, why are other containers not decorated, why is this type of tomb or this technique of production absent from this area?

In what ways can archaeologists describe similarities and differences? In the fibula example given above, we already have a typological difference (between the fibula and the brooch) and a depositional similarity (the fibula occurs in graves with women). We have also referred to similarities and differences along the functional dimension. We shall see that the interweaving and networking of different types and levels of similarity and difference support interpretation. For the moment, however, we wish to discuss each type of dimension of similarity/difference separately. Each type of similarity and difference can occur at more than one level and scale.

The first type of similarity and difference with which archaeologists routinely deal is the *temporal*. Clearly if two objects are close in time, that is, they are similar along the temporal dimension, as seen in stratigraphy, absolute dating, or otherwise, then archaeologists would be more likely to place them in the same context and give them related meanings. In chapter 7 we made it clear that the archaeologist's understanding of time might differ markedly from the understandings of time held in ancient societies. Also, the temporal dimension is closely linked to other dimensions – if two objects are in the same temporal context but widely distant in space or in other dimensions, then the similar temporal context may be irrelevant. Diffusion is a process that takes place over time and space and also involves the typological dimension.

The concern along the temporal dimension is to isolate a period or phase in which, in some sense, inter-related events are occurring. So within a phase there is continuity of structure, and/or meaning content, and/or systemic processes etc. But what scale of temporal analysis is necessary for the understanding of any particular object? In chapter 7 examples were noted of continuities over millennia. It was also suggested (p. 138) that, ultimately, it is necessary to move backwards, 'peeling off the onion skins', until the very first cultural act is identified. This is not a practical or necessary solution in most instances; in most cases one simply wants to identify the historical context which has a direct bearing on the question at hand.

Archaeologists already have a battery of quantitative techniques for identifying continuities and breaks in temporal sequences (Doran and Hodson 1975), and such evidence is used in identifying the relevant context, but many breaks which appear substantial may in fact express continuities or transformations at the structural level, and they may involve diffusion and migration, implying that the relevant temporal context has to be pursued in other spatial contexts. In general, archaeologists have been successful in identifying the relevant systemic inter-relationships for the understanding of any one object (artifact, site or whatever). These are simply all the factors in the previous system state which impinge upon the new state. But in the imposition of meaning content, when the archaeologist wishes to evaluate the claims that two objects are likely to have the same meaning content because they are contemporary, or that the meanings are unlikely to have changed within the same phase, the question of scale becomes even more important. So, from considering temporal similarities and differences, we are left with the question: what is the scale on which the relevant temporal context is to be defined? This question of scale will reappear and will be dealt with later, but it seems to depend on the questions that are being asked and the attributes that are being measured.

Similarities and differences can also be noted along the *spatial* dimension. Here the archaeologists are concerned with identifying functional and symbolic meanings and structures from the arrangements of objects (and sites, etc.) over space. Space, like time, is also qualitatively experienced, as we saw in chapter 6, and therefore should not be understood simply as a neutral variable. Normally analysis along this dimension assumes that the temporal dimension has been controlled. The concern is to derive meanings from objects because they have similar spatial relationships (e.g. clustered, regularly spaced). Again, a battery of techniques already exists for such analysis. It can be claimed that many of these spatial techniques involve imposing externally derived hypotheses without adequate consideration of context; however, new analytical procedures are now emerging which allow greater sensitivity to archaeological data. For example, Kintigh and Ammerman (1982) have described contextual, heuristic methods for the description of point distributions, and related techniques have been described for assessing the association between distributions (Hodder and Okell 1978), and for determining the boundaries of distributions (Carr 1984). Indeed, it is possible to define a whole new generation of spatial analytical techniques in archaeology, which are less concerned to impose methods and theories, pre-packaged, from other disciplines or from abstract probability theory, and are more concerned with the specific archaeological problem at hand (Hodder 1985).

In these various ways the archaeologist seeks to define the spatial context which is relevant to an understanding of a particular object. In many cases this is fairly straightforward – the origins of the raw material can be sought, the spatial extent of the style can be mapped, the boundaries of the settlement cluster can be drawn. Often, however, the relevant scale of analysis will vary depending on the attribute selected (raw material, decorative style, shape). This is similar to the variation found if an individual is asked 'where do you come from?' The response (street, part of town, town, county, country, continent) will depend on contextual questions (who is being talked to and where, and why the question is being asked). Thus there is no 'right' scale of analysis.

This problem is particularly acute in the archaeological concern to define 'regions' of analysis. This is often done *a priori*, based on environmental features (e.g. a valley system), but whether such an imposed entity has any relevance to the questions being asked is not always clear. The 'region' will vary depending on the attributes being discussed. Thus there can be no one *a priori* scale of spatial context – the context varies from the immediate environment to the whole world if some relevant dimension of variation can be found linking objects (sites, cultures or whatever) at these different scales. As was made clear in the case of the temporal dimension, the definition of context will depend on identifying relevant dimensions of variation along which similarities and differences can be measured, and this will be discussed further below.

It is perhaps helpful to identify a third type of similarity and difference – the *depositional unit* – which is in fact a combination of the first two. We mean here closed layers of soil, pits, graves, ditches and the like, which are bounded in space and time. To say that two objects may have associated meanings because they come from the same pit is just as subjective as saying that they have related meanings because they are linked spatially and temporally, but there is also an additional component of interpretation in that it is assumed that the boundaries of the unit are themselves relevant for the identification of meaning. Archaeologists routinely accept this premiss; indeed co-occurrence in a pit, or on a house floor, may be seen as more important than unbounded spatial distance. Once again, similarities and differences in depositional unit can be claimed at many scales (layer, post-hole, house, site) and the question of identifying the relevant scale of context will have to be discussed.

The *typological* dimension also could be argued to be simply a variant of the two primary dimensions. If two artifacts are said to be similar typologically, this really means that they have similar arrangements or forms in space. However it is helpful to distinguish the notion of 'type', as is usual in archaeology, since typological similarities of objects over space and time are different from the distances (over space and time) between them. Indeed, the notion of typological similarities and differences is central to the definition of temporal contexts (incorporating periods, phases) and spatial contexts (incorporating cultures, styles). Thus typology is central to the development of the contextual approach in archaeology. It is also the aspect which most securely links archaeology to its traditional concerns and methods.

At the basis of all archaeological work is the need to classify and categorize, and the debate as to whether these classifications are 'ours' or 'theirs', 'etic' or 'emic', is an old one. On the whole, however, this stage of analysis, the initial typology of settlements, artifacts or economies, is normally separated from the later analysis of social process. Most archaeologists recognize the subjectivity of their own typologies and have focussed on mathematical and computer techniques which aim to limit this subjectivity. After having 'done the best they can' with the initial, unavoidably difficult stage, archaeologists then move on to quantify and compare and to arrive at social process.

For example it may be claimed that there is more uniformity or diversity in one area or period than another, or that one region has sites in which 20% of potsherds have zig-zag designs while another adjacent region also has 20% zig-zag designs, indicating close contact, lack of competition, trade etc. But how can we be sure that the initial typology is valid? As in the example of the bird/rabbit drawing on p. 18, how can we be sure that the zig-zags, though looking the same, are not different?

To get at such questions, a start can be made with the structure of decoration (chapter 3). Do the zig-zags occur on the same parts of the same types of pot, or in the same structural position in relation to other decorations? But also, what is the culture-historical context of the use of zig-zag (and other) decoration in the two areas? Going back in time, can we see the zig-zags deriving from different origins and traditions? Have they had different associations and meanings?

In defining 'types', archaeologists need to examine the historical association of traits in order to attempt to enter into the subjective meanings they connote. To some degree, archaeologists have traditionally been sensitive to such considerations, at least implicitly. For example, through much of the Neolithic in north and west Europe, pots tend to have horizontally organized decoration near the rim, and vertical decoration lower down. Sometimes, as in some beaker shapes, this distinction is marked by a break in the outline of the pot between neck and body. In discussing and categorizing types of Neolithic pottery, this particular historical circumstance can be taken into account, with the upper and lower zones of decoration being treated differently.

Of course it can be argued that such differences, between upper horizontal and lower vertical decoration, are entirely imposed from the outside and would not have been recognized by Neolithic individuals. Certainly this possibility will always remain, but it is argued here that archaeologists have been successful, and can have further success, in recovering typologies which approximate indigenous perceptions (always remembering that such perceptions would have varied according to social contexts and strategy). Success in such endeavours depends on including as much information as is available on the historical contexts and associations of traits, styles and organizational design properties, as well as on a reconstruction of the active use of such traits in social strategies.

Thus, one contextual approach to typology is to obtain as much information as possible about the similarities and differences of individual attributes before the larger typologies are built. A rather different approach is to accept the arbitrariness of our own categories and to be more open to alternative possibilities. For example, the plant typologies used by palaeoethnobotanists tend to be restricted to the established species lists. It would be possible, however, to class plant remains according to height of plant, stickiness of leaves, period of flowering, and so on. These varied classifications can be tested for correlations with other variables, with the aim of letting the data contribute to the choice of appropriate typology. A similar procedure could be followed for bone, pottery or any other typology.

Four dimensions of variation (temporal, spatial, depositional and typological) have been discussed, and functional variation has been briefly mentioned. One general point can be emphasized. An important aspect of contextual history is that it allows for dimensions of variation which occur at 'deeper' levels than in much archaeology. In other words, similarities and differences are also sought in terms of abstractions which draw together the observable data in ways which are not immediately apparent. For example, an abstract opposition between culture and nature may link together the degree to which settlements are 'defended' or bounded, and the relative proportions of wild and domesticated animals found in those settlements. Thus, where the culture/nature dichotomy is more marked, the boundaries around settlements (separating the domestic from the wild) may be more substantial, houses too may be more elaborate, and even pottery may be more decorated (as marking the 'domestication' of food products as they are brought in, prepared and consumed in the domestic world). The bones of wild animals, especially the still wild ancestors or equivalents of domesticated stock, may not occur in settlement sites. As the culture/nature dichotomy becomes less marked, or as its focus is changed, all the above 'similarities' may change together if the hypothesis that the culture/nature dichotomy is a relevant dimension of variation is correct. It is not immediately apparent that boundaries around settlements, pottery decoration and the proportions of wild and domesticated animal bones have anything to do with each other. The provision of a 'deep' abstraction suddenly makes sense of varied pieces of information as they change through time.

Relevant dimensions of variation

In any set of cultural data there are perhaps limitless similarities and differences that can be identified. For example, all pots in an area are similar in that they are made of clay, but different in that the detailed marks of decoration vary slightly or in that the distributions of temper particles are not identical. How do we pick out the relevant similarities and differences, and what is the relevant scale of analysis?

We wish to argue initially that the relevant dimensions of variation are identified heuristically in archaeology by finding those dimensions of variation (grouped into temporal, spatial, depositional and typological etc.) which show significant patterns of similarity and difference. Significance itself is largely defined in terms of the number and quality of coincident similarities and differences in relation to a theory. An important safeguard in interpreting past meaning content is the ability to support hypotheses about meaningful dimensions of variation in a variety of different aspects of the data (see, for example, Deetz 1983, Hall 1983). For example, if the orientation of houses is symbolically important in comparing and contrasting houses (see above, p. 71) does the same dimension of variation occur also in the placing of tombs? There are numerous ways in which archaeologists routinely seek for significant correlations, associations and differences, but the inferred pattern increases in interest as more of the network coincides. Since the definition of such statistically significant patterning depends on one's theory, guidelines are needed for the types of significant similarities and differences that can be sought.

Here it is helpful to return to the distinction between systemic and symbolic meanings. As already noted, it is in the realm of systemic processes that most archaeological theory and method have been developed. Given such work, it is recognized that consideration of the sources of raw materials is significant and relevant to a discussion of the exchange of the items made from those raw materials. In discussing subsistence economies it is relevant and significant to study bones and seeds from a variety of functionally inter-related sites. But immediately, we are drawn in such accounts to the need to consider the symbolic meaning content of bones (see above, p. 15), which has been less well researched and is less easy to define.

In discussing the content of symbolic meanings a range of different theories from structuralism and post-structuralism to Marxist and structuration theories concerned with ideology, power, action and representation are used. But such theories can always be tied to particular similarities and differences. A start can be made with an example. Imagine we are concerned with the meaning of the occurrence of red pots on a site. What are the relevant dimensions of variation for determining the meaning of this attribute? With what should the red pots be compared in order to identify similarities and differences? A second, contemporary site has no red pots, but it does have bronze fibulae (which do not occur on the first site). Is the difference between the pots and the fibulae relevant for an understanding of the pots? Such a difference would be relevant if it were part of a more general difference in historical tradition between the two sites or regions, but since it is on its own we cannot say that the fibulae are relevant to the red pots unless there is some dimension along which we can measure the variation and see significant patterning. Thus, we might find that the red pots and fibulae occurred in the same spatial location within houses or graves – in such a case they would be alternative types when measured in terms of spatial location; or red pots on the first site might be contrasted with black pots on the second site, with the fibulae only found in the black pots. Once some dimension is found along which distinctively patterned similarities and differences occur, then the fibulae do become relevant to an understanding of the red pots. Our theories about the way material culture 'texts' work, including the notion of structural oppositions, allow statistical significance to be defined. In the case of the red pots, if we find statistically significant patterning with the fibulae, then the pots and the fibulae are part of the same context and must be described together. A lack of significant contextual patterning between two artifact classes does not mean an absence of meaning: each depositional event, whether it involves a pot alone, a fibula alone or both together, has operational meaning. Importantly, the lack of a clear pattern may indicate that instead of consensus, there was a cacophony of voices and acts in this area, or perhaps chaos as a result of post-depositional processes. In the example given on p. 174, the fibula and the brooch are relevant to each other because they occur as alternative dress items.

As another hypothetical example, we can take the design in Fig. 8. If we want to compare this pottery design with other designs on pots in order to identify similarities and differences, we have to describe it in some way. But, *a priori*, there are very many ways of describing the same design, some of which are provided in the diagram. What is the relevant dimension of variation on which the designs can be described and compared? It might be thought, and it is often claimed, that decisions by archaeologists about which is the 'right' description are entirely arbitrary. Yet we have already seen that much other information within the 'same' context can be used to aid the decision. For example, lozenge shapes (as in description '*f*' in Fig. 8) made of beaten gold might be found in the same graves as the decorated pots, apparently worn on male bodies as items of prestige. In fact lozenges might be found frequently in different but significant contexts within the same culture as the pots. This evidence for statistical association might lead the archaeologist to suggest that the '*f*' description in Fig. 8 was the 'best' in this particular context.

Reading the past

Design:

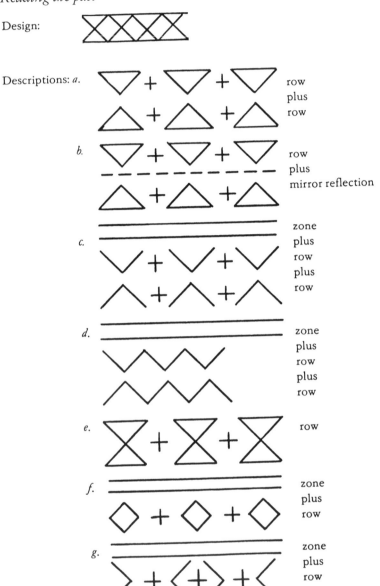

Descriptions: *a.* ▽ + ▽ + ▽   row
                                  plus
              △ + △ + △   row

b. ▽ + ▽ + ▽   row
     – – – – – – – – –   plus
                          mirror reflection
     △ + △ + △

c. ═══════════   zone
                    plus
     ∨ + ∨ + ∨   row
                    plus
     ∧ + ∧ + ∧   row

d. ═══════════   zone
                    plus
     ∨∨∨∨   row
                    plus
     ∧∧∧∧   row

e. ⋈ + ⋈ + ⋈   row

f. ═══════════   zone
                    plus
     ◇ + ◇ + ◇   row

g. ═══════════   zone
                    plus
     〉+ 〈+〉+ 〈   row

Fig. 8.

186

In this example we can continue further to define what is a relevant similarity or difference – along which dimension and at what scale. For example, at some point the lozenge used as comparison may be so distorted in shape that we doubt its relevance, or there may be such a gap in space or time between the lozenges being compared that we say that they are unlikely to have any relevance to each other; they have no common meaning. We can of course argue that the gold lozenges in graves are dress items, on a different depositional dimension to the pots, and therefore with different and unrelated meanings. Such an argument would have to demonstrate a lack of theoretically plausible dimensions on which significant patterning occurred in the similarities and differences between pots and graves.

It is, then, by looking for significant patterning along dimensions of variation that the relevant dimensions are defined. The symbolic meaning of the object is an abstraction from the totality of these cross-references. Yet, each event that helps establish (or strays from) the pattern has its own operational meaning which we can only make sense of by seeing how it conforms to the precedent established by each of the other previous events. The specific meanings may differ and conflict along different dimensions of variation and our acceptance and understanding of this complexity will be closely related to the theories with which we are equipped. None of these procedures can take place without simultaneous abstraction and theory. To note a pattern is simultaneously to give it meaning, as one describes dimensions of variance as being related to dress, colour, sex and so on. The aim is simply to place this subjectivity within a careful consideration of the data complex.

Definition of context

Each object exists in many relevant dimensions at once, and so, where the data exist, a rich network of associations and contrasts can be followed through in building up towards an interpretation of meaning. The totality of the relevant dimensions of variation around any one object can be identified as the context of that object.

The relevant context for an object 'x' to which we are trying to give meaning (of any type) is all those aspects of the data which have relationships with 'x' which are significantly patterned in the ways described above. A more precise definition for the context of an archaeological attribute is *the totality of the relevant environment*, where 'relevant' refers to a significant relationship to the object – that is, a relationship necessary for discerning the object's meaning. We have also seen that the context will depend on the operational intention (of past social actors and present analysts).

It should be clear from this definition of context that the boundaries around a group of similarities (such as a cultural unit) do not form the boundaries of the context, since the differences *between* cultural units may be relevant for an understanding of the meaning of objects *within* each cultural unit. Rather, the boundaries of the context only occur when a lack of significant similarities *and* differences occurs. It should also be made clear that the definition is object-centred and situation specific. The 'object' may be an attribute, artifact, type, culture or whatever; however – unlike the notions of a unitary culture or type – the context varies with the specifically located object and the dimensions of variation being considered, and with the operational intention. 'Cultures', therefore, are components or aspects of contexts, but they do not define them.

In the interpretation of symbolic meanings, the significant dimensions of variation define structures of signification. One of the main and immediate impacts of the contextual approach is that it no longer becomes possible to study one arbitrarily defined aspect of the data on its own (Hall 1977). Over recent years research has come to be centred upon, for example, the settlement system, or the ceramics, or the lithics, or the seeds, from a site or region or even at a cross-cultural scale. Now, however, it is claimed that decorated pots can only be understood by comparison with other containers and/or with other items made of clay, and/or with other decorated items – all within the same context. In this example, 'containers', 'clay' or 'decoration' are the dimensions of variation along which similarities and differences are sought. Burial can only be understood through its contextual relationships to the contemporary settlements and non-burial rituals (Parker Pearson 1984a, b). Lithic variation can be examined as structured food procuring process alongside bone and seed variation. The focus of research becomes the context, or rather the series of contexts involved in 'a culture' or 'a region'.

Within a context, items have symbolic meanings through their relationships and contrasts with other items within the same text. But if everything only has meaning in relation to everything else, how does one ever enter into the context? Where does one start? The problem is clearly present in the original definition of attributes. In order to describe a pot we need to make decisions about the relevant variables – should we measure shape, height, zonation or motif? The contextual answer is that one searches for other data along these dimensions of variation in order to identify the relevant dimensions which make up the context. Thus, in the example given above concerning lozenge decoration (p. 185), one searches along the dimension of 'motif' to identify similar motifs (as well as differences and absences – if the gold lozenges are only found in male graves we might be encouraged to think they are 'male' symbols when used on the pots, in contrast to 'female' symbols), and one finds the gold lozenge. But the lozenge on the pots and on the gold item of dress may mean different things because on one scale they occur in different contexts. One could only support the theory that the two sets of lozenges had similar meanings by finding other aspects of similarity between them (for example, other motifs used in male dress items which also occur as pot decoration). So everything depends on everything else, and the definition of attributes depends on the definition of context which depends on the definition of attributes!

There seems to be no easy answer to this problem. However, if it were truly the case that we had no way of knowing what context was relevant or how the context should be described, then even the most basic forms of communication would be impossible. The problem is surely not as insurmountable as it looks. In the course of living, one learns which contexts are relevant (Asad 1986, p. 149). Nevertheless, it is important to be aware that even though we cannot have any understanding without delineating a context, the act of delineating that context forecloses certain kinds of understanding (Yates 1990, p. 155). We must always stop the chain of context somewhere, but in doing so we close down certain possibilities. This closure is a strategic act of control, committed by archaeologists as well as actors in the past whose strategies of power depended on controlling the meaning of encounters and events. These closures do not end interpretation, but they do create power relations.

Thus, in the past as in the present, the creation of context is an intentional act. The goal of interpretation, however, is to move beyond one's starting point, to have one's intentions reformed and reconstituted as they fuse with the object of interpretation. In this sense, it is important to know all the data as thoroughly as possible, and gradually to accommodate theory to data by trial-and-error searching for relevant dimensions of variation, cross-checking with contextual information, and so on. The procedure certainly implies that interpretation of meaning will be more successful where the data are more richly networked. It was often implied, during the period of the New Archaeology, that archaeology would develop, not from the collection of more data, but from advances in theory. While such notions have their own historical context, the contextual approach is very much dependent on data. We have seen, throughout the descriptions above, that theory, interpretation and subjectivity are involved at every stage. Yet at the same time, the emphasis is placed on interpreting what the data can 'tell' us, and the more networked the data, the more there is to 'read'. As already noted, an object out of context is not readable; and a symbol painted on a cave wall when there are no deposits in the cave, when there are no deposits in the region that contain other depictions of the symbol on other objects, and when there are no graves containing the symbol, is scarcely more readable.

It is partly for this reason that historical archaeology is an 'easier' approach. Here the data are richly networked, much survives, and there are many leads that can be followed through, even in the absence of the literary texts, which themselves only provide another context in which to look for similarities and differences. The same problems remain – of having to define whether the written context is relevant to the other contexts (e.g. archaeological layers), and of deciding whether similarities between two contexts (written and non-written) imply the same or different meanings. Yet there is more possibility of facing these issues because the richer data allow more similarities and differences to be sought along more relevant dimensions of variation.

In prehistoric archaeology, the further one goes back in time, so that survival rates diminish, the more difficult it becomes to ground hypotheses in data. Here the rare site with detailed information may often act as a key for numerous less well-excavated or poorly surviving sites. In many areas contextual archaeology can hardly begin until more data have been collected.

Explanation and description

Does all this mean that explaining and understanding the past are simply a matter of describing the contextual data in the fullest way possible? Much damage has been done in archaeology by the opposition of the words 'description' and 'explanation': 'descriptive' became little more than a pejorative term to throw at archaeologists who were not 'scientists'. It can be argued, however, that adequate explanation involves little more than a description in answer to a question. For example, consider the following sequence of questions and explanations:

1.	Why was this site abandoned?	Because the population increased.
2.	What is the relevance of population increase to site abandonment?	The site grew too large.
3.	Too large for what?	The people had overused the environment.

In each case the explanation is simply a description of some events, although of course there is also an asumption that the response is in some way relevant to the question. So, in the response given in 3, it is assumed that people need to live off their local environment. These are the unexamined theories used within the explanation, but if we push and ask questions about these theories, we will again be faced by descriptions, either particular or general:

4.	Why does it matter that they overuse their environment?	Because people live off the resources near them.
5.	Why can they not use distant resources?	Because too much energy is expended.

It is always possible, therefore, to step in at some point along this chain of question and answer and ask another question, arguing that previous work has been too descriptive. Indeed, this has been the format of much of this volume, in comparing different approaches in archaeology. The alternatives offered may be more satisfactory in that they are broader and take into account important factors which had previously been neglected, and they may be more explanatory in that sense, but the explanations are only further descriptions. The example above concerns a settlement process, but the same can be said of interpretations of meanings and texts. The symbolic meaning given to an object is simply a description of aspects of its context and use. For example:

Contextual archaeology

| 6. | What is the meaning of this crown? | The person who wears it is king. |

Thus, in many ways, explanation is description and description *is* explanation. In contextual archaeology it is necessary continually to ask questions in order to see whether the general assumptions are relevant in the particular context; this leads to full and detailed description of the total context as the whole network of associations and contrasts is followed through. This is a never ending process as new links are sought and old ones re-evaluated. The archaeologist plays on these data, bringing them to life as the composer combines the varied instruments of an orchestra in his or her score.

Contextual archaeology thus links adequate explanation to full description, as all the numerous influences impinging on any one trait or object are followed through. This is the point made by Case (1973) in introducing contextual archaeology. In history there is only a stream of continuous events, no absolute hiatus, so the only explanation of change is a full account of change.

It need hardly be said, given the discussion in this chapter, that full description of contexts is not opposed to theory and generalization. All description involves theories, meaning, subjectivity, generalization, and historical imagination. This is why the archaeologist is more like the composer than the conductor of music. The ultimate aim of our detailed accounts may well be generalization and universal laws, but initially, as scientists rather than as musicians or artists, our concern must be to question whether the theories, generalizations and imaginative insights have the meaning we assume them to have in past historical contexts. Contextual archaeology links question and data in a controlled way, governed by some general principles about how we read texts, but even these general principles must be open to critique. We must leave open the possibility that societies may have existed in the past with specific and unique cultural formations which are not well described in our standard categories and terms derived from, for example, Marx, Weber or Foucault.

A comment is needed here on the use of ethnographic analogy in archaeology. At one level ethnographic knowledge simply contributes to the historical imagination, inciting new perspectives and alternative theories. But usually rather more is meant by the term analogy: the past is interpreted in the light of the present because of some similarity between them. Information is transferred from the present to the past because of observed similarities. This procedure is simply another instance of the general approach already outlined. In order to use analogy one has to assess similarities and differences between contexts (Wylie 1985; Hodder 1982d). In comparing a present society with one in the past, the procedures are similar to those used in a comparison of two neighbouring sites or cultures in the past. In both cases it is a matter of evaluating similarities and differences between two contexts and discerning whether information can be transferred from one to the other.

In both cases the main problem is to decide whether the similarities and differences in the two contexts are relevant to each other; thus archaeologists have greater confidence in direct historical analogies where the spatial context is constant and the temporal gap is slight. Where cross-cultural analogies are made, the problem becomes one of finding some relevant dimension of variation along which the similarities and differences can be examined, but over great distances and time periods, and when comparing societies in vastly different social and economic environments, it is difficult to know whether relevant relationships in the present were equally relevant in the past. For example, settlement size may be relevant to population size today, but it is not easy to say that it was so in the past. The use of analogy thus tends to depend on general theories which can provide arguments of relevance. It is the task of contextual archaeology to be critical of such general, cross-cultural theories, to examine more fully their contexts, present and past. Without the general theories there would be few questions asked of the past and fewer answers given. Without a contextual approach, the present and past become reduced to an assumed sameness.

Critical hermeneutics

Throughout this chapter we have given the impression that a contextual approach involves building up towards interpretation from the similarities and differences in the data. We have, however, increasingly tempered this view with the alternative position that even the identification of similarities and differences and relevant dimensions of variation depends on theory. In fact a contextual analysis involves moving back and forth between theory and data and trying different theories to see which accounts for the data best.

The model of meaning and understanding described here draws from a philosophical tradition called hermeneutics. In this section, we focus more closely on the methods of interpretation: the hermeneutic method.

Since its beginnings with Dilthey, there have been considerable developments in hermeneutic understanding and this recent discussion of hermeneutics has been introduced into archaeology. Hermeneutics is the science of interpretation, traditionally applied to the discovery of the real but hidden meanings of sacred texts, specifically the gospels, but given a more general and modern meaning by a range of writers from Schleiermacher, Dilthey and Heidegger to Gadamer and Ricoeur. Hermeneutics involves understanding the world not as a physical system, but as an object of human thought and action.

Thus the primary hermeneutic rule (Gadamer 1975, p. 258), as in contextual archaeology, is that we must understand any detail such as an object or word in terms of the whole, and the whole in terms of the detail. As an interpreter, one plays back and forth between part and whole until one achieves the harmony of all the details with the whole. In this case, the 'part' includes the plans and intentions of past actors. The 'whole' involves the wider context of historical meanings (social, economic, cultural, technological, etc.) within which the actor's subjectivities are formed. Thus, for Gadamer and others (Taylor 1985, p. 24), the hermeneutic circle involves moving back and forth from a particular action and its operational meanings to the wider context of historical meanings.

But there is also a second kind of back and forth motion. As we noted above, in coming to understanding, we relate the informant's opinions and views to our own opinions and views. This involves a playing back and forth between the social and theoretical context of the interpreter, and the historical or cultural context of the object of interpretation. Both the interpreter and the object of interpretation contribute to understanding, always generating a new, hybridised meaning. In this sense, whether we like it or not, we think ourselves into the past. We need to be aware that we are doing this and we need to do it critically.

If, in going back and forth between part and whole and between past and present, interpretation is in some sense circular, where does it begin? How do we start? Since interpretation incorporates our own values and theories, even those that we are not fully conscious of, interpretation has already begun even as we think about a problem for the first time. Rather than asking where to begin, we should instead ask how to get interpretation going in a direction that will move us beyond our initial position. Hermeneutic science recognises that we can only understand the human world through asking questions of it. Nothing has meaning except in relation to a question. Interpretation involves the logic of question and answer. One cannot sit back and observe the data; they must be brought into action by asking questions – why should anyone want to erect a building like that, what was the purpose of the shape of this ditch, why is this wall made of turf and that of stone? And the question must not be vague ('let us see what is here') but definite ('are these loose stones a ruined wall?'). Indeed it is the process of question and answer which operationalises the part–whole insight, as will be shown further below. Question and answer continue in an endless spiral since every question expects an answer and every answer frames and creates new questions.

Every question is shaped by the interests and biographical experiences – the operational meanings – of the researcher, which means that every question 'prefigures' the answer to some extent. Interpretation of the past is therefore bound into a question and answer procedure which is rooted in the present. Analogy with the present thus underlies our interpretation of the past. The cycle of question and answer leads to new questions and a new understanding of self in relation to other (the past).

Nevertheless it might appear from this account that an object needs to be understood simultaneously in terms of its own time and in terms of our present world. It is as if the object has to be understood in terms of two separate 'wholes' or contexts: 'theirs' and 'ours' (though the separation itself will eventually be dissolved). We have already discussed how an object in its own time can be understood by moving back and forth from the particular action to the general historical context. To understand the object in our own culture, we will need to carry out a similar kind of back and forth. Wylie (1989a), who felicitously characterises this back and forth movement as 'tacking', makes a similar point about how the analyst must tack vertically between particular and general in both 'our' context and 'their' context, not to mention a horizontal tack across the two contexts (see also the 'fourfold hermeneutic': Shanks and Tilley 1987a, pp. 107–8; Shanks and Hodder 1995, p. 10).

The interpretive work within our own context should include more voices than that of the archaeologist alone. No one person can speak for the dead, and archaeologists are not the only ones qualified for interpretation (La Roche and Blakey 1997). If there are descendent communities, archaeologists should extend the interpretive process to include the input of those communities. In some situations, legislation (such as the Archaeological Resources Protection Act in the US) mandates the opening and broadening of dialogue between archaeologists and communities who have historic ties to the area under investigation (Watkins 2000). Incorporating descendent communities with close cultural affiliation to the past society being studied can help blur the distinction between the present context and the past context. The possibility of blurring the two contexts, past and present, is in fact a necessity and brings us back to Gadamer.

Gadamer's (1975, p. 29) equivalent to our discussion of context is his notion of horizon – everything that is relevant from a particular perspective, asking a particular question. How is it possible to link the hermeneutic principles, past and present, both with the finite contextual boundaries and with closed horizons? Gadamer deals elegantly with this problem by arguing that both contexts or horizons are continually moving for those who live in them and construct them. The answer to a question immediately changes the perspective and the horizon. And the two contexts are continually moving in relation to each other since the answer to a question about the 'other' leads to new self-awareness and new questions. Properly, there is only one horizon, from the present perspective. What the interpreter tries to do is attain an understanding that overcomes 'our' particularity and that of the 'other'. An attempt is made at the fusion of horizons. But the scientific process involves at the same time trying to distinguish between those horizons or contexts as best we can, and as critically as we can.

Once we have achieved this understanding of the meanings of a situation, how do we then proceed to validate this understanding? In the contextual method described here, the idea of testing of theory against data is seen as an inexact description of archaeological interpretation because theory and data are partly interdependent. Since data are perceived within a theory, they cannot be used as an 'independent' test of theory.

This does not mean that the hermeneutic circle is vicious. Rather, we achieve validation through different methods. We can be rigorous in our reconstructions of the past if we use the criteria of coherence and correspondence to judge between theories. By coherence, we refer to the internal coherence of the argument: a coherent reconstruction must make sense at least in terms of the archaeologist's picture of the world. By correspondence, we mean correspondence between an understanding and the evidence at hand. Although the evidence does not exist with absolute objectivity, it does nevertheless exist in the real world – it is tangible and it is there, like it or not. Whatever our perceptions of the world, we are constrained by the evidence, and brought up against its consequences. We reiterate that there is no test for correspondence: it is instead a matter of accommodating part to whole, or, better yet, fitting (Hodder 1999a, pp. 59–62). As the fit becomes tighter and as our understanding begins to fit more and more cases, our interpretation gains ground. The hermeneutic circles become spirals (Hodder 1992).

It is in our dialogue with each other about the success or failure of such fusions that we learn about ourselves so that the past contributes to the present. The attempt to fuse with the other, as long as it is done critically and with an awareness of difference and contextuality, changes our experience and therefore changes our perspective. We would argue for a critical hermeneutics in which interpretations are situated historically in the past and present. But the end result is not a debilitating relativism in which the past is viewed as largely constructed in the present. We resist the notion that archaeological data represent only 'networks of resistance' to our hypotheses (Shanks and Tilley 1987a, p. 104).

Nevertheless, interpretive methods for getting better and better understandings of the past – of evaluating theories with rigour in a post-positivist framework – have often provoked an incredulous outcry. Many critics claim that if we accept that data and theory are interdependent and if we encourage multiple perspectives of the past, we will open the floodgates of relativism and create a maelstrom in which 'anything goes': in which all firm grounds for contesting abominable (fascist, racist, sexist, etc.) interpretations and uses of the past are washed away. For the most part, these claims are rudderless: they result in some cases from blatant misreadings of key post-positivist texts and in other cases from the purposefully ambiguous, shifty nature of the post-positivist texts themselves. However, the spectre of relativism endures (Renfrew 2001), perhaps because it is not easy, even for the most epistemologically astute, to explain how the dichotomy between relativism and objectivism can be overcome.

The hermeneutic method described above is but one of a number of ways to navigate between the Scylla of relativism and the Charybdis of objectivism. Alison Wylie (1992a, b; 1993) outlined a separate route when she demonstrated that engaging in archaeology from a political perspective, such as feminism, can 'enhance the conceptual and empirical integrity of archaeological inquiry'. An overtly political engagement does not compromise a commitment to objectivity and value neutrality. Wylie argues that feminist archaeology succeeds because it is more responsive to the facts. According to Fotiadis, Wylie thus appears to return to a form of objectivism. This stance, 'feminist empiricism' (Engelstad 1991; Harding 1986), is problematic because it resurrects a dichotomy between the *formation* of hypotheses (where political interests gain voice) and the *evaluation* of hypotheses (where only the facts speak) (Fotiadis 1994). The mitigated objectivism that Wylie attempts to create is, in the end, not mitigated enough.

One of Wylie's solutions to this criticism is to remember that the facts, theories and background assumptions of any archaeological argument are quite heterogeneous, and that this disunity can be exploited (Wylie 1992b; 2000). Certain facts, such as radiocarbon dates, are laden by theories (in this case physics) entirely different from the social theories for which they are being used as evidence. This degree of independence between evidence and theory makes the interpretation more compelling. Arguments also gain credibility if the different lines of evidence in support of an argument are constituted by independent bodies of theory. For example, the law of superposition, stylistic change in pottery and radiocarbon each contribute to chronological reconstructions, but they each depend on unique auxiliary theories. By exploiting multiple types of evidence, archaeological arguments become like cables with many evidential strands (Bernstein 1983; Wylie 1989a).

Another solution is to emphasise that the strands of the cable do not all need to be evidential. Interpretations should also be evaluated in terms of ethics, politics, aesthetics, relevance and more (Lampeter Archaeology Workshop 1997; 1998). This solution is close to a solution on which both Fotiadis and Wylie agree: to document the role played by politics in the use of the data themselves (the context of evaluation), not just in the formation of theories. In the feminist example, we must always acknowledge that contemporary political causes – combating androcentrism – motivate the reinterpretation of already existing data or the digging of new data. By reattaching facts to the political circumstances that inspired them to be gathered, we strengthen them against future attack. In other words, facts attached to a crusade against androcentrism are more difficult to assail than facts standing alone. A statement thus derives its strength by holding onto things more solid than itself. Shanks and Hodder (1995) note that a skilfully crafted objectivity holds onto a heterogeneous assemblage of resources, people and energies (see also Latour 1999, p. 151). To undermine such an assemblage may require not just the snipping of cables, but the mustering and mobilisation of equal or more resources, people and energies. Though Shanks and Hodder use a network metaphor in place of a cable metaphor, the connections in their network (coherence of argument, aesthetics of site report) are similar to the strands of the cable.

Reattaching facts to politics and networks reminds us that facts have a point (Wylie 1994). As Brumfiel (1991; see also Fotiadis 1994) has argued, archaeological argumentation is allegorical, and it is the allegorical nature of our arguments – the way they point to values and struggles in the present – that gives them force. Facts are thus timely. Some people despair at the way that the same body of data (Upper Palaeolithic cave paintings, for example) has been used to support multiple generations of different and even contradictory interpretations. But the despair will disappear if we let go of the mistaken assumption that the data themselves have some abstract, immutable essence, independent of time. Data are thus plural, capable of being *spoken for* in many different ways, but also *looked at* in many different ways: with the naked eye, in thin section under the microscope, as grouped by statistics, etc. (Shanks and Hodder 1995, p. 20).

In sum, to accept the post-positivist critique of objectivity is not to embrace a rabid, anything goes, relativism. Rather, it is to accept that facts and data are always relative to a particular historical context and are always mustered in relation to a network of other forces and institutions. This means that the interpretations that seem to fit best and the criteria used to judge the closeness of fit cannot exist outside of historical time (Lampeter Archaeology Workshop 1997; Wylie 1989b; Hutson 2001; Shanks and Hodder 1995). Our conclusions closely match a recent discussion by Bruno Latour (1999), who also rejects the choice between a timeless, unconnected objectivity and the mob-rule threat of relativism. Latour embraces a 'sturdy relativism' (p. 5), in which we can be relatively sure of many things and in which we improve our science by reconnecting it and relating it to the multiple goals, groups and gadgets of our social collective (pp. 16–18).

Having offered these suggestions – 'sturdy' relativism, mitigated objectivity, critical hermeneutics, etc. – we back away from recommending anything more specific. The paths beyond objectivism and relativism will lead to different outcomes in each archaeological case (Hodder 1999a, p. 24). Which strands of argumentation and networks or resources will prove decisive cannot be predicted in advance, only settled in practice. We join Donna Haraway (1991, p. 195), whose comments on relativism and objectivism mirror many of the points made above, in 'arguing for politics and epistemologies of location, positioning, and situating, where partiality and not universality is the condition of [making] rational knowledge claims'.

Sometimes there may be no common ground between knowledge claims, no agreement as to what type of information is meaningful or acceptable as evidence. In these cases, where two or more contemporary groups that have a stake in the past hold irreconcilably different – incommensurable – understandings of the past, archaeologists can still halt the slide to moral relativism so feared by the guardians of unmitigated objectivism. Incommensurability does not absolve us from responsible intervention in such confrontations, though the appropriate intervention will depend on a local and unpredictable mix of personal conviction and the circumstances of the situation (Lampeter Archaeology Workshop 1997). In the next chapter we present examples of the increasingly common encounters and engagements between archaeologists and other groups that bring quite different meanings to the archaeological record.

In our view the above account of the hermeneutic, contextual exercise describes what archaeologists can do in interpreting the past. We have simplified the process, but we believe we have described its essential characteristics. We can only accommodate as best and as critically as we can, and choose between theories by seeing which accommodates best. We have to accept both the rigour and objectivity of contextual analysis and the fact that our interpretations are moments in a stream of learning and social practice.

Conclusion

In the discussion in this chapter an emphasis has been placed on methods of identifying and studying contexts in order to interpret meaning. It was noted that various types of meaning can be sought, varying from the systematic processes of social and economic relations, to the structured contents of symbolic codes, to the conjuncture of these two, as mediated by the embodied experiences and strategic intentions, in the context of everyday life. Because the first two types of meaning are produced and reproduced in these daily operations, it is impossible to separate the three types of meaning except for heuristic purposes. When based on contextual analysis, these meanings can be termed contextual (for other discussions of contextual methods, and application, see articles in Hodder 1987a and, for example, Parkington 1989).

The first type of contextual meaning refers to the environmental, technological and behavioural context of action. Understanding of an object comes about through placing it in relation to the larger functioning whole. Processual and Marxist archaeology have tended to concentrate on the larger scales of this type of context, but the moment-by-moment context of situationally expedient action also needs to be incorporated.

Second, context can be taken to mean 'with-text'. Just as a written word can be more easily understood when it is embedded within a sentence, an object of material culture is more easily understood if it is situated in place and time and in relation to other archaeological objects. This network of relationships can be read, by careful analysis as outlined in this chapter, in order to reach an interpretation of meaning content. When possible, archaeologists should share the labour of interpretation with descendent communities. Of course, our readings may be incorrect, but misreading of the language does not imply that the objects must remain mute.

Reading text is not an appropriate analogy for reading material culture because text is a different sort of sign than material culture. Nevertheless, when we remember that text, like material culture, can be both a sign and an object (a book, a newspaper), we realise that text is a better metaphor for material culture than language. This is because material culture is the product of action, and, as Ricoeur (1971) argues, human action is best discussed by using the model of text rather than language (see Hodder 1989a; Moore 1990). A text is a concrete product written to do something. It is the product of discourse – situated communication (Barrett 1987). Yet the text as product of discourse loses some of the force of the original communication (Ricouer 1971; see also Austin 1962; Searle 1970). The meanings may become distanced from the intentions of the 'writer' of the text and may depend very much on the context in which the text is read. In the same way, as time elapses between action and the encounter of its residues, the meaning of material culture often depends on the context of use rather than solely on the context of production or on the 'author'. Even more than a written text, material culture meanings embody pragmatic and functional concerns. Text, rather than language, is thus an appropriate metaphor for the dual nature of material culture (as technological and functional object and as sign) which has been argued throughout this book (but see pp. 167–8).

These two types of contextual meaning have a common characteristic also found in other uses of the term in archaeology (see pp. 162–6). All such uses refer to a concern with particular data rather than general theory. One of the aims of this volume is certainly to argue that general terms and theories must be better grounded in the particular context of study. Yet 'contextualism' does not equate with 'particularism', a term which has come to be associated in archaeology with the rejection of or lack of interest in general theory. Within contextual archaeology a recognition of the need for general theory and for theoretical archaeology remains, but rather, the concern is to demand a closer relationship between theory and data, placing one in terms of the other, and emphasizing inductive as well as deductive procedures.

Contextual archaeology involves the study of contextual data, using contextual methods of analysis, in order to arrive at two types of contextual meaning which are discussed in relation to general theory. But in discussing contextual archaeology it has frequently been found necessary throughout this volume to refer in passing to another type of context – the particular contexts of archaeologists themselves. This latter type of context seems intimately connected with the others, in a relationship which it is no longer possible to ignore. The context of the archaeologist is discussed in the next chapter, as part of a widespread series of changes in archaeology that can be termed post-processual.

9 Post-processual archaeology

Processual archaeology made contributions to archaeological theory by encouraging the notion of culture as adaptive, and by applying systems theory, information exchange theory and a host of other general theories. Many of these ideas had existed in some form in earlier approaches in archaeology, and the extent of this continuity will be further examined below. Yet perhaps the major contribution made by the New Archaeology was methodological (Meltzer 1979; Moore and Keene 1983, p. 4). Archaeologists became more concerned about problems of inference, sampling and research design. Quantitative and statistical techniques were used more frequently; procedures were questioned and made more explicit. Contextual archaeology is an attempt to develop archaeological methodology further.

In the realm of theory, there have been a number of developments since the early 1960s which, it can be argued, indicate movement from the initial stance of processual archaeology as represented by the early papers of Binford (1962; 1965) and Flannery (1967). In the 1980s, what we now call post-processual archaeology encouraged an engagement with the theoretical turns taken in other fields, particularly anthropology, which had explored many new directions not foreseen by the first wave of anthropological archaeology in the 1960s. In the new millennium, as the debate between processualism and post-processualism gives way to a thousand archaeologies (Preucel 1995; Schiffer 2000), the usefulness of this debate is as questionable as the demand for a resolution (Hutson 2001; cf. VanPool and VanPool 1999). In this chapter we summarise the ways in which archaeology benefits from the dismissal of this and other dichotomies and suggest areas in which archaeology can export theory to fields from which it once only imported.

Post-processual archaeology

Beyond engaging with new theories, post-processual archaeology also valued engagements with society. The centrepiece of the positivist methods introduced into archaeology in the 1960s and 1970s was a strict separation between the object of research and the social context of the subjects conducting the research. Theory could come from anywhere but if it contaminated the data, any chance of clean hypothesis testing would be ruined. As mentioned in chapter 1, most archaeologists have since backed away from this stance. In the previous chapter, we stressed how understanding comes from the mesh between present political contexts and past 'data'. The politics of the present are therefore part of archaeological inquiry. We must therefore dissolve one final dichotomy: that between subject and object. To show how archaeology is a contemporary social process, we conclude the chapter by illustrating a series of recent engagements between archaeologists and other communities who have a stake in the archaeological record.

Variability and materiality

Throughout this volume it has been noted that most current archaeological theory, of whatever hue, retains a normative component, in that explanation assumes ideas held in common and rules of behaviour. Adequate accounts of individual variation and perception were encountered most frequently in those studies based on modern theories of social action and practice (chapter 5), embodiment (chapter 6) and history (chapter 7).

This finding is in direct opposition to the commonly stated aim of the New Archaeology to be concerned with variability. Certainly in some of Binford's later work (cf. 1984) the notion of expedient, situational behaviour comes to the fore. As was noted in chapter 2, such interests have not made their way into archaeological consideration of ideology and symbolic meanings. Even in Binford's studies, individuals appear bound by universal rules concerned with what individuals will do 'if other things are equal'. Because Binford does not recount a meaning-laden process, the ability of individuals to create change and to create their culture as an active social process is minimized.

Norms and rules do exist. The argument here is rather that, in order to allow for change, innovation and agency, the relationships between norms, rules and individuals need to be examined more fully. In the practice of daily life, 'other things' never are 'equal'. It is always necessary to improvise expediently, yet through the framework of the norms and rules, changing them in the process (see p. 91). In this volume such questions have been discussed in the context of the relationships between the individual and society, and between practice and structure.

The first development that is found, then, in the post-processual phase, is the inclusion, under the heading 'process', of an adequate consideration of agency. For example, it is necessary to develop approaches to typology which are concerned less with defining 'types' and more with describing multi-dimensional surfaces of variability on which the 'type' can be seen to vary with context. More generally, archaeologists tend to force their material into styles, cultures, systems, structures, preferring to ignore the 'random' noise of individual variability. Leach's (1954) insight that various stages of development may be expressions of a common underlying structure is an important one for archaeologists who have tended to disregard variability: for example, there has been little account of how individual sites in a region may go through similar trajectories but at different, overlapping times (but see Frankenstein and Rowlands 1978).

The concern with variability is of particular importance in relation to social and cultural change. For example, it may prove to be the case in a particular area that most individual variability is allowed in areas outside the direct control of dominant groups.

The recognition of variability in individual perception leads to a curious twist in the tale of the reconstruction of the content of historical meanings. In chapter 8 we discussed meaning content and how it can be attained in contextual archaeology, but we also showed that there is not *one* meaning in the past. The same object can have different or conflicting meanings along different dimensions of variation and from different perspectives. Ethnographers too often assume that there is some authoritative account of meaning that can be achieved. Certainly one has to allow for different perspectives from different interest groups in society (chapter 4), yet the problem goes far deeper than this. If material culture is a 'text', then a multiplicity of readings could have existed in the past. An example is the varied meanings given in British society to the use of safety pins by punks. It seemed to Hodder (1982d) that individuals would create verbal reasons for such items but that these verbal reasons were not 'correct' or 'incorrect' – they were all interpretations of a text in different verbal contexts, and in different social contexts. Individuals seemed to be making up the verbal meanings of things as Hodder talked to them, contradicting and varying their responses as a social ploy.

The fragmentation of holistic notions such as culture, society and origin, and the dispersal of meaning along chains of signifiers (p. 67) provide the main thrust of much post-structuralist archaeology (e.g. Tilley 1990a; Bapty and Yates 1990). Much of the post-structuralist critique emphasizes the different pasts we produce in the present and the plurality of views that should be opened to debate. We will return to this point below, but for the moment we can focus on the plurality of meanings within past societies. At first sight this notion of cultures as heterogeneous assemblages of overlapping, conflicting interpretations and representations of those interpretations, in an endless spiral of movement and variation, is disturbing to the archaeologist. Given the difficulty of interpreting *any* meaning in the past, how can the archaeologist ever approach this complexity of meaning? In fact, however, the potentials introduced by this insight are considerable. Archaeologists no longer need to force their data into well-bounded categories, and overlapping multiple dimensions of meaning can be sought using a contextual methodology. The *real* complexity of the archaeological data can be faced. An example of the way in which material culture can be interpreted as having different meanings to different groups, at different times in the past, is provided by Greene (1987).

Perhaps more important is the link between variability of text interpretations and the discussion of power in chapter 4. The potential of individuals to 'see' things from different and contradictory perspectives may, in theory, be almost limitless. How, then, is meaning controlled by interest groups within society? Strategies might include placing events and their meanings in nature, making them 'natural', or placing them in the past, making them appear inevitable. More generally, material culture has a number of distinctive aspects which suggest that it may play a major role in the control of meaning variation. In particular, it is durable and it is concrete. All the dimensions of material culture elaboration discussed under the heading of 'contextual archaeology' – all the associations, contrasts, spatial and temporal rhythms and so on – can be used in attempts to 'fix' meanings. Much, if not all, material culture production can be described as a process in which different interest groups and individuals try to set up authoritative or established meanings in relation to conflicting interests and in the face of the inherent ability of individuals to create their own, shifting, foot-loose schemes.

The 'fixing' of meanings may be most apparent at centres of control, and in public rituals. The various domains of culture, the opposing strands, may here be brought together, and the dominant structures re-established. A small contemporary example of the relationship between perspective and control may help to clarify the point. Walking in large, formal gardens one is often aware of some larger pattern. Glimpses are obtained of long lines of trees, shrubs, statues, lawn, ponds. In many parts of the garden one is not allowed to walk, and the individual understanding of the overall pattern remains partial and personal, dependent on the particular trajectory taken in the garden. Many of the formal gardens of which we are thinking are arranged around a large house, itself raised up or at the centre of radiating alignments. It is only from here, the centre of control, that the overall organization becomes apparent. Suddenly, from the centre, the scheme makes sense and the individual understandings can be placed within their context – a context constructed by the centre.

All aspects of cultural production, from the use of space, as in the above example, to the styles of pots and metal items, can be seen to play a part in the negotiation and 'fixing' of meaning by individuals and interest groups within society, whether child, mother, father, chief or commoner. Rather than assuming norms and systems, in the attempt to produce bounded entities, archaeologists can use their material to examine the continual process of interpretation and reinterpretation in relation to interest, itself an interpretation of events.

Many great continental thinkers of the 20th century – Freud, Benjamin, Lacan, Foucault – have appropriated archaeology in some form. However, the 'archaeology' referred to by these writers consists of little more than shallow metaphors – the idea that archaeologists work with silent traces and fragments or the idea that the past is concealed and that we have to dig deep down, one layer at a time, to get to it – for which no archaeologists would take credit. We cannot claim that the actual work of archaeology has made an impact on the conceptual repertoire of any of the theorists listed above. Nevertheless, archaeology's focus on material culture positions it as a potential contributor to any field – anthropology, sociology, cultural studies, history of science and technology – that takes seriously the interaction between people and things.

Early work by Rathje (1979), Miller (1984) and Shanks and Tilley (1987a) showed that archaeology could contribute to an understanding and critique of the present by paying attention to objects that are usually taken for granted. The success of the cross-disciplinary *Journal of Material Culture*, founded in 1996, demonstrates that many fields besides archaeology recognise the importance of objects (Shanks 2001) and underscores the perceived need for a forum on the topic. Archaeology, a field which concerns itself with the production, consumption, discard, style, context and historicity of objects, has much to contribute to the dialogue on material culture, and it is perhaps no surprise that some of the path-breaking works on the subject have come from writers trained in archaeology (Miller 1987; 1995; 1998; Schiffer 1991; 1995).

There are many reasons to be interested in the material world. As we noted in the previous chapter, the material world is the substance out of which people create their own meaningful, biographical texts. In chapter 6 we stressed that one's memories and sense of self are closely tied to the people, landscapes and things that fill a life. And in chapter 5 we presented the possibility that things are more than just props in the creation of meaningful lives: they acquire lives of their own. Bruno Latour has discussed this point in a number of contexts. In his ethnographic and historical studies of science (1999), he argues that when scientists isolate new substances in labs, such as the fermenting microorganisms studied by Pasteur, they do not simply reveal things that were always there, but give those substances the conditions in which they can act and prove their mettle. Thus, rather than seeing matter as a passive substance waiting to create a fuss, matter is active and can help scientists gain medals.

Even though things have lives, it is not quite correct to say they have lives 'of their own'. Matter is not a sort of bedrock unaffected by the transient biographies of the people that skitter across its surface. Rather, the reality of a thing depends in part on the actions of people. Latour refers to this mutually constitutive interrelationship as circulating reference: a network of associations and collaborations between people and things. In his analysis of a failed attempt to create a Personal Rapid Transit system in Paris, Latour shows that one 'cannot conceive of a technological object without taking into account the mass of human beings with all their passions and politics and pitiful calculations' (1996, p. xiii). Latour's point, then, is that the lives of people are so thoroughly interwoven with the lives of objects that a human science can no longer be the science of humans alone. Machines, like texts and human actions, must also be interpreted.

Post-processual archaeology

A case of intertwining of people and things to which archaeology has recently contributed is the house society approach to social organisation. Lévi-Strauss (1987) conceived of the house society to help characterise social structures that elude explanations based on kinship alone. At the core of such ambiguous social groups, ranging from the noble houses of medieval Europe to the Kwakiutl of the Pacific Northwest, he and other ethnographers (see papers in Carsten and Hugh-Jones 1995) found 'a spiritual and material heritage, comprising dignity, origins, kinship, names and symbols, wealth and power' (Lévi-Strauss 1987, p. 174). Since material heritage such as heirlooms and landed estates have deep histories and play an active role in constituting these social groups, the archaeological approach has made substantial contributions to the understanding of ancient, historic and contemporary societies (Joyce and Gillespie 2000).

Historians and anthropologists have come to recognise in particular that monuments and material heritage play an active role in society, and that archaeologists can contribute to wider debates from the perspective of their theoretical understanding of material monuments (e.g. Bradley 1993). For example, Rowlands (1993) has discussed different ways in which societies develop relationships with monuments and memory. In a highly politicised context, Jerusalem, Nadia Abu El-Haj focuses on the materiality of archaeology as being constitutive of a new reality. She argues that 'in the case of archaeology, it is not only historiographies or narratives of and for past and present that are made. Rather, in excavating the land archaeologists produce material culture – a new material culture that inscribes the landscape with the concrete signs of particular histories and historicities. It is through the making of those objects that archaeology most powerfully "translates" past and present, that it is able not simply to legitimize existing cultural and political worlds, but also to reinvent them' (1998, p. 168). Archaeology not only can contribute to the study of the relationships between materiality and memory, but also plays an active part in forming those memories.

As we have noted throughout the book (see chapters 3 and 9), material culture is often not the focus of conscious reflection or conversation. Our feel for our landscape and our bodily adjustments or reactions to things are not constituted in discourse. This condition creates what Buchli and Lucas (2001) refer to as an absent present. The unconstituted or nondiscursive nature of material culture makes it an especially attractive site for attempts by special-interest groups to control meaning in society.

Process and structure

Archaeologists have in the past been concerned with two main types of process, historical processes (such as diffusion, migration, convergence, divergence) and adaptive processes (population increase, resource utilization, social complexity, trade and so on). Although the work of Grahame Clark and Gordon Childe, for example, shows that both types of process have been studied for a long time in archaeology, it was the processual archaeology of the 1960s and 1970s that introduced a special emphasis on the latter form.

In essence, the two types of process are very similar. If a culture changes, we might say that this is because of the process of diffusion or because of the processes of population increase and environmental deterioration. Of course, as was discussed in the first part of this chapter, we can argue about whether diffusion is an adequate explanation, in the same way that we can argue about whether any processual account is adequate. Yet the manner of argument is always the same – visible event is related causally to visible event. It was on the inter-relationships, correlations and covariations between such events that a positivist New Archaeology was able to build.

The notion that there might be structures, codes of presences and absences, that lie behind historical and adaptive processes, cannot exist comfortably with the empiricism and positivism that have dominated archaeology since its inception. In this sense, post-processual archaeology, in so far as it incorporates structuralism and Marxism, is a far more radical break than that which has occurred before.

There are dangers in talking of 'structure' as if a unified concept is widely accepted for this term. There are major differences between the types of social structure studied in Marxist archaeology, and the formal and meaning structures studied in structuralist archaeology. Yet despite these fundamental differences, all such uses of the term imply something not visible at the surface – some organizational scheme or principle, not necessarily rigid or determining, that is immanent, visible only in its effects. Thus a new level of reality is proposed in archaeology, often described as 'deeper' than, 'behind' or 'beneath' the measurable evidence.

Yet rather than talking about these deeper structures as underlying the historical and adaptive processes, it is more appropriate to talk of how each of these elements contributes to an integrated view of society that is always in the process of becoming. From the practice theories and dialectics of domination and resistance discussed in chapter 5, from the intersections of historical events and structures in chapter 7, and from the operational meanings in chapter 8, there emerges the familiar idea that society is never a given: its reproduction or transformation is contingent on historical actions that draw upon various unpredictable combinations of structures. The structures and processes mentioned are fluid and constituted in their performance. Because of the passage of time, which allows for the reformulation of context, these structures can be differently reproduced even if the performance is a reiteration of the previous performance.

Historical meaning content: the ideal and the material

The third aspect of post-processual archaeology that can be identified is an increasing acceptance within archaeology of the need for, and possibility of, the rigorous reconstruction of contextual meanings. Within traditional archaeology the 'ladder of inference' (see p. 43) leading to the ideational realm could scarcely be scaled, and the New Archaeology often operated with the same attitude. For example, Binford (1965; 1982, p. 162) has claimed that archaeology is essentially materialist and poorly equipped to carry out 'palaeopsychology'.

We have seen throughout this book, however, an increasing readiness on the part of archaeologists to deal with the ideational sub-system, meaning and operational intentions. All such developments have played an important part in suggesting to archaeologists that systematic links can be identified between the material and the ideal.

We have also seen, in all realms of archaeology, an increasing awareness that the particular historical context needs to be taken into account in applying general theories. The older law-and-order attitude has been faced with its own inability to deliver valid and interesting general laws.

Yet the ideational realm is, in most of archaeology, still studied largely in terms of the functions of symbols and rituals. And the historical context is no more, usually, than the specific conditions in phase *A* that affect phase *B*. In traditional archaeology too, meaning content was rarely examined; material symbols were seen as indicators of contact, cultural affiliation and diffusion. Only in chapter 7 were a few studies noted of an emerging explicit interest in meaning content as the 'cog-wheel' for the inter-relationships between structure and process.

Insofar as post-processual archaeologists recognize that all archaeologists necessarily impose meaning content, and that such meanings form the core of archaeological analyses which must be made explicit and rigorous, the concern with meaning content is a third marked break with most recent and traditional archaeology.

Initially, the linking of meaning contents with historical particularism appears to have pernicious results for archaeology. A dangerous and negative pessimism lurks. How can archaeologists understand these particular other worlds, coherent only to themselves? In the discussion of contextual archaeology in chapter 8 we have attempted to demonstrate that increasingly plausible approximations to this 'otherness', in all its particularity, can be achieved. This is ultimately because historical meanings, however 'other' and coherent to themselves, are nevertheless real, producing real effects in the material world, and they are coherent, and thereby structured and systematic. In relation to the real, structured system of data, archaeologists critically evaluate their theories. The data are real but are both objective and subjective; and the theories are always open to further questions and new perspectives. Better and better accommodations and new insights can be achieved in a continuing process of interpretation.

Such discussions open up a debate about the relationship between subject and object. And if every society and time can be expected to produce their own prehistory, what are the responsibilities of archaeologists to the worlds in which they live?

Archaeology and society

Object and subject

Processual archaeology was not characterized by a detailed examination of the social contexts of archaeologists, since the main emphasis was to be placed on independent testing of theories against ethnographic and archaeological data. In the 1980s, however, archaeologists began to show a greater interest in the subjectivity of the pasts we reconstruct in relation to contemporary power strategies (Patterson 1986; Gibbon 1989; Meltzer 1983; Kristiansen 1981; Rowlands 1984; Wilk 1985; Leone *et al.* 1987; Trigger 1980). Archaeologists engaging in critical theory have been the most vocal in exploring this issue.

Although the archaeologist can be rigorous and scientific in the accommodation of theory and data, much of our definition of those data depends on ourselves. It is writers such as Childe and Collingwood who, from their Marxist and historical idealist positions respectively, discussed most fully the contemporary social basis of archaeological knowledge. The discussion of power and ideology in chapter 4 raises the issue of whether archaeological interpretations are ideological in relation to sectional interests.

Critical Theory

'Critical Theory' is the umbrella term given to a diversity of European authors, particularly those of the 'Frankfurt school', centred around the Institute of Social Research established in Frankfurt in 1923 (Held 1980). The main figures are Horkheimer, Adorno and Marcuse. More recently Habermas and his associates have reformulated the notion of Critical Theory. The approaches followed in Critical Theory derive from the tradition of German idealist thought, and incorporate a Marxist perspective. Critical Theorists claim on the one hand that all knowledge is historically conditioned, but at the same time suggest that truth can be evaluated and criticism can be conducted independently of social interests – in short, that Critical Theory has a privileged position in relation to theory.

Among the various aspects of the work of Critical Theory that might be of most interest to archaeology, the analysis of aesthetics and contemporary culture is immediately relevant to the presentation of the archaeological past in museums, on television and so on. In their *Dialectic of the Englightenment* Horkheimer and Adorno (1973) use the term 'culture industry'. Contrasting, for example, 'serious' and 'popular' music, they show that modern culture is standardized according to the rationalization of production and distribution techniques. Individuals do not 'live' art and culture any more – they consume its performance. The culture industry impedes the development of thinking, independent individuals; it conveys a message of adjustment, obedience. People are diverted, distracted and made passive. While there are many exceptions, archaeology in television documentaries and in museum displays is often presented as ordered, to be passively viewed. It is consumed as the cultural component of the leisure industry, rarely challenging and participatory. Archaeological scientists can place this sense of order and control and the supremacy of science (their own science and that of all dominant social groups) in a long-term historical perspective involving escape from the disordered primeval past through technological innovation. The result is a powerful ideological message.

Another relevant aspect of the work of Critical Theorists is their discussion of the philosophy of history. Habermas argues that it is inadequate to rest with the idealist interpretative understanding of contextual meanings, and the analyst must move towards the explanation of systematically distorted communication. In other words, one must see how the ideas of an age relate to domination and power. Similar points are made by Marcuse, Horkheimer and Adorno. In the *Dialectic of the Enlightenment*, the aim is to 'break the grip of all closed systems of thought; it is conceived as a contribution to the undermining of all beliefs that claim completeness and encourage an unreflected affirmation of society' (Held 1980, p. 150).

Following Hegel, the Enlightenment is seen as the rise of universal science in which the control of nature and human beings is the main aim. Within positivism, the world was seen as made up of material things which could be commanded and ordered according to universal laws, and the laws of history were equated with the laws of nature. It can certainly be argued (Hodder 1984b) that archaeological use of the natural science model, positivism and systems theory supports an 'ideology of control' whereby the 'apolitical' scientist is presented as essential for the control of society in past and future time and space.

In contrast, Critical Theory seeks a new enlightenment, an emancipation in which critical reason leads to liberation from all forces of domination and destruction. With writers such as Lukacs, the insight which leads to this liberation is that the structure of the social process constrains, dominates and determines the social totality, including thought and consciousness.

The ideals of objectivity and value-freedom are described by critical theorists as being themselves value-laden. Critical Theory seeks to judge between competing accounts of reality and to expose realms of ideology, and thus to emancipate people from class domination. By emphasizing the material and social conditions, ideological distortions can be revealed, leading to self-awareness and emancipation.

A materialist approach to history as ideology has been taken most clearly in archaeology by Leone (1982; Leone *et al.* 1987; see also Handsman 1980 and 1981). Leone notes that when the past is interpreted and made history it tends to become ideology, and he suggests that the consciousness or revelation of that process may help those who write or are told about the past to become aware of the ideological notions that generate modern everyday life. Through, for example, locating the origins of individualism or modern notions of time in the growth of capitalism in eighteenth-century America, visitors to museums could be made aware of their own ideology as historically-based, and their taken-for-granteds could be revealed as sources of domination.

While the notions of self-critique, and awareness of the social and political value of what we write, are of prime importance in the further development of archaeology, the position held by Critical Theory – as exemplified by Leone and Handsman's publications in the 1980s – seems to us to be difficult, although undoubtedly attractive and important, for two main reasons.

First, such work embodies an unsatisfactory notion of domination both in the past and in the present. Leone has acknowledged that the early stages of his collaborative work on the archaeology of Annapolis focused too heavily on dominant ideologies and did not account for the possibility of resistance (see chapter 5). Additional oral history and archaeology of residences of both free and enslaved African Americans in Annapolis strove to give voice to alternative experiences of the past (Leone *et al.* 1995). Whether or not the new phase of work succeeds in granting agency to these voices is a matter of debate (Wilkie and Bartoy 2000).

As for the present, society is represented as being ridden with all embracing, unified systems of representation. 'Society appears in their writings as steered from above rather than as the outcome, as I believe it to be, of a continuous process of struggle over rules and resources' (Held 1980, p. 365). However, there is evidence that different people in the contemporary public view the past in very different ways, and it is not at all clear that archaeology contributes to the maintenance of a universal Western ideology that prevents people from understanding their social conditions of existence. Indeed it seems that the past as constructed and experienced in contemporary life may reveal as much about the present as it masks.

Surveys of the general public in England conducted by Merriman (1991) suggested that individuals and subordinate groups in contemporary Britain are not easily duped by dominant interpretations of the past: although dominated groups including the working class appeared to have least scientific knowledge about the past, they scored highest in responses to questions about the need for the past. Individuals in such categories do think that the past and archaeology are necessary and worthwhile in giving meaning to the present. Yet individuals frequently showed a scepticism about the manipulation of the past by the media or by national governments; many people felt that little of what was said about the past by archaeologists and scientists could be proved in any way.

The second problem with current critical approaches in archaeology concerns the critique of those approaches themselves as historically generated. How can Critical Theory on the one hand claim that all knowledge is historical, distorted communication, and on the other hand be a critical means of enlightenment and emancipation? By what right or procedures does it accord itself a special theoretical status? The dilemma of critical theory in archaeology is: why should anyone accept a Marxist or critical analysis of our reconstructions of the past including the origins of capitalism? If the past is ideology, how can we presume to argue that only certain intellectuals can see through ideology to identify the social reality?

More recently, Leone has avoided the premise of the existence of a single social reality. Instead, since understanding history requires multiple views, the goal is to produce a variety of perspectives on the past, particularly those that have gone unrecorded historically. In this approach there is a willingness to give interviews and oral history equal weight to the material data (Leone *et al.* 1995, p. 122).

The special theoretical status which Leone claims in order to avoid the above dilemma is an avowedly 'materialist archaeology'. But if, for example, we do not accept the basic tenets of materialism, for reasons outlined in this book, we can claim that materialism is itself a false ideology – that it is just another universal theory developed by the academic community in order to maintain privileged control of the 'correct' interpretation of the past.

An alternative response to the second criticism made above is to argue that the past is not knowable with any integrity. The task of the archaeologist is, then, to choose any political stance he or she likes as a member of society, and to write the past so as to further that political viewpoint. This is certainly an honest reply which many may find attractive, but the potential results are disturbing. If the past has no integrity, and anyone's interpretation is as good as anyone else's, then archaeology is completely open to political manipulation by governments, elite interest groups, and fascist dictatorships. With the data described as totally subjective, the archaeologist would have no recourse to the data in objecting to 'misuses' of the past. The past which was disseminated would depend entirely on power, and the ability to control theory, method and communication. In this volume, however, we have argued that the data from the past do have a contextual reality in relation to theory (see p. 200).

Another important source of critique in archaeology is provided by post-structuralist writers such as Derrida (1975; see Bapty and Yates 1990; Tilley 1990a). The underlying idea here (see chapter 3 and p. 65) is that meaning is dispersed along chains of signifiers. Thus the validity of terms like truth or origin is undermined by the dependence of these terms on other terms in an endless sequence. One useful result of this critique is that it encourages archaeologists to examine their own writing and show how it is imbued with style and rhetoric (e.g. Hodder 1989b; Tilley 1989). In other words, the objectivity and truth claims can be shown to be constructed using various mechanisms (such as choice of words, appeal to authority, impersonal descriptions, avoidance of the 'I', the experienced and the contingent). Another useful result is that attempts are made to think of ways in which the past and our writing about the past can be opened up to alternative perspectives. However, difficulties similar to those encountered with Critical Theory approaches recur. The fragmentation of the past and the dispersal of meaning, distinctive characteristics of post-modern thought, can be seen as entirely consistent with dominant interests within later or high capitalism (Eagleton 1983). In the post-modern world in which individuals, time and place are fragmented and commodified, the directed interests of subordinate groups are undermined and their 'truth' dispersed. This is why we have resisted a radical decentring of the subject and embraced a theory of agency and why we have retained an account which puts faith in the reality and modified objectivity of the past. Ultimately a fully critical and responsible archaeology must be able to use the objectivity and reality of the experience of its data to shape and transform the experience of the world.

Although critical theory in archaeology emerged partly as a result of initiatives taken by academic archaeologists alone, it can be argued that some movement in the direction of critical perspectives has resulted from recent confrontations between 'established' and 'alternative' archaeologies and from engagements between archaeologists and non-archaeologists. By 'established' we mean the archaeology written by Western, upper middle class and largely Anglo-Saxon males. We wish to identify three examples of the kind of confrontations and engagements that have had an emergent impact on the practice of archaeology. In all these cases, two points can be made: first, the past is subjectively constructed in the present, and second, the subjective past is involved in power strategies today.

African burial grounds

The African Burial Ground project in New York City can be read as part of a critical tradition in archaeology as well as a paradigm case of how the goals and motivations of scientific archaeology can be successfully coordinated with the goals and motivations of other communities who have a stake in the past (La Roche and Blakey 1997; cf. Langford 1983).

In the summer of 1991, a CRM firm contracted by the US government began excavating the construction site of a proposed office building near City Hall in Manhattan. Eighteenth-century maps referred to an African cemetery in the vicinity, and within less than a year more than 400 burials were disinterred. Upset by the disturbance of the burials and osteological analyses that focused mainly on racial classification, a broad coalition of concerned citizens, artists, clergy members, activists, anthropologists, and city, state and federal politicians succeeded in stopping the excavation and transferring the artifacts and human remains to a team of African-American anthropologists whose research design was supported by the descendent community. Thereafter, the African Burial Ground project consisted of not only osteology and forensics (stable isotope analysis, molecular genetics, morphology, morphometrics, etc.), but also African and African-American history, art history and ethnology, a public education and interpretation programme, plans to rebury the human remains and determine the future fate of the site, and more.

The research conducted by the African Burial Ground project has addressed a number of Eurocentric distortions and omissions in the historical record that, if left uncorrected, would deny northern racism and locate enslavement primarily in the southern United States (Pittman 1998). During the 18th century, the vast majority of Africans in New York were enslaved. Evidence of malnutrition and excessive physical strain demonstrate the abhorrent quality of life for many New York slaves (Blakey 1998). Disrespect for the humanity of New York city's Africans continued after death. Not allowed to bury their dead in church cemeteries, Africans had to use a plot of land in a ravine outside of the palisades that marked the edge of the city. The burial ground was desecrated by dumping of refuse from nearby tanning and pottery industries, grave robbing by medical students, executions in retribution for alleged revolts, and, once the burial grounds were closed, the digging of privies and cisterns as part of Dutch American occupation of the site in the 19th century. Ironically, now that we know much more about the African Burial Ground, distortion continues today in artistic portraits that picture the burial grounds as a lush, flat pastoral landscape rather than a hilly ravine on the margin of noxious industries. Such inaccuracies negate the actual hardships faced by New York's early African community and defuse the raw power of the Burial Ground (La Roche and Blakey 1997, p. 98).

Beyond providing evidence that confronts a whitewashed past, the African Burial Ground is 'an avenue leading to spiritual rebirth and renewal', a possibility that 'slavery's wounds might finally be tended' (La Roche and Blakey 1997, p. 100; Blakey 1998, p. 58). In other words, the African Burial Ground project, along with other examples of African-American historical archaeology (Franklin 1997; Leone *et al.* 1995; McDavid and Babson 1997), empowers contemporary descendants by giving them tangible, material evidence of their heritage and of the contributions and suffering of their once ignored, silenced and disenfranchised ancestors.

As an example of an archaeology engaged in contemporary politics, the African Burial Ground project also serves as a model for the potential benefits of collaboration between archaeologists and non-archaeologists. Despite the fact that archaeology, physical anthropology and history have traditionally abused or demeaned African-Americans, systematic consultation between the descendent community and the team that replaced the original CRM firm led the descendent community to endorse wholeheartedly a scientific research design. Because of a shared affinity for African-American culture, past and present, it helped that the archaeologists and descendent communities were both African-American (La Roche and Blakey 1997, p. 93). However, the recent history of engagements between archaeologists and native Americans, to which we now turn, shows that a successful collaboration does not require ethnic homogeneity of the participants.

Indigenous archaeologies

Western archaeologists working in non-industrialized societies, particularly in the post-colonial era, became increasingly confronted both with the idea that the pasts they were reconstructing were 'Western' and with an articulate rejection of those pasts as being politically and ideologically motivated (Layton 1989a and b). The secure rocks of objective data began to seem more like shifting sands of subjective impressions. In many parts of the Middle East and of Africa, for example, Western archaeological interpretations have been rejected or reassessed and the Western archaeologists themselves excluded.

It can be suggested that the Australian government publicized anthropological and archaeological interpretations of Aborigines as 'natural', primitive and isolated. By processes such as these, the Australian Aborigines were denied another identity and their access to Western knowledge about disease, health, the law and power was restricted. On the other hand, Aborigines make use of archaeological interpretations in land claims, and similar strategies are used elsewhere, for example by the Canadian Inuit. In Europe, too, archaeology makes legitimate claims about long-term residence in certain areas. For example, in Norway, debate about archaeologists' abilities to identify ethnic groups in prehistory is heightened by political issues concerned with Sami (Lapp) rights.

The United States of America, a country which has grown up through the relatively recent mass genocide of indigenous American peoples and which has even developed high positive values in relation to 'the frontier', has complex attitudes to the archaeology of the peoples it displaced (Watkins 2000). These attitudes have changed through time, but they have always portrayed America's native people as unprogressive (Trigger 1980). Thus in the nineteenth century native peoples were seen as unprogressive savages, a view resulting in the 'Mound Builder' myth according to which spectacular earthworks in North America were described as produced by non-native Americans. In the early twentieth century, the same disrespect for native Americans led to a lack of interest in explaining their cultural developments; a descriptive and static picture was painted. In processual archaeology, native Americans were treated as laboratories for the testing of general statements of interest to non-native American archaeologists but of little relevance to the history or concerns of the native Americans themselves (Trigger 1980). In all these ways, the native Americans' place in America, and the Euro-American destruction of that place, are minimized, and archaeology contributes to an 'historical amnesia'. Recently, however, liberal tendencies and environmental resource concerns in Western society, coupled with native American land claims, have led to Western archaeologists working on behalf of groups in the United States and Canada. Indeed recent legislation in the United States (including NAGPRA) attempts to safeguard the interests of native Americans in regard to their heritage. This has led to closer cooperation between archaeologists and native Americans (Swidler *et al.* 1997; Watkins 2000), and even to changes in archaeological method which involve native American oral traditions and ritual observances within the scientific process (e.g. Dowdall and Parrish 2003).

The differences between Western and indigenous perceptions of non-Western pasts are often difficult to handle in practice. There is often considerable mistrust, misunderstanding and resentment. But it is difficulties such as these which have begun to push Western archaeologists to consider their own biases and to confront the issue of whether differences in interpretation can be resolved by testing theories against objective data. In many cases the doctrines of verification are themselves perceived as political (Langford 1983). The temptation is to withdraw from the confrontation and the debate, rather than to expose the apolitical nature of Western empiricism and positivism to erosion.

Feminist archaeologies

It is this ability of Western archaeologists to note but ignore the confrontation with indigenous archaeologies which emphasizes the importance of a feminist perspective in archaeology. By 'feminist' we mean here a critical perspective from the point of view of women in contemporary society, which goes beyond 'gender archaeology' – the study of the relations between men and women in the past. Since this perspective in archaeology derives from a contemporary current within the West it is potentially less easy to ignore than the archaeology of distant countries. This potential (Conkey and Spector 1984) is rapidly being realized (Barstow 1978; Claassen 1994; Conkey and Gero 1997; Engelstad 1991; Gero 1985; Gero and Conkey 1991; Gilchrist 1993; Meskell 2002; Sørensen 1988; 2000; Wright 1996).

We do not intend to discuss the imbalance in the representation of women in the archaeological profession or the use of sexist language in archaeological publications, although both matters are linked to the main aspect of feminist archaeology to be discussed here as relevant to the theme of this chapter. Rather, we shall concentrate on two important points made by feminist archaeologists (Conkey and Spector 1984). The first is that archaeologists have tended to view the past sexual division of labour as similar to that of the present. For example, hunting and trade are often seen as male pursuits, while gathering and weaving are female. Projectile points and well-made tools are linked to men, while non-wheel-made pots are linked to women. This sex-linking of past activities makes present sexual relations seem inevitable and legitimate.

Second, greater interest is shown in the 'dominant' male activities. Males are generally portrayed as stronger, more aggressive, more dominant, more active and more important than women, who often appear as weak, passive and dependent. The past is written in terms of leadership, power, warfare, the exchange of women, man the hunter, rights of inheritance, control over resources, and so on.

These two androcentric strands of archaeological analysis have been critically examined, in particular, in relation to the debate about the 'origins of man' and 'man the hunter' (Conkey and Spector *ibid.*), and reinterpretations of the 'origins of man' have been made in which women play a more positive role (e.g. Tanner 1981). The impact of the debate is equally relevant for the adoption of agriculture (Draper 1975; Gero and Conkey 1990) and for the rise of the state (Gailey 1987; Hastorf 1990).

In relation to the two points made above, feminist archaeologists argue that, first, we cannot assume universally equivalent divisions of labour and sex-linking of activities. Rather than assuming that the term 'woman' has universal cultural characteristics, there is a need to examine the way in which gender constructions can vary. Archaeological data are rife with evidence of the cultural constructions of gender relations. Objects can be linked to women in graves, the nutritional aspect of gender relations can be examined in comparing female and male skeletons (Hastorf 1990), the representation and non-representation of women in art and symbolism can be studied. Indeed, it is often the absence of women from certain domains of representation that will support insight into gender constructions.

In relation to the second point made above, it is argued by feminist archaeologists that women can play an active role in society (see Tanner 1981). For example, pottery decoration has been seen by archaeologists largely as a cultural indicator – it is a passive indexing device. Even when viewed in terms of information flow, exchange and interaction, the decoration remains passive and unrelated to women. Feminist perspectives, however, suggest that in certain situations pottery decoration may be involved in the covert discourse of women who are 'muted' in the dominant modes of discourse (Braithwaite 1982). Indeed, decoration and elaboration in the domestic context may often have much more to do with the negotiation of power between men and women than they have with symbolizing contact and interaction between local groups (see Hodder 1984a for an application of this notion to European prehistory).

One of the most important aspects of the feminist critique relates to the discussion of power in chapter 4, where it was argued that there are different types of power which overlap and conflict and are continually being negotiated between different interest groups. Power is not simply a 'reality' of force or the control of resources but is also closely linked to meanings, values and prestige. Control of a prestigious resource can only be used as the basis of power when the resource has been given cultural and social values. Moore (1988, p. 35) argues that 'most feminist scholars would now agree, I think, that the cultural valuations given to women and men in society arise from something more than just their respective positions in the relations of production'. The representation of gender relations in material culture (in burials, dress, art, use of space, etc.) may tell us more about the attempts made to value or devalue men and women than it tells us about the 'real' power of men and women in the control of resources. We cannot simply read off gender dominance from the material representation of gender relations (Hodder 1990c). Rather, we are forced, in discussing the representation of gender dominance, to interpret symbolic meanings. For this reason, we would argue that the overall theoretical shift being outlined in this volume is needed in the discipline before many of the most exciting aspects of feminism can take hold in archaeology. As Michelle Rosaldo said of this shift in anthropology, we must pursue not universal, general causality but meaningful explanation. 'It now appears to me that woman's place in human social life is not in any direct sense a product of the things she *does*, but of the *meaning* her activities acquire through concrete social interaction' (Rosaldo 1980, p. 400).

If we want to show how gender relations are experienced and given meaning, how they are used to define personhood and how they are involved in subtle ways in multidimensional relations of power, a critical hermeneutic or contextual approach may be necessary. In so far as issues of meaning are part of feminist archaeology, positivism is not an appropriate framework. Feminism has had a very late impact in archaeology in comparison with related disciplines. Stacey and Thorne (1985) claim that feminist approaches have succeeded least in disciplines (like sociology, psychology, economics) more deeply anchored in positivism. It is in fields with a strong interpretive approach (history, literature, sociocultural anthropology) that feminism has advanced furthest. It may be archaeology's recent positivist history coupled with its increasing resource base in the sciences that impeded the development of feminist archaeology for so long.

In recent years there has been internal debate within feminist archaeology about the overall emphasis on women rather than on gender relations, and on various forms of sexuality that counter dominant modes of discourse (Voss and Schmidt 2000). Indeed, one of the main issues at the heart of a 'third wave' of feminism and feminist archaeology is that not enough attention has been paid to different categories of men and women. Rather than talking of women as a whole in a particular society, the focus is on differences in class, age, occupation and so on which may be just as important in defining identity as sex or gender (Joyce 2000; Meskell 1999). This emphasis on difference radically undermines claims for an essential character for men and women. Even the biological basis of sexual difference is now seen as embedded in discourse (Foucault 1981b). Cultural 'gender' cannot be set against biological 'sex' because the latter too is discursive and historically changing. This type of 'third wave' approach leads to attempts to describe individual and private lives (Meskell 2002). It leads to a focus on difference and social agency, but also to a situating of sex and gender as components in wider social fields which vary historically and spatially.

Other alternative Western archaeologies

From Creationists and readers of Von Daniken to metal detector users (Gregory 1983) and ley-line hunters (Williamson and Bellamy 1983), alternative and often extremely popular pasts are derived which establishment archaeologists may try to ignore, or dismiss as 'fringe'. Increasingly, however, direct confrontation occurs, particularly in Western societies in which the past as a resource has now to be used more effectively for the general public, as a commodity, well-packaged and responsive to demand.

In many Western countries archaeology has long been linked to the upper and middle classes. To what extent is this true today, how is the past used to legitimate established interests, and what are the effects on interpretations of the past? A survey of the British public's knowledge of and attitudes to archaeology was carried out by Merriman (1989a, b; 1991).

From the surveys, it is clear that certain groups of people in contemporary Britain know more about the past than others. They have a broader and more accurate knowledge of what archaeologists write. They watch more archaeological documentaries on television, go more to museums and visit sites and churches, and read more about the past. Not surprisingly, these people have often had more education (stayed at school longer, or had some form of further education) than those with less archaeological knowledge. They also often have higher-valued jobs with more control over people and resources.

How exactly do these different groups in society interpret the past? The survey results suggested that less educated, lower income groups tended to be relatively more interested in their local past, in archaeology as history. Most individuals in the general public find it extremely difficult to develop their ideas about an alternative past in relation to the data from the past. They are excited by Von Daniken and films such as *One Million Years B.C.* and *Raiders of the Lost Ark*, and they develop their personal views about what the past must have been like, but they are kept at a distance from archaeological artifacts by glass cases, systems analyses and the jargon of social theory. Where they *do* manage to gain some access to an immediately experienced past, they are often directly confronted by the archaeological establishment, or else their views are studiously ignored. For example, metal detector users and the archaeological establishment in Britain have entered into a heated and acrimonious debate which serves only to widen social divisions (Hodder 1984b). Those archaeologists who do try to work with, rather than against, metal detector enthusiasts have found ways of encouraging cooperation and understanding (Gregory 1983).

The same can be said for the various forms of New Age archaeology that are burgeoning world-wide. In particular, the interactions between archaeology and the various goddess communities have been explored by a number of archaeologists (e.g. Meskell 1995; 1998b; Tringham and Conkey 1998). Locations such as the Neolithic temples in Malta, the Bronze Age sites on Crete, or Çatalhöyük in Turkey have become pilgrimage sites for such groups (Rountree 1999; 2001; 2002). The individuals involved in these tours are often well educated. Their aim is often to engage in sites more deeply than most tourists, and this can lead to conflict with local communities (Rountree 2001). There is often a desire to perform circle dances and other rituals on sites. Some goddess groups are very sensitive to local interests and to the preservation of sites, but other groups may be antagonistic towards archaeologists whom they see as male-biased and secular, unresponsive to the presence of the goddess. But attempts can be made to enter into a dialogue with these groups (see www.catalhoyuk.com), and successful collaborative programmes at sites can be developed in which the new religions, archaeological science and local communities are accommodated to each other.

There is, then, great potential for archaeologists to encourage and help to create different views of and ways of participating in the past (Willey 1980). Attempts could be made to explain how the past is excavated (Leone 1983) and how it is reconstructed. Many museums, such as the Jorvik Viking Centre in York, are now more concerned with providing living versions of the past that can be experienced by the public. This is equally true of some well-established museums.

Conclusion

In the latter part of this chapter we have discussed the actual and potential archaeological viewpoints of a number of groups which can be described as subordinate on a global or intra-societal scale. These alternative, but by no means 'minority', viewpoints confront establishment perspectives and imply that the pasts we reconstruct are both partly subjective and involved in the negotiation of power.

It does not seem possible to react to this discussion of the contextuality of archaeological knowledge by claiming that 'method' will allow differentiation between the alternative interpretations of the past. Positivism, independent Middle Range Theories, materialist analysis, all can be seen to be tied to particular contemporary social assumptions; method too is ideological.

An open relativism appears at first to be the only solution, whereby 'anything goes'. Certainly there are some attractive aspects of this solution, if it allows greater debate between different viewpoints and a fuller involvement of archaeology in contemporary social and political issues. Yet most archaeologists feel that this solution is too extreme. Most feel that some interpretations of the past are not as good as others, that not everything can be said with equal integrity.

The contemporary social basis of our reconstructions of the past does not necessitate a lack of validity for those reconstructions. Our interpretations may be biased, but they may still be 'right'. Clearly, however, it is important to understand where our ideas come from, and why we want to reconstruct the past in a particular way.

There is a dialectical relationship between past and present: the past is interpreted in terms of the present, but the past can also be used to criticize and challenge the present. In this view it is possible critically to evaluate past and present contexts in relation to each other, so as to achieve a better understanding of both. There is a human mental ability to conceive of more than one subjective context and critically to examine the relationship between varied perspectives. This discussion returns us to earlier statements in this volume about the relationship between the larger whole (structure, system) and the individual part (action, practice, the individual). Structures and taken-for-granteds may well be the media for thought and action, yet they can themselves be changed by critical thought and action.

Thus the data are not objective or subjective but real. And there are no universal instruments of measurement, but it is possible to understand 'otherness'. Even the notions of the universality of meaning construction must be subject to critical evaluation, especially in periods prior to *Homo sapiens sapiens*. We always translate 'their' meanings into 'our' language, but our language is flexible and rich enough to identify and perceive differences in the way the same 'words' are used in different contexts. The subjectivity of other objects can be comprehended without imposing our own 'objective' subjectivities; the subject/object division that has dominated archaeology can be broken down.

Post-processual archaeology, then, involves the breaking down of established, taken-for-granted dichotomies, and opens up study of the relationships between norm and individual, process and structure, material and ideal, object and subject. Post-processual archaeology does not espouse one approach or argue that archaeology should develop an agreed methodology. It is about opening up, not shutting down, and therefore welcomes the proliferation of archaeologies. Though we endorse the hermeneutic method, our endorsement should not be taken as a rejection of other methods or approaches. In fact, we argue that the hermeneutic approach is extremely broad, subsuming modes of inquiry that prioritise both the laboratory sciences and the humanities. Finally post-processual archaeology is about engagements with social theory and social groups. Though in the next chapter we maintain that archaeology is archaeology is archaeology, it is strongest when most broadly networked with other disciplines and most relevant when interwoven with social issues.

10 Conclusion: archaeology as archaeology

The archaeology for which we have been advocating attempts to capture a new openness to debate in archaeology – a broadening to include a variety of influences including Marxism, structuralism, practice theories, embodiment, feminist critiques and public archaeology. At the same time, the aim is to establish archaeology as a discipline able to contribute an independent voice to both intellectual and public debates. The contextual approach discussed in chapter 8 is one way of doing this which we personally find attractive, given our own views of the society in which we live and of what ought to happen to it, and given our opinion of the development of archaeology over the last 20 years.

In contributing to and being involved in broader interdisciplinary debate, archaeologists read various types of general meaning in their data. We have discussed three overlapping types of meaning. One is the meaning of objects as physical, involved in exchanges of matter, energy and information; the concern here is with the object as a resource, functioning after its production, to facilitate organizational needs. A second is the meaning of objects in relation to the structured contents of historical traditions. A third kind of meaning – operational meaning – resides in the specifics of the context of each event or expression. Operational meaning is shaped by the previous two meanings but also takes into account (1) the specific intentions underlying the discrete actions of people in the past and (2) the unique lived, embodied experience of each actor. In claiming that these views (object as object, object as meaningfully constituted, object as product of situated intentions, object in relation to personal experience) are necessary in archaeology, we do not espouse a live and let live policy in which these approaches can exist separately, side by side. There is little one can do by focussing only on the object as physical object. Perhaps distance from the source of an exchanged object, the amount of meat on bones, the efficacity of tools for cutting skin and so on, can be assessed without reference to historical meanings; but we have shown in numerous examples that most statements about the past involve making assumptions about such meanings – whether one is talking of prestige exchange, the economy or the population size of a settlement. Even words like 'wall', 'pit' and 'settlement' denote purpose. We cannot always assume that 'figurine' and 'agriculture' mean the same thing in different contexts. Archaeologists have always worked by thinking themselves into past cultural contexts – one cannot get very far otherwise. The three approaches cannot exist separately because each is necessary to the other and is routinely involved in the other. The concern of this volume has been to argue for the necessity of this relationship, to argue that we should be more explicit and rigorous in our reconstructions of historical meanings, and that we should discuss the theoretical and methodological issues which result.

However, the reaction against such discussion in archaeology has been remarkably persistent. Much of Binford's writing centres on this theme. In an account of resin-processing activities amongst the Ayawara Australian Aborigines, Binford (1984) notes variation between Aboriginal groups. He asks whether this variation is expedient and situational or cultural, thus continuing the old split between process and norm, and framing the question on the assumption that such a split exists. Binford argues that variation in resin-processing depends on whether processing is carried out by mixed-sex groups using female-curated items, or whether it is done by all-male groups away from the residential camp. He concludes that resin-processing is situational and not culturally determined.

Clearly resin-processing may vary depending on whether women are present, and on where it is carried out. But to describe this variation and covariation is to do an adequate analysis of *neither* of Binford's two concerns – situational adaptation and culture. We have argued that situational decision making is a central part of context (chapter 8); but to examine situational variability we need to have a clear idea of why women do certain tasks and men others, and we need to examine the active social context of male and female strategies in relation to each other. What are women or men trying to do in refusing to do this task in this residential camp, but not in that camp, and so on? Binford provides no answers to such questions. To examine the role of culture, we need to examine indigenous attitudes to the particular tools used in resin-processing, to those tools which can or cannot be used inside and outside the residential camp, to resin and resin-processing themselves, to men and women. We would need to examine such attitudes and strategies by observing more of the cultural context (what else do men and women do, what else are the different locations used for, and so on).

Rather than seeing culture and situational decision making as divorced, we can see them both as closely intertwined in each social 'action'. In Collingwood's terms, we need to get at the 'inside' of the Ayawara events. As in his Nunamiut study, Binford provides us with inadequate information to examine culture as the medium of action – the situational decisions, as described, occur in a cultural vacuum so that we cannot explain their specificity, their causes or their effects. The poverty of the argument is clear. Binford is more interested in making some general contribution to an abstract theoretical debate about which 'ism' is correct than he is in understanding the particular event in all its richness and complexity. The contemporary game of power is played out, but the cause of science is not necessarily advanced. Of course, we would return to the larger theoretical issues after having discussed Ayawara resin-processing in full, and general theories are necessary in the initial approach to and interpretation of the data, but in Binford's account the dialectical relationship between theory and data, the critical comparison of contexts, never takes place. Binford short-circuits the argument by 'testing' theories against pre-selected criteria, rather than trying to place the theories more fully in their contexts. Binford does not 'read' the Ayawara resin-processing 'text'. Discussion about 'isms' therefore becomes confrontational, based on *a priori* assumptions and on power. The contribution that the Ayawara could make to debate between the 'isms' is never realized.

Testing interpretations

We do not wish to give the impression in the above account of Binford's work that we cannot 'test' theories. A dichotomy sometimes emerges between testing and interpretation. In fact the dichotomy should concern different approaches to testing. Some processual archaeologists have built up an inaccurate and contradictory picture of how archaeologists test their theories.

Instead of testing, we come to an understanding. Though our understandings are contingent on our contemporary engagements with the world and are therefore subject to change, it is indeed possible to show that certain understandings fit the data better than others. There are two aspects of this fitting procedure. First, we may show that the theories feeding our interpretations are incomplete, self-contradictory or perhaps unconscionable given the contemporary context of the work. This context includes the relations of power impacting and impacted by archaeology and the interests of other communities that claim connections to the past. Second, we show that previous theories leave much of the data unaccounted for in comparison with new theories, or we show that earlier theories used incorrect data (such as incorrect dates) or that they were based on the recognition of patterns which were not statistically significant, and so on.

It is easy to confuse scientific procedures with the hypothesis-testing approach. But in fact the use of scientific means of analysis, whether involving the use of statistics, quantification, chemical or physical studies, is equally relevant with a hermeneutic approach. Such scientific methods are used for discerning and testing patterns (for example against the notion of randomness), relationships, dates and sources. The methods help us to find patterns against which we can evaluate our claims. But they do not provide a way of avoiding the hermeneutic circle. They allow us to describe pattern more accurately and to look for more dimensions of variability, but the pattern still has to be interpreted. We still have to appeal to coherence and correspondence. However much we use statistical and scientific methods, whether we are primarily concerned with ecological or with cultural issues, we all follow a hermeneutic enterprise as outlined in chapter 8.

This description of archaeology is decried by some archaeologists as unscientific because it argues that we use ad hoc accommodative arguments (Binford 1982). Such archaeologists feel that a properly scientific argument needs to reach a greater degree of certainty, stability and universality and that the social construction of archaeological knowledge can be discounted. They argue for universal instruments of measurement which are not historically variable.

We would agree that Middle Range Theory can be built with some success in relation to the various non-cultural processes which affect the archaeological record. For example, knowledge about the responses of types of stone, bone and clay to different forces allows us to evaluate the validity of hypotheses about the past. They provide a test which is based on universal non-cultural processes and which is independent because based on theories unrelated to those being evaluated. It is not possible to make the same claims for cultural processes. We would accept that we need to generalise about cultural processes in order to form abstractions and construct theories. An example of an attempt to generalise about cultural processes includes Cowgill's sketch of a Middle Range Theory of the Mind (1993). These generalisations include inferences about meaning, emotion, ideology and power. Cowgill claims that his Middle Range Theory is similar to other Middle Range Theories in that its assumptions should be independent of the evidence. However, Cowgill explicitly states that Middle Range Theory can pertain to local situations, which means that his approach is in fact contextual and therefore significantly different from traditional Middle Range Theory.

Conclusion: archaeology as archaeology

Traditional Middle Range Theory, which works best for non-cultural processes and assumes strict independence of context, creates a contradiction when it is applied to the testing of hypotheses about mind, meaning and representation. On the one hand, it is argued by some processual archaeologists that universal relationships in the organization of, for example, ritual and religion (Renfrew 1985) allow the archaeologist to test theories against the data. Various predictions are made on the basis of Middle Range theoretical understanding and the data are examined to see if they fit. For this procedure to be scientific in the way that is often claimed, the hypothesis about the past, the Middle Range Theory and the data should all be independent of each other and the Middle Range knowledge should be universal. On the other hand, as was noted in chapter 2, writers such as Renfrew, Flannery and Marcus and Binford and Sabloff argue that each culture has its own 'cognitive phylogeny' or each approach its own paradigm. These two positions simply do not compute. The contextuality of knowledge undermines the dependence on universal measuring devices, the independence of theories and the objective confrontation of theory and data.

The alternative is to move backwards and forwards between theory and data, trying to fit or accommodate one to the other in a clear and rigorous fashion, on the one hand being sensitive to the particularity of the data and on the other hand being critical about assumptions and theories. Much damage has been done in archaeology by the crudity of hypothesis-testing and narrow 'scientific method', although in practice most archaeologists have continued to find that what they discover is of greater interest and complexity than their expectations. There is always a surplus of meaning which requires a more sensitive, hermeneutic interpretation. A properly scientific approach accepts the need to account for all the data, in all its particularity, and the need for the critical probing of the only partial independence of theory and data.

However much they would like to think otherwise, archaeologists rarely work as positivist natural scientists. We would argue that on the whole what they tend to do is follow simple hermeneutic procedures within a stream of changing interpretation. This realization has been clarified by the need to interpret internal meanings but it is equally relevant to all types of archaeology.

Any discussion of 'reading' the past or of internal meanings has hints of empathy and a lack of science, so that the statement 'it makes sense to me' appears to become the final arbiter of any debate. Archaeology thus becomes prey to special interests. Post-processual archaeologists would, however, reject empathy and would reject the notion that anyone's interpretation of the past, however unrelated to the data, is equally valid. Some would emphasize the contribution made by debate between different perspectives on the past as one mechanism for the critique of vested interests and invalid interpretations. Others (e.g. Shanks and Tilley 1987a and b) would describe the archaeological data as 'networks of resistances' which constrain what can be said about the past. Our own view is that even this is too 'presentist' and does not allow that our conception of the present is partly built out of the reality of the past. For example, it is undoubtedly the case that our present ideas about evolution and progress have been contributed to by the hard findings of archaeologists. Equally, archaeology is what it is today in each country partly because of what has been found. What has been found is a product of what has been looked for but it also affects the way we look (for example, concentrating our researches on certain wealthy or visible sites, regions or periods). Archaeology, the present and the past, subject and object, are in a dialectical relationship which is always in movement. They, we, depend on each other and bring each other into existence.

Archaeology and its distinctive role

In order for a broader, post-processual archaeology to be achieved, studies of the three types of meaning of material objects (as object, as signs and as operational contexts) need to be incorporated. In this way the four general issues of post-processual archaeology (the relationships between norm and individual, process and structure, ideal and material, subject and object) can be addressed. It might seem that in becoming part of such debates, and using theories from other disciplines, archaeology would lose some of its distinctiveness and independence. Post-processual archaeology is part of wider concerns within social theory, and contextual analysis derives much of its methods and theory from linguistic analysis.

Yet it has also been argued in this book that contextual archaeological data can be examined in their own terms, and that the specificity of past meanings can be approached. Perhaps archaeology can contribute its own data to the general debates, using its own methods and theories to do so, as an independent discipline. We wish now to examine the proposal, again different from traditional and processual archaeology, that archaeology is neither history nor anthropology, but just archaeology.

The claim that 'archaeology is archaeology is archaeology' was forcefully made by David Clarke. His *Analytical Archaeology* (1968) is the most significant attempt to develop a peculiarly archaeological methodology based on archaeological contexts. In his later Glastonbury study (1972; see above, p. 68), Clarke conducted a detailed contextual analysis incorporating a structural element. Apart from his non-alignment with the view that 'archaeology is anthropology or it is nothing', Clarke differed from much processual or 'New' archaeology because he retained a concern with cultural entities, their diffusion and continuities. Despite a strong natural science element in his work, he was suspicious of too easily imposing and 'testing' general laws. There are clearly many similarities, therefore, with the more limited account of a contextual approach provided in this volume. The major difference, apart from the detailed type of methodology embraced, is in Clarke's failure to identify ways of moving beyond the data to interpret them. In *Analytical Archaeology* his scheme is analytical and empirical. The social and cultural meanings of his archaeological patterns are far from clear.

Simple cross-cultural interpretations were imposed (for example regarding the significance of regional cultural groupings), and there is little concern with meaning content and 'history from the inside' in this or any of his later works.

Taylor too had claimed (1948) that 'archaeology is neither history nor anthropology' (*ibid.*, p. 44). Again there are many similarities between the view put forward in this volume and his conjunctive approach, which had as its primary goal 'the elucidation of cultural conjunctives, the associations and relationships, the "affinities", *within* the manifestation under investigation' (*ibid.*, pp. 95–6). The aim was to examine contextual information in each unit or site as a discrete entity within its own cultural expression, with an emphasis on the cultural context in contrast to the comparative method. Further, 'culture is a mental phenomenon, consisting of the content of minds, not of material objects or observable behaviour' (*ibid.*, p. 98). In applied examples, Taylor demonstrates the ability of archaeologists to reconstruct ideas in the covert culture of past societies. For example, in an examination of cloth decoration Taylor notes whether cords are twisted to the left or right, and goes on to identify structuring principles, one being that Coahuila textile shows 'unconcern with regularized decorative wholes' (*ibid.*, p. 182).

Despite these clear similarities with the viewpoints discussed in chapter 9, there are some important limitations in his approach, recalling the critical comments made earlier in this volume. First, Taylor claims a categoric distinction between idea and practice: 'Culture itself consists of ideas, not processes' (*ibid.*, p. 110). This is the opposite to Binford's claim, and it is equally inadequate.

Second, Taylor's view is normative, although not in the sense that 'societies' somehow share an outlook on the world. Taylor suggested that culture can be either shared or individual and idiosyncratic. However, we would take issue with Taylor in regard to the second meaning of normative – that behaviour is rule-bound. Individuals or groups are so controlled by systems or codes or structures that they cannot usurp them. Taylor appears to talk of culture as made up of rules of this kind, rather than of contextual decisions informed by rules and dispositions. In this sense his approach is not contextual (situationally contextual) but normative.

Despite these and other differences with Taylor's approach (in particular Taylor does not develop a socially self-conscious and critical stance in relation to the subjectivity of data description and interpretation), it is clear that Taylor, in common with Collingwood, has much to offer contemporary archaeologists. It is not our concern to deny links to earlier archaeologists – indeed it seems necessary to rebuild the bridges which were so harshly broken by processual archaeology, and to re-evaluate what has been termed the 'long sleep of archaeological theory' (Renfrew 1983b).

In this volume, the notion that archaeology should have an independent existence, despite its involvements in general theory and method, has the following components. First, we have already commented in chapter 9 that archaeology can be distinguished from antiquarianism by its concern with the contexts of material objects. It has been argued that archaeologists can incorporate inductive methods in building up from contextual associations and contrasts towards a critical understanding of specific historical meanings. These readings and interpretations are translations in a different time; they make universal assumptions, but the results are not wholly dependent on the present. The readings inform and contribute to the present through critical evaluation of the past. How much archaeologists can interpret depends on the richness of their data networks and on their knowledge and abilities, yet there is a clear potential for independent archaeological contribution.

Second, while archaeologists may read material culture, we do not read it as if it were text. There are distinct differences between material culture and spoken or written language, differences which need to be researched further. Material culture often appears to be a simpler but more ambiguous language, and, in comparison to speech, it often seems more fixed and durable. In addition, most words are arbitrary signifiers of the concepts signified: thus, the relationship between the word 'tree', as opposed to 'arbre' or 'tarm', and the concept 'tree' is conventional, and historical. But a material culture 'word', such as a photograph or sculpture of a human being, is not an arbitrary representation of that which is signified: thus, in contrast to the majority of words, many material culture signs are iconic or indexical. These and other differences imply that archaeologists have to develop their own theory and method for reading their own particular data.

Third, archaeology can avail itself of evidence of human cultural activity that covers enormous spans of time. This long-term perspective has the potential for leading to new insights into the four main issues in post-processual archaeology. For example, over the long term, what role is played by the individual event in the general processes of social and cultural change, and what is the relationship between structure and process? In the short term, it may appear that social and economic determinants are more important, but over the long term the social and economic decisions may be seen to form repeated patterns that have an underlying structural or cultural rhythm. Initial archaeological work in this direction was discussed in chapter 5.

In these various ways, archaeology can be seen as an independent discipline groping towards independent method and theory, but necessarily linked to and contributing to general social theory. The problem of the relationship between the particular and the general, which underlies the three points discussed in the previous paragraphs, is itself a wide issue to which archaeology can make a particular contribution.

Archaeological objects raise questions about the relationship between the specific and the general, in an extreme and evocative form. This relationship, apparently ignored in much recent academic archaeology, has been captured by Mags Harries in her public art on the streets of Boston (frontispiece). We claim that her art is archaeological, first because she recognizes the close immediacy of everyday mundane objects, their historical specificity. Often produced to be left behind, unintended and unnoticed, the objects capture a fleeting moment in concrete form. Second, however, we feel that we understand the objects, that there is a commonality and nearness, even over great expanses of time. We are confronted by the enormity of time and the generality of experience. In this volume we have tried to argue that we can understand this distance and generality only by exploiting to the full the concrete everydayness of the artifacts themselves, in all their specificity.

On the streets of Boston, Mags Harries creates archaeological objects. Her art is archaeological in the two senses just defined. For archaeology itself to become archaeological once again, it must involve more than digging up more artifacts and putting them in museums and into socio-cultural sub-systems – we need to examine the specific contexts of objects in the past, in order to debate our own contexts in the face of the generality of the long term.

In discussing tentative steps in these directions, this volume intentionally raises more questions than it answers – about the relationships between individuals and societies, about the existence of general laws, about the role of archaeologists in society, and so on. The meaning of the past is more complex than we might have thought. However, rather than taking the line that archaeology now appears hopelessly difficult, we have in fact suggested that archaeologists can return to basic principles in translating the meaning of past texts into their own contemporary language. The methods of excavation and interpretation based on the notion of context are well-developed. Using such methods – Collingwood's question-and-answer procedure, notions of coherence and correspondence, the idea that meaning is constructed through structured sets of differences – and recognizing the importance of critical analysis, it is argued that contextual information from the past can lead to understanding of functional and ideational meanings. In this way long-term history can be reconstructed and can contribute to debate within modern social theory and within society at large.

Bibliography

Abercrombie, N., Hill, S., and Turner, B., 1980, *The Dominant Ideology Thesis*, London: George Allen and Unwin

Abu El-Haj, N., 1998, 'Translating Truths: Nationalism, the Practice of Archaeology and the Remaking of Past and Present in Contemporary Jerusalem', *American Ethnologist* 25(2), 168–88

Althusser, L., 1977, *For Marx*, London: New Left Books

Ames, K., 1996, 'Archaeology, Style, and the Theory of Coevolution', in H. Maschner (ed.), *Darwinian Archaeologies*, New York: Plenum

Ammerman, A., 1979, 'A Study of Obsidian Exchange Networks in Calabria', *World Archaeology* 11, 95–110

Anati, M.-J., 1994, 'Archetypes, Constants, and Universal Paradigms in Prehistoric Art', *Semiotica* 100(2/4), 124–41

Appadurai, Arjun, 1986, 'Introduction: Commodities and the Politics of Value', in Arjun Appadurai (ed.), *The Social Life of Things*, Cambridge University Press

Arnold, Bettina, 1990, 'The Past as Propaganda: Totalitarian Archaeology in Nazi Germany', *Antiquity* 64, 464–78

2001, 'The Limits of Agency in the Analysis of Elite Iron Age Celtic Burials', *Journal of Social Archaeology* 1(2), 210–24

Arnold, D., 1983, 'Design Structure and Community Organisation in Quinua, Peru', in D. Washburn (ed.), *Structure and Cognition in Art*, Cambridge University Press

Asad, Talal, 1986, 'The Concept of Cultural Translation in British Social Anthropology', in J. Clifford and G. Marcus (eds.), *Writing Culture*, Berkeley: University of California Press

Austin, J., 1962, *How to Do Things with Words*, Cambridge, MA: Harvard University Press

Bailey, G. (ed.), 1983, *Hunter-Gatherer Economy in Prehistory: A European Perspective*, Cambridge University Press

Bapty, I., and Yates, T. (eds.), 1990, *Archaeology after Structuralism: Introductory Readings in Post-Structuralism and Archaeology*, London: Routledge

Barrett, J. C., 1981, 'Aspects of the Iron Age in Atlantic Scotland: A Case Study in the Problems of Archaeological Interpretation',

Proceedings of the Society of Antiquaries of Scotland 111, 205–19

1987, 'Contextual Archaeology', *Antiquity* 61, 468–73

1988, 'Food, Gender and Metal: Questions of Social Reproduction', in M. L. Sørensen and R. Thomas (eds.), *The Transition from Bronze Age to Iron Age in Europe*, Oxford: British Archaeological Reports

1994, *Fragments from Antiquity: An Archaeology of Social Life in Britain, 2900–1200 B.C.*, Oxford: Blackwell

2000, 'A Thesis on Agency', in Marcia-Anne Dobres and John Robb (eds.), *Agency in Archaeology*, London: Routledge

and Kinnes, I. (eds.), 1988, *The Archaeology of Context in the Neolithic and Bronze Age: Recent Trends*, University of Sheffield: J. Collis

Barstow, A., 1978, 'The Uses of Archaeology for Women's History: James Mellaart's Work on the Neolithic Goddess at Catal Huyuk', *Feminist Studies* 4, 7–18

Barthes, Roland, 1975, *S/Z*, New York: Hill and Wang

Bayard, Donn, 1969, 'Science, Theory, and Reality in the New Archaeology', *American Antiquity* 34, 376–84

Beaudry, M., Cook, L. J., and Mrozowski, S. A., 1991, 'Artifacts and Active Voices: Material Culture as Social Discourse', in R. H. McGuire and R. Paynter (eds.), *The Archaeology of Inequality*, Oxford: Blackwell

Bekaert, Stefan, 1998, 'Multiple Levels of Meaning and the Tension of Consciousness', *Archaeological Dialogues* 5, 7–29

Bender, B., 1978, 'Gatherer–Hunter to Farmer: A Social Perspective', *World Archaeology* 10, 204–22

1985, 'Emergent Tribal Formations in the American Midcontinent', *American Antiquity* 50, 52–62

1993, 'Stonehenge: Contested Landscapes (Medieval to Present Day)', in B. Bender (ed.), *Landscape: Politics and Perspectives*, Oxford: Berg

Benjamin, W., 1969, *Illuminations*, New York: Schocken

Berard, C., and Durand, J.-L., 1984, 'Entrer en imagerie', in *La Cité des images*, Paris: Fernand Nathan

Bermudez, José Luis, 1995, 'Ecological Perception and the Notion of a Nonconceptual Point of View', in J. L. Bermudez, A. Marcel, and N. Eilan (eds.), *The Body and the Self*, Cambridge, MA: MIT Press

Bernstein, Richard J., 1983, *Beyond Objectivism and Relativism: Science, Hermeneutics, and Praxis*, Philadelphia: University of Pennsylvania Press

Bettinger, R. L., Boyd, R., and Richerson, P. J., 1996, 'Style, Function and Evolutionary Processes', in H. Maschner (ed.), *Darwinian Archaeologies*, New York: Plenum

Binford, L. R., 1962, 'Archaeology as Anthropology', *American Antiquity* 28, 217–25

1965, 'Archaeological Systematics and the Study of Cultural Process', *American Antiquity* 31, 203–10

1967, 'Smudge Pits and Hide Smoking: The Use of Analogy in Archaeological Reasoning', *American Antiquity* 32, 1–12

1971, 'Mortuary Practices: Their Study and Their Potential', in J. Brown (ed.), *Approaches to the Social Dimensions of Mortuary Practices*, Memoirs of the American Archaeology Society 25

(ed) 1977, *For Theory Building in Archaeology*, New York: Academic Press

1978, *Nunamiut Ethnoarchaeology*, New York: Academic Press

1982, 'Meaning, Inference and the Material Record', in A. C. Renfrew and S. Shennan (eds.), *Ranking, Resource and Exchange*, Cambridge University Press

1983, *In Pursuit of the Past*, London: Thames and Hudson

1984, 'An Ayawara Day: Flour, Spinifex Gum, and Shifting Perspectives', *Journal of Anthropological Research* 40, 157–82

and Sabloff, J. A., 1982, 'Paradigms, Systematics and Archaeology', *Journal of Anthropological Research* 38, 137–53

Bintliff, J. L., 1984, 'Structuralism and Myth in Minoan Studies', *Antiquity* 58, 35–8

(ed.), 1991, *The Annales School and Archaeology*, New York: New York University Press

Blakey, Michael L., 1998, 'The New York African Burial Ground Project: An Examination of Enslaved Lives, A Construction of Ancestral Ties', *Transforming Archaeology* 7, 53–8

Blanton, R. E., Feinman, G. M., Kowalewski, S. A., and Peregrine, P. N., 1996, 'A Dual-Processual Theory for the Evolution of Mesoamerican Civilization', *Current Anthropology* 37, 1–14

Bloch, M., 1995, 'Questions Not to Ask of Malagasy Carvings', in I. Hodder, M. Shanks, A. Alexandri, V. Buchli, J. Carman, J. Last, and G. Lucas (eds.), *Interpreting Archaeology: Finding Meaning in the Past*, London: Routledge

Boas, F., 1940, *Race, Language and Culture*, New York: Macmillan Press

Bouissac, P., 1994, 'Prehistoric Signs', a special issue of *Semiotica* 100(2/4)

Bibliography

Bourdieu, P., 1977, *Race, Language and Culture*, New York: Macmillan Press

 1977, *Outline of a Theory of Practice*, Cambridge University Press

 1988, *Homo Academicus*, Stanford: Stanford University Press

 1990 [1987], *In Other Words: Essays towards a Reflexive Sociology*, London: Polity Press

 1991 [1984], *Language and Symbolic Power*, Cambridge, MA: Harvard University Press

Bradley, R., 1984, *The Social Foundations of Prehistoric Britain*, London: Longman

 1990, *The Passage of Arms: An Archaeological Analysis of Prehistoric Hoards and Votive Deposits*, Cambridge University Press

 1993, *Altering the Earth: The Origins of Monuments in Britain and Continental Europe*, Edinburgh: Society of Antiquaries of Scotland

Braithwaite, M., 1982, 'Decoration as Ritual Symbol: A Theoretical Proposal and an Ethnographic Study in Southern Sudan', in I. Hodder (ed.), *Symbolic and Structural Archaeology*, Cambridge University Press

 1984, 'Ritual and Prestige in the Prehistory of Wessex c. 2200–1400 BC: A New Dimension to the Archaeological Evidence', in D. Miller and C. Tilley (eds.), *Ideology, Power and Prehistory*, Cambridge University Press

Braudel, F., 1973, *The Mediterranean and the Mediterranean World in the Age of Philip II*, London: Collins

Braun, D. P., and Plog, S., 1982, 'Evolution of "Tribal" Social Networks: Theory and Prehistoric North American Evidence', *American Antiquity* 47, 504–25

Brown, M., 1996, 'On Resisting Resistance', *American Anthropologist* 98, 729–34

Brück, J., 2001, 'Monuments, Power and Personhood in the British Neolithic', *Journal of the Royal Anthropological Institute* 7, 649–67

Brumfiel, Elizabeth, 1991, 'Weaving and Cooking: Women's Production in Aztec Mexico', in J. M. Gero and M. Conkey (eds.), *Engendering Archaeology: Women in Prehistory*, Oxford: Blackwell

 1996, 'Figurines and the Aztec State: Testing the Effectiveness of Ideological Domination', in R. P. Wright (ed.), *Gender and Archaeology*, Philadelphia: University of Pennsylvania

Buchli, V., 1995, 'Interpreting Material Culture: The Trouble with Text', in I. Hodder, M. Shanks, A. Alexandri, V. Buchli, J. Carman, J. Last, and G. Lucas (eds.), *Interpreting Archaeology: Finding Meaning in the Past*, London: Routledge and Lucas, Gavin, 2001, 'The Absent Present: Archaeologies of the Contemporary Past', in V. Buchli and G. Lucas (eds.), *Archaeologies of the Contemporary Past*, London: Routledge

Burgière, A., 1982, 'The Fate of the History of Mentalités in the Annales', *Comparative Studies in Society and History* 24, 424–37

Butler, J., 1990, *Gender Trouble: Feminism and the Subversion of Identity*, New York: Routledge

1993, *Bodies That Matter*, New York: Routledge

1998, *Excitable Speech*, London: Routledge

Butterworth, George, 1995, 'An Ecological Perspective on the Origins of the Self', in J. L. Bermudez, A. Marcel, and N. Eilan (eds.), *The Body and the Self*, Cambridge, MA: MIT Press

Butzer, K., 1982, *Archaeology as Human Ecology*, Cambridge University Press

Campbell, Ewan, 2000, 'The Raw, the Cooked and the Burnt: Interpretation of Food and Animals in the Hebridean Iron Age', *Archaeological Dialogues* 7, 185–98

Capone, P. H., and Preucel, R. W., 2002, 'Ceramic Semiotics: Women, Pottery and Social Meanings at Kotyiti Pueblo', in R. W. Preucel (ed.), *Archaeologies of the Pueblo Revolt*, Albuquerque: University of New Mexico Press

Carr, C., 1984, 'The Nature of Organisation of Intrasite Archaeological Records and Spatial Analysis Approaches to their Investigation', in M. Schiffer (ed.), *Advances in Archaeological Method and Theory*, vol. 7, New York: Academic Press

Carsten, J., and Hugh-Jones, S., 1995, *About the House: Lévi-Strauss and Beyond*, Cambridge University Press

Case, H., 1973, 'Illusion and Meaning', in A. C. Renfrew (ed.), *The Explanation of Culture Change*, London: Duckworth

Chapman, R. W., 1981, 'The Emergence of Formal Disposal Areas and the "Problem" of the Megalithic Tombs in Prehistoric Europe', in R. Chapman, I. Kinnes and K. Randsborg (eds.), *The Archaeology of Death*, Cambridge University Press

Chesson, Meredith S., 2001, 'Social Memory, Identity, and Death: An Introduction', in Meredith S. Chesson (ed.), *Social Memory, Identity, and Death: Anthropological Perspectives on Mortuary Rituals*, Arlington, VA: American Anthropological Association

Childe, V. G., 1925, *The Dawn of European Civilisation*, London: Kegan Paul

1936, *Man Makes Himself*, London: Collins

1949, *Social Worlds of Knowledge*, Oxford University Press

Bibliography

1951, *Social Evolution*, New York: Schuman

Chippindale, C., 1993, 'Ambition, Deference, Discrepancy, Consumption: The Intellectual Background to a Post-Processual Archaeology', in N. Yoffee and A. Sherratt (eds.), *Archaeological Theory: Who Sets the Agenda?* Cambridge University Press

Claassen, C. (ed.), 1994, *Women in Archaeology*, Philadelphia: University of Pennsylvania

O'Neal, M., Wilson, T., Arnold, E., and Lansdell, B., 1999, 'Hearing and Reading Southeastern Archaeology: A Review of the Annual Meetings of the SEAC from 1983 through 1995 and the Journal *Southeastern Archaeology*', *Southeastern Archaeology* 18(2), 85–97

Clark, J. G. D., 1939, *Archaeology and Society*, London: Methuen

Clarke, D. L., 1968, *Analytical Archaeology*, London: Methuen

1972, 'A Provisional Model of an Iron Age Society and its Settlement System', in D. L. Clarke (ed.), *Models in Archaeology*, London: Methuen

1973, 'Archaeology: The Loss of Innocence', *Antiquity* 47, 6–18

Coe, M. D., 1978, 'Supernatural Patrons of Maya Scribes and Artists', in N. Hammond (ed.), *Social Process in Maya History*, New York: Academic Press

Collet, D. P., 1993, 'Metaphors and Representations Associated with Precolonial Iron-Smelting in Eastern and Southern Africa', in T. Shaw, P. Sinclair, B. Andah, and A. Okpoko (eds.), *The Archaeology of Africa: Foods, Metals and Towns*, London: Routledge

Collingwood, R. G., 1939, *An Autobiography*, Oxford University Press

1946, *The Idea of History*, Oxford University Press

and Myres, J., 1936, *Roman Britain and the English Settlements*, Oxford University Press

Colwell, Rita, 1998, 'Balancing the Biocomplexity of the Planet's Living Systems: A Twenty-First Century Task for Science', *Bioscience* 48(10), 787

Conkey, Margaret, 1984, 'To Find Ourselves: Art and Social Geography of Prehistoric Hunter Gatherers', in Carmel Schrire (ed.), *Past and Present in Hunter Gatherer Studies*, New York: Academic Press

1989, 'The Structural Analysis of Paleolithic Art', in C. C. Lamberg-Karlovsky (ed.), *Archaeological Thought in the Americas*, Cambridge University Press

1997, 'Beyond Art and Between the Caves: Thinking about Context in the Interpretive Process', in M. Conkey, O. Soffer, D. Stratmann, and N. G. Jablonski (eds.), *Beyond Art: Pleistocene*

Image and Symbol, San Francisco: California Academy of Arts and Sciences

2001, 'Structural and Semiotic Approaches', in David S. Whitley (ed.), *Handbook of Rock Art Research*, Walnut Creek, CA: Altamira

and Gero, J., 1997, 'From Program to Practice: Gender and Feminism in Archaeology', *Annual Review of Anthropology* 26, 411–37

and Spector, J., 1984, 'Archaeology and the Study of Gender', in M. Schiffer (ed.), *Advances in Archaeological Method and Theory*, vol. 7, New York: Academic Press

with Williams, S., 1991, 'Original Narratives: The Political Economy of Gender in Archaeology', in M. di Leonardo (ed.), *Gender at the Crossroads of Knowledge: Feminist Anthropology in the Postmodern Era*, Berkeley: University of California Press

Conrad, G. W., and Demarest, A. A., 1984, *Religion and Empire*, Cambridge University Press

Cowgill, G., 1993, 'Distinguished Lecture in Archaeology: Beyond Criticizing New Archaeology', *American Anthropologist* 95, 551–73

Cresswell, R., 1972, 'Les Trois Sources d'une technologie nouvelle', in J. M. C. Thomas and L. Bernot (eds.), *Langues et techniques, nature et société*, Paris: Klinksieck

Csordas, T. J., 1990, 'Embodiment as a Paradigm for Anthropology', *Ethos* 18, 5–47

1995, 'Introduction: The Body as Representation and Being-in-the-World', in T. J. Csordas (ed.), *Embodiment and Experience: The Existential Ground of Culture and the Self*, Cambridge University Press

Daniel, G. E., 1962, *The Idea of Prehistory*, Harmondsworth: Penguin

Darnton, Robert, 1984, *The Great Cat Massacre and Other Episodes in French Cultural History*, New York: Vintage

Davis, D. D., 1984, 'Investigating the Diffusion of Stylistic Innovations', in M. Schiffer (ed.), *Advances in Archaeological Method and Theory*, vol. 6, New York: Academic Press

Davis, W., 1982, 'Canonical Representation in Egyptian Art', *Res* 4, 21–46

1984, 'Representation and Knowledge in the Prehistoric Rock Art of Africa', *African Archaeological Review* 2, 7–35

de Certeau, M., 1984, *The Practice of Everyday Life*, Berkeley: University of California Press

Bibliography

Deetz, James, 1967, *Invitation to Archaeology*, New York: Natural History Press

1977, *In Small Things Forgotten*, New York: Anchor Books

1983, 'Scientific Humanism and Humanistic Science: A Plea for Paradigmatic Pluralism in Historical Archaeology', *Geoscience and Man* 23, 27–34

1988a, 'History and Archaeological Theory: Walter Taylor Revisited', *American Antiquity* 53, 13–22

1988b, 'Material Culture and Worldview in Colonial Anglo-America', in M. Leone and P. B. Potter (eds.), *The Recovery of Meaning*, Washington: Smithsonian

Demarrais, Elizabeth, Castillo, Jaime Luis, and Earle, Timothy, 1996, 'Ideology, Materialization and Power Strategies', *Current Anthropology* 37, 15–31

Derrida, J., 1976, *Of Grammatology*, Baltimore: Johns Hopkins University Press

Digard, J.-P., 1979, 'La technologie en anthropologie: fin de parcours ou nouveau siffle?', *L'Homme* 19, 73–104

Dobres, Marcia-Anne, and Robb, John (eds.), 2000a, *Agency in Archaeology*, London: Routledge

2000b, 'Agency in Archaeology: Paradigm or Platitude?', in Marcia-Anne Dobres and John Robb (eds.), *Agency in Archaeology*, London: Routledge

Donley, L., 1982, 'House Power: Swahili Space and Symbolic Markers', in I. Hodder (ed.), *Symbolic and Structural Archaeology*, Cambridge University Press

1990, 'A Structuring Structure: The Swahili House', in S. Kent (ed.), *Domestic Architecture and the Use of Space*, Cambridge University Press

Doran, J., and Hodson, F. R., 1975, *Mathematics and Computers in Archaeology*, Edinburgh: Edinburgh University Press

Douglas, M., 1969, *Purity and Danger*, London: Routledge and Kegan Paul

1970, *Natural Symbols*, New York: Vintage

Dowdall, K., and Parrish, O., 2003, 'A Collaborative Approach to Archaeology on the Sonoma Coast, California', unpublished paper

Draper, P., 1975, '!Kung Women: Contrasts in Sexual Egalitarianism in Foraging and Sedentary Contexts', in R. R. Reiter (ed.), *Toward an Anthropology of Women*, New York: Monthly Review Press

Drennan, R., 1976, 'Religion and Social Evolution in Formative Mesoamerica', in K. Flannery (ed.), *The Early Mesoamerican Village*, New York: Academic Press

Dreyfus, Hubert L., 1991, *Being-in-the-World: A Commentary on Heidegger's Being and Time, Division I*, Cambridge, MA: MIT Press

Drummond, L., 1983, 'Jonestown: A Study in Ethnographic Discourse', *Semiotica* 46, 167–209

Duby, G., 1980, *The Three Orders*, Chicago: University of Chicago Press

Duke, Philip, 1992, 'Braudel and North American Archaeology: An Example from the Northern Plains', in A. B. Knapp (ed.), *Archaeology, Annales and Ethnohistory*, Cambridge University Press

Dumezil, G., 1977, *Les Dieux-Souverains des Indo-Européens*, Paris: Gallimard

Dunnell, Robert, 1986, 'Methodological Issues in Americanist Artifact Classification', in M. B. Schiffer (ed.), *Advances in Archaeological Method and Theory 9*, New York: Academic Press

Eagleton, T., 1983, *Literary Theory*, Oxford: Blackwell

Earle, T. K., 1990, 'Style and Iconography as Legitimisation in Complex Chiefdoms', in M. W. Conkey and C. A. Hastorf (eds.), *The Uses of Style in Archaeology*, Cambridge University Press

and Ericson, J. (eds.), 1977, *Exchange Systems in Prehistory*, New York: Academic Press

and Preucel, R. M., 1987, 'Processual Archaeology and the Radical Critique', *Current Anthropology* 28, 501–38

Edmonds, M., 1999, *Ancestral Geographies of the Neolithic: Landscapes, Monuments and Memories*, London: Routledge

Elias, N., 1994 [1936], *The Civilizing Process: The History of Manners*, Oxford: Blackwell

Elliott, Anthony, 1994, *Psychoanalytic Theory*, Oxford: Blackwell

Engelstad, Ericka, 1991, 'Images of Power and Contradiction: Feminist Theory and Post-Processual Archaeology', *Antiquity* 65, 502–14

Ericson, J., and Earle, T. (eds.), 1982, *Contexts for Prehistoric Exchange*, New York: Academic Press

Faris, J., 1972, *Nuba Personal Art*, London: Duckworth

1983, 'From Form to Content in the Structural Study of Aesthetic Systems', in D. Washburn (ed.), *Structure and Cognition in Art*, Cambridge University Press

Fausto-Sterling, Anne, 1985, *Myths of Gender: Biological Theories about Women and Men*, New York: Basic Books

Bibliography

1989, 'Life in the XY Corral', *Women's Studies International Forum* 12(3), *Special Issue on Feminism and Science: In Memory of Ruth Bleier*, ed. Sue Rosser

Ferguson, L., 1991, 'Struggling with Pots in South Carolina', in R. H. McGuire and R. Paynter (eds.), *The Archaeology of Inequality*, Blackwell: Oxford

Fink, Bruce, 1995, *The Lacanian Subject: Between Language and Jouissance*, Princeton: Princeton University Press

Flannery, K. V., 1967, 'Culture History v. Culture Process: a Debate in American Archaeology', *Scientific American* 217, 119–22

1973, 'Archaeology with a Capital S', in C. Redman (ed.), *Research and Theory in Current Archaeology*, New York: Wiley

1982, 'The Golden Marshalltown: A Parable for the Archaeology of the 1980's', *American Anthropologist* 84, 265–78

and Marcus, J., 1976, 'Formative Oaxaca and the Zapotec Cosmos', *American Scientist* 64, 374–83

1983, *The Cloud People*, New York: Academic Press

Fletcher, R., 1977, 'Settlement Studies (Micro and Semi-Micro)', in D. L. Clarke (ed.), *Spatial Archaeology*, New York: Academic Press

1992, 'Time Perspectivism, Annales, and the Potential of Archaeology', in A. B. Knapp (ed.), *Archeology, Annales and Ethnohistory*, Cambridge University Press

Fotiadis, Michael, 1994, 'What is Archaeology's "Mitigated Objectivism" Mitigated By? Comments on Wylie', *American Antiquity* 59, 545–55

Foucault, Michel, 1970 [1966], *The Order of Things*, New York: Vintage Books

1972, *The Archaeology of Knowledge*, New York: Pantheon

1977, *Discipline and Punish*, New York: Vintage Books

1979, 'What is an Author?', in J. Harari (ed.), *Textual Strategies: Perspectives in Post-Structuralist Criticism*, Ithaca: Cornell University Press

1981a, *The History of Sexuality, Volume 1: An Introduction*, London: Penguin

1981b [1970], 'The Order of Discourse', in R. Young (ed.), *Untying the Text*, Boston: Routledge and Kegan Paul

1986, *The Use of Pleasure*, New York: Vintage

Frankenstein, S., and Rowlands, M., 1978, 'The Internal Structure and Regional Context of Early Iron Age Society in South-Western Germany', *Bulletin of the Institute of Archaeology* 15, 73–112

Franklin, Maria, 1997, 'Why Are There So Few Black American Archaeologists?', *Antiquity* 71, 799–801

Friedman, J., 1974, 'Marxism, Structuralism and Vulgar Materialism', *Man* 9, 444–69

1975, 'Tribes, States and Transformations', in M. Bloch (ed.), *Marxist Analyses in Social Anthropology*, London: Association of Social Anthropologists

and Rowlands, M. (eds.), 1978, *The Evolution of Social Systems*, London: Duckworth

Fritz, J., 1978, 'Paleopsychology Today: Ideational Systems and Human Adaptation in Prehistory', in C. Redman *et al.* (eds.), *Social Archaeology: Beyond Dating and Subsistence*, New York: Academic Press

Gadamer, H.-G., 1975, *Truth and Method*, New York: Seabury Press
1981, *Reason in the Age of Science*, Cambridge, MA: MIT Press

Gailey, C. W., 1987, *Kinship to Kingship*, Austin: University of Texas Press

Gazzaniga, Michael S., 1998, *The Mind's Past*, Berkeley: University of California Press

Geertz, Clifford, 1973, *The Interpretation of Cultures*, New York: Basic Books

Gell, Alfred, 1998, *Art and Agency*, Oxford: Clarendon

Gellner, Ernest, 1970, 'Concepts and Society', in B. R. Wilson (ed.), *Rationality*, Oxford: Basil Blackwell

1982, 'What is Structuralism?', in C. Renfrew, M. Rowlands and B. Seegraves (eds.), *Theory and Explanation in Archaeology*, London: Academic Press

Gero, J., 1985, 'Socio-Politics and the Woman-at-Home Ideology', *American Antiquity* 50, 342–50

2000, 'Troubled Travels in Agency and Feminism', in Marcia-Anne Dobres and John Robb (eds.), *Agency in Archaeology*, London: Routledge

and Conkey, M. (eds.), 1990, *Engendering Archaeology: Women and Prehistory*, Oxford: Blackwell

Lacy, David M., and Blakey, Michael L. (eds.), 1983, *The Socio-Politics of Archaeology*, Research Reports 23, Amherst: Department of Anthropology, University of Massachusetts

Gibbon, G., 1989, *Explanation in Archaeology*, Oxford: Blackwell

Gibbs, L., 1987, 'Identifying Gender Representation in the Archaeological Record: A Contextual Study', in I. Hodder (ed.),

Bibliography

The Archaeology of Contextual Meaning, Cambridge University Press

Gibson, James J., 1966, *The Senses Considered as Perceptual Systems*, Boston: Houghton Mifflin

Giddens, A., 1976, 'Introduction', in M. Weber, *The Protestant Ethic and the Spirit of Capitalism*, London: George Allen and Unwin

1979, *Central Problems in Social Theory*, London: Macmillan

1981, *A Contemporary Critique of Historical Materialism*, London: Macmillan

Gilchrist, R., 1993, *Gender and Material Culture: The Archaeology of Religious Women*, London: Routledge

Gilman, A., 1984, 'Explaining the Upper Palaeolithic Revolution', in M. Spriggs (ed.), *Marxist Perspectives in Archaeology*, Cambridge University Press

Glassie, J., 1975, *Folk Housing of Middle Virginia*, Knoxville: University of Tennessee Press

Gledhill, J., 1989, 'Formative Development in the North American South West', *British Archaeological Report* 47, 241–84

Gosden, C., 1994, *Social Being and Time*, Oxford: Blackwell

Gottdeiner, M., 1993, *Postmodern Semiotics*, Oxford: Blackwell

Gould, R., 1980, *Living Archaeology*, Cambridge University Press

Graves, M., and Ladefoged, T. N., 1995, 'The Evolutionary Significance of Ceremonial Architecture in Polynesia', in P. A. Teltser (ed.), *Evolutionary Archaeology: Methodological Issues*, Tucson: University of Arizona Press

Greene, G., 1987, 'Gothic Material Culture', in I. Hodder (ed.), *Archaeology as Long-Term History*, Cambridge University Press

Gregory, T., 1983, 'The Impact of Metal Detecting on Archaeology and the Public', *Archaeological Review from Cambridge* 2, 5–8

Hall, R. L., 1976, 'Ghosts, Water Barriers, Corn, and Sacred Enclosures in the Eastern Woodlands', *American Antiquity* 41, 360–4

1977, 'An Anthropocentric Perspective for Eastern United States Prehistory', *American Antiquity* 42, 499–517

1983, 'A Pan-continental Perspective on Red Ochre and Glacial Kame Ceremonialism', in R. C. Dunnell and D. K. Grayson (eds.), *Lulu Linear Punctuated: Essays in Honour of George Irving Quimby*, University of Michigan Anthropological Papers, 72

Hamann, Byron, 2002, 'The Social Life of Pre-Sunrise Things: Indigenous Mesoamerican Archaeology', *Current Anthropology* 43, 351–82

Hamilakis, Y., Pluciennik, M., and Tarlow, S. (eds.), 2002, *Thinking through the Body: Archaeologies of Corporeality*, New York: Plenum

Handsman, R., 1980, 'Studying Myth and History in Modern America: Perspectives for the Past from the Continent', *Reviews in Anthropology* 7, 255–68

    1981, 'Early Capitalism and the Centre Village of Canaan, Connecticut, a Study of Transformations and Separations', *Artifacts* 9, 1–21

    and Leone, Mark, 1989, 'Living History and Critical Archaeology in the Reconstruction of the Past', in Valerie Pinsky and Alison Wylie (eds.), *Critical Traditions in Contemporary Archaeology*, Cambridge University Press

Haraway, D., 1991, *Simians, Cyborgs and Women*, New York: Routledge

Hardin, M., 1970, 'Design Structure and Social Interaction: Archaeological Implications of an Ethnographic Analysis', *American Antiquity* 35, 332–43

Harding, S., 1986, *The Science Question in Feminism*, Ithaca, NY: Cornell University Press

Harris, M., 1979, *Cultural Materialism: The Struggle for a Science of Culture*, New York: Random House

Hastorf, G., 1990, 'Gender, Space and Food in Prehistory', in J. Gero and M. Conkey (eds.), *Engendering Archaeology: Women and Prehistory*, Oxford: Blackwell

Haudricourt, A. G., 1962, 'Domestication des animaux, culture des plantes et traitement d'autrui', *L'Homme* 2, 40–50

Hawkes, C., 1942, 'Race, Prehistory and European Civilisation', *Man* 73, 125–30

    1954, 'Archaeological Theory and Method: Some Suggestions from the Old World', *American Anthropologist* 56, 155–68

    1972, 'Europe and England: Fact and Fox', *Helinium* 12, 105–16

    1976, 'Celts and Cultures: Wealth, Power, Art', in C. Hawkes and P.-M. Duval, *Celtic Art in Ancient Europe*, London: Seminar Press

Hawkes, J., 1968, 'The Proper Study of Mankind', *Antiquity* 42, 255–62

Hebdige, Dick, 1979, *Subculture: The Meaning of Style*, London: Methuen

Heidegger, M., 1971, *Poetry, Language and Thought*, trans. A. Hofstadter, New York: Harper and Row

    1996, *Being and Time*, trans. J. Stambaugh, Albany: SUNY Press

Held, D., 1980, Introduction to *Critical Theory*, London: Hutchinson

Bibliography

Helskog, K., 1995, 'Maleness and Femaleness in the Sky and the Underworld – and in between', in K. Helskog and B. Olsen (eds.), *Perceiving Rock Art: Social and Political Perspectives*, Oslo: The Institute for Comparative Research in Human Culture

Herzfeld, Michael, 1992, 'Metapatterns: Archaeology and the Uses of Evidence Scarcity', in Jean-Claude Gardin and Christopher Peebles (eds.), *Representations in Archaeology*, Bloomington: Indiana University Press

Higgs, E. S., and Jarman, M., 1969, 'The Origins of Agriculture: A Reconsideration', *Antiquity* 43, 31–41

Hill, J. D., 1995, *Ritual and Rubbish in the Iron Age of Wessex*, Oxford: BAR British Series

Hillier, B., Leaman, A., Stansall, P., and Bedford, M., 1976, 'Space Syntax', *Environment and Planning* Series B3, 147–85

Hingley, Richard, 1990, 'Domestic Organization and Gender Relations in Iron Age and Romano-British Households', in Ross Samson (ed.), *The Social Archaeology of the House*, Edinburgh University Press

    1997, 'Iron, Ironworking, and Regeneration: A Study of the Symbolic Meaning of Metalworking in Iron Age Britain', in A. Gwilt and Colin Haselgrove (eds.), *Reconstructing Iron Age Societies: New Approaches to the British Iron Age*, Oxford: Oxbow

Hobsbawn, E., and Ranger, T. (eds.), 1984, *The Invention of Tradition*, Cambridge University Press

Hodder, I., 1979, 'Social and Economic Stress and Material Culture Patterning', *American Antiquity* 44, 446–54

    1981, 'Towards a Mature Archaeology', in I. Hodder, G. Isaac and N. Hammond (eds.), *Pattern of the Past*, Cambridge University Press

    1982a, *Symbols in Action*, Cambridge University Press

    1982b, 'Sequences of Structural Change in the Dutch Neolithic', in I. Hodder (ed.), *Symbolic and Structural Archaeology*, Cambridge University Press

    1982c, 'Theoretical Archaeology: A Reactionary View', in I. Hodder (ed.), *Symbolic and Structural Archaeology*, Cambridge University Press

    1982d, *The Present Past*, London: Batsford

    1984a, 'Burials, Houses, Women and Men in the European Neolithic', in D. Miller and C. Tilley (eds.), *Ideology, Power and Prehistory*, Cambridge University Press

    1984b, 'Archaeology in 1984', *Antiquity* 58, 25–32

1985, 'New Generations of Spatial Analysis in Archaeology', in F. Burillo (ed.), *Arqueologia Espacial*, Tervel: Colegio Universitario

1986, *Reading the Past*, 1st edn, Cambridge University Press

(ed.), 1987a, *The Archaeology of Contextual Meanings*, Cambridge University Press

(ed.), 1987b, *Archaeology as Long-Term History*, Cambridge University Press

1989a, 'This is not an Article about Material Culture as Text', *Journal of Anthropological Archaeology* 8, 250–69

1989b, 'Writing Archaeology: Site Reports in Context', *Antiquity* 63, 268–74

1990a, *The Domestication of Europe*, Oxford: Blackwell

1990b, 'Post-Processual Archaeology: The Current Debate', in R. Preucel (ed.), *Processual and Postprocessual Archaeologies: Multiple Ways & Knowing the Past*, Carbondale: Southern Illinois University Press

1990c, 'Gender Representation and Social Reality', Proceedings of the 1989 Chacmool Conference, University of Calgary

1991, 'The Decoration of Containers; an Ethnographic Study', *American Antiquity* 56, 7–18

1992, 'Towards Radical Doubt: A Dialogue', in Ian Hodder (ed.), *Theory and Practice in Archaeology*, London: Routledge

1999a, *The Archaeological Process*, Oxford: Blackwell

1999b, 'British Prehistory: Some Thoughts Looking in', *Cambridge Archaeological Journal* 9, 376–80

2000, 'Agency and Individuals in Long-Term Process', in Marcia-Anne Dobres and John Robb (eds.), *Agency in Archaeology*, London: Routledge

and Evans, C., 1984, 'Report on the Excavations at Haddenham, Cambs.', *Cambridgeshire Archaeological Committee Annual Report* 3, 11–14

and Lane, P., 1982, 'A Contextual Examination of Neolithic Axe Distribution in Britain', in J. Ericson and T. Earle (eds.), *Contexts for Prehistoric Exchange*, New York: Academic Press

and Okell, E., 1978, 'An Index for Assessing the Association between Distributions of Points in Archaeology', in I. Hodder (ed.), *Simulation Studies in Archaeology*, Cambridge University Press

and Orton, C., 1976, *Spatial Analysis in Archaeology*, Cambridge University Press

Bibliography

Parker Pearson, M., Peck, N., and Stone, P., 1985, *Archaeology, Knowledge and Society: Surveys in Britain* (typescript)

Horkheimer, M., and Adorno, T., 1973, *Dialectics of the Enlightenment*, London: Allen Lane

Huffman, T. N., 1981, 'Snakes and Birds: Expressive Space at Great Zimbabwe', *African Studies* 40, 131–50

1984, 'Expressive Space in the Zimbabwe Culture', *Man* 19, 593–612

Hutson, Scott, 1998, 'Strategies for the Reproduction of Prestige in Archaeological Discourse', *Assemblage* 4: http://www.shef.ac.uk/~assem/4/

2001, 'Synergy through Disunity, Science as Social Practice: Comments on Vanpool and Vanpool, *American Antiquity* 66, 349–60

2002a, 'Built Space and Bad Subjects: Domination and Resistance at Monte Albán, Oaxaca, Mexico', *Journal of Social Archaeology* 2(1), 53–80

2002b, 'Gendered Citation Practices in *American Antiquity* and Other Archeology Journals', *American Antiquity* 67, 331–42

and Markens, Robert, in press 'Rethinking Emic Pottery Classification', *Kroeber Anthropological Society Papers* 89, Department of Anthropology, University of California, Berkeley

Iannone, Giles, 2002, 'Annales History and the Ancient Maya State: Some Observations on the "Dynamic Model"', *American Anthropologist* 104, 68–78

Ingold, T., 1986, *The Appropriation of Nature*, Manchester: Manchester University Press

1995, 'Building, Dwelling, Living: How Animals and People Make Themselves at Home in the World', in M. Strathern (ed.), *Shifting Contexts: Transformations in Anthropological Knowledge*, London: Routledge

2000, *The Perception of the Environment: Essays on Livelihood, Dwelling and Skill*, London: Routledge

Isbell, W. H., 1976, 'Cosmological Order Expressed in Prehistoric Ceremonial Centres', *Andean Symbolism Symposium*, Paris: International Congress of Americanists

Jameson, Fredric, 1984, 'Postmodernism, or the Cultural Logic of Late Capitalism', *New Left Review* 196, 53–92

Jochim, T., 1983, 'Palaeolithic Cave Art in Ecological Perspective', in G. Bailey (ed.), *Hunter-Gatherer Economy in Prehistory*, Cambridge University Press

Johnson, G., 1982, 'Organisational Structure and Scalar Stress', in A. Renfrew, M. Rowlands and B. Seagrave (eds.), *Theory and Explanation in Archaeology*, New York: Academic Press

Johnson, M. H., 1989, 'Conceptions of Agency in Archaeological Interpretation', *Journal of Anthropological Archaeology* 8, 189–211

Joyce, A. A., Bustamante, Laura A., and Levine, Marc N., 2001, 'Commoner Power: A Case Study from the Classic Period Collapse on the Oaxaca Coast', *Journal of Archaeological Method and Theory* 8(4), 343–85

Joyce, R. A., 1993, 'Women's Work: Images of Production and Reproduction in Prehispanic Southern Central America', *Current Anthropology* 34(3), 255–74

1994, 'Dorothy Hughes Popenoe: Eve in an Archaeological Garden', in C. Claassen (ed.), *Women in Archaeology*, Philadelphia: University of Pennsylvania Press

1998, 'Performing the Body in Prehispanic Central America', *Res* 33, 147–65

1999, 'Girling the Girl and Boying the Boy', *World Archaeology* 31, 473–83

2000, *Gender and Power in Ancient Mesoamerica*, Austin: University of Texas Press

2001, 'Burying the Dead at Tlatilco: Social Memory and Social Identities', in Meredith S. Chesson (ed.), *Social Memory, Identity, and Death: Anthropological Perspectives on Mortuary Rituals*, Arlington, VA: American Anthropological Association

2002, *The Languages of Archaeology*, Oxford: Blackwell

and Gillespie, S. D. (eds.), 2000, *Beyond Kinship: Social and Material Reproduction in House Societies*, Philadelphia: University of Pennsylvania Press

Kearney, Michael, 1996, *Reconceptualizing the Peasantry*, Boulder: Westview

Kehoe, A. B., 1979, 'The Sacred Heart: A Case for Stimulus Diffusion', *American Ethnologist* 6, 763–71

1998, *The Land of Prehistory*, New York: Routledge

and Kehoe, T. F., 1973, 'Cognitive Models for Archaeological Interpretation', *American Antiquity* 38, 150–4

1977, 'Stones, Solstices and Sun Dance Structures', *Plains Anthropologist* 22, 85–95

Keller, Evelyn Fox, 1985, *Reflections on Gender and Science*, New Haven: Yale University Press.

Bibliography

Kent, S., 1984, *Analysing Activity Areas*, Albuquerque: University of New Mexico Press

Kintigh, K., and Ammerman, A. J., 1982, 'Heuristic Approaches to Spatial Analysis in Archaeology', *American Antiquity* 47, 31–63

Kirch, P. V., 1992, *Anahulu, vol. 2: The Archaeology of History*, Chicago: University of Chicago Press

Knapp, A. Bernard (ed.), 1992a, *Archaeology, Annales and Ethnohistory*, Cambridge University Press

1992b, 'Archaeology and Annales: Time, Space and Change', in A. B. Knapp (ed.), *Archaeology, Annales and Ethnohistory*, Cambridge University Press

Kohl, P. L., 1981, 'Materialist Approaches in Prehistory', *Annual Review of Anthropology* 10, 89–118

Kohn, Marek, and Mithen, Steven, 1999, 'Handaxes: Products of Sexual Selection', *Antiquity* 73, 518–26

Kramer, C. (ed.), 1979, *Ethnoarchaeology*, New York: Columbia University Press

Kristiansen, K., 1981, 'A Social History of Danish Archaeology (1805–1975)', in G. Daniel (ed.), *Towards a History of Archaeology*, London: Duckworth

1984, 'Ideology and Material Culture: An Archaeological Perspective', in M. Spriggs (ed.), *Marxist Perspectives in Archaeology*, Cambridge University Press

1989, 'Value, Ranking and Consumption in the European Bronze Age', in D. Miller, M. Rowlands and C. Tilley (eds.), *Domination and Resistance*, London: Unwin Hyman

and Rowlands, M., 1998, *Social Transformations in Archaeology*, London and New York: Routledge

Kroeber, A. L., 1963, *Anthropology: Culture, Patterns and Processes*, New York: Harcourt Brace Jovanowich

Kus, Susan, 1992, 'Toward an Archaeology of Body and Soul', in Chris Peebles and Jean Claude Gardin (eds.), *Representations in Archaeology*, Bloomington: University of Indiana Press

Kushner, Gilbert, 1970, 'A Consideration of Some Processual Designs for Archaeology as Anthropology', *American Antiquity* 2, 125–32

La Roche, Cheryl J., and Blakey, Micheal L., 1997, 'Seizing Intellectual Power: The Dialogue at the New York African Burial Ground', *Historical Archaeology* 31, 84–106

Ladurie, E., 1980, *Montaillou*, London: Penguin

Lakoff, George, and Johnson, Mark, 1999, *Philosophy in the Flesh: The Embodied Mind and Its Challenge to Western Thought*, New York: Basic Books

Lampeter Archaeology Workshop, 1997, 'Relativism, Objectivity and the Politics of the Past', *Archaeological Dialogues* 4, 166–75

1998, 'Relativism, Politics, and Debate', *Archaeological Dialogues* 5, 43–53.

Langford, R. F., 1983, Our Heritage – Your Playground, *Australian Archaeology* 16, 1–6

Laqueur, T., 1990, *Making Sex: Body and Gender from the Greeks to Freud*, Cambridge, MA: Harvard University Press

Last, Jonathan, 1995, 'The Nature of History', in I. Hodder, M. Shanks, A. Alexandri, V. Buchli, J. Carman, J. Last, and G. Lucas (eds.), *Interpreting Archaeology*, London: Routledge

Lathrap, D. W., 1977, 'Our Father the Layman, our Mother the Gourd: Spinden Revisited, or a Unitary Model for the Emergence of Agriculture in the New World', in C. Reed (ed.), *Origins of Agriculture*, The Hague: Mouton

Latour, Bruno, 1996, *Aramis, or, the Love of Technology*. Cambridge, MA: Harvard University Press

1999, *Pandora's Hope: Essays on the Reality of Science Studies*, Cambridge, MA: Harvard University Press

Layton, R. (ed.), 1989a, *Conflict in the Archaeology of Living Traditions*, London: Unwin Hyman

(ed.), 1989b, *Who Needs the Past? Indigenous Values and Archaeology*, London: Unwin Hyman

Leach, E., 1954, *Political Systems of Highland Burma: A Study of Kachin Social Structure*, London: Bell

1973, 'Concluding Address', in A. C. Renfrew (ed.), *The Explanation of Culture Change*, London: Duckworth

Lechtmann, H., 1984, 'Andean Value Systems and the Development of Prehistoric Metallurgy', *Technology and Culture* 25, 1–36

Leenhardt, M., 1979 [1947], *Do Kamo*, Chicago: University of Chicago Press

Le Goff, J., 1985, *The Medieval Imagination*, Chicago: University of Chicago Press

Lemonnier, P., 1976, 'La Description des chaines opératoires: contribution à l'étude des systèmes techniques', *Techniques et Culture* 1, 100–5

1983, 'L'Etude des systèmes techniques, une urgence en technologie culturelle', *Techniques et Culture* 1, 11–26

1984, 'L'Ecorce battue chez Les Anga de Nouvelle-Guinée, *Techniques et Culture* 4, 127–75

Lenssen-Erz, T., 1994, 'The Rock Art Paintings of the Brandberg, Namibia, and a Concept of Textualization for Purposes of Data Processing', *Semiotica* 100(2/4), 169–200

Leone, M., 1978, 'Time in American Archaeology', in C. Redman *et al*. (eds.), *Social Archaeology: Beyond Subsistence and Dating*, New York: Academic Press

1982, 'Some Opinions about Recovering Mind', *American Antiquity* 47, 742–60

1983, 'The Role of Archaeology in Verifying American Identity', *Archaeological Review from Cambridge* 2, 44–50

1984, 'Interpreting Ideology in Historical Archaeology: The William Paca Garden in Annapolis, Maryland', in D. Miller and C. Tilley (eds.), *Ideology, Power and Prehistory*, Cambridge University Press

1988, 'The Georgian Order as the Order of Merchant Capitalism in Annapolis', in M. Leone and P. B. Potter (eds.), *The Recovery of Meaning*, Washington: Smithsonian Institution Press

Mullins, Paul R., Creveling, Marian C., Hurst, Laurence, Jackson-Nash, Barbara, Jones, Lynn, Jopling Kaiser, Hannah, Logan, George C., and Warner, Mark S., 1995, 'Can an African-American Historical Archaeology be an Alternative Voice?', in I. Hodder, M. Shanks, A. Alexandri, V. Buchli, J. Carman, J. Last, and G. Lucas (eds.), *Interpreting Archaeology*, London: Routledge

and Potter, Parker B., 1988, *The Recovery of Meaning: Historical Archaeology in the Eastern United States*, Washington, Smithsonian Institution Press

Potter, P. B., and Shackel, P., 1987, 'Toward a Critical Archaeology', *Current Anthropology* 28, 251–82

Leroi-Gourhan, A., 1943, *L'Homme la mattère*, Paris: Albin Michel

1945, *Milieu et techniques*, Paris: Albin Michel

1965, *Préhistoire de l'art occidental*, Paris: Mazenod

1982, *The Dawn of European Art*, Cambridge University Press

Lévi-Strauss, C., 1963, *Structural Anthropology*, New York: Basic Books

1987, *The Way of the Masks*, trans. S. Modelski, Seattle: University of Washington Press

Levin, Michael E., 1973, 'On Explanation in Archaeology: A Rebuttal to Fritz and Plog', *American Antiquity* 38, 387–95

Little, Barbara, 1997, 'Expressing Ideology without a Voice, or Obfuscation and the Enlightenment', *International Journal of Historical Archaeology* 1, 225–41

Longacre, W., 1970, *Archaeology as Anthropology*, Tucson: Anthropological Papers of the University of Arizona, 17

McCafferty, S. D., and McCafferty, G. A., 1988, 'Powerful Women and the Myth of Male Dominance in Aztec Society', *Archaeological Review from Cambridge* 7(1), 45–59

1991, 'Spinning and Weaving as Female Gender Identity in Postclassic Mexico', in M. B. Schevill, J. C. Berlo and E. B. Dwyer (eds.), *Textile Traditions of Mesoamerica and the Andes: An Anthology*, New York: Garland

1994, 'Engendering Tomb 7 at Monte Albán: Respinning an Old Yarn', *Current Anthropology* 35, 143–66

McDavid, C., and Babson, D. (eds.), 1997, *In the Realm of Politics: Prospects for Public Participation in African-American and Plantation Archaeology*, *Historical Archaeology* 31(3)

McGhee, R., 1977, 'Ivory for the Sea Woman: The Symbolic Attributes of a Prehistoric Technology', *Canadian Journal of Archaeology* 1, 141–59

McGuire, R. H., 1988, 'Dialogues with the Dead: Ideology and the Cemetery', in M. Leone and P. B. Potter (eds.), *The Recovery of Meaning*, Washington: Smithsonian Institution Press

1992, *A Marxist Archaeology*, New York: Academic Press

and Howard, A. V., 1987, 'The Structure and Organization of Hohokam Shell Exchange', *The Kiva* 52, 113–46

and Paynter, R. (eds.), 1991, *The Archaeology of Inequality*, Oxford: Blackwell

McKellar, Judith, 1983, 'Correlates and the Explanation of Distributions', *Atlatl, Occasional Papers 4*, Tucson: Anthropology Club, University of Arizona

Maquet, Jacques, 1995, 'Objects as Instruments, Objects as Signs', in Stevan Lubar and W. David Kingery (eds.), *History from Things: Essays on Material Culture*, Washington: Smithsonian Institution Press

Marx, K., 1971, *A Contribution to the Critique of Political Economy*, London: Lawrence and Wishart

1977 [1852], 'The Eighteenth Brumaire of Louis Bonaparte', in D. McLellan (ed.), *Karl Marx, Selected Writings*, Oxford University Press and Engels, F., 1970, *German Ideology*, London: Lawrence and Wishart

Mauss, M., 1973 [1935], 'Techniques of the Body', *Economy and Society* 2, 70–88

Meltzer, D., 1979, 'Paradigms and the Nature of Change in Archaeology', *American Antiquity* 44, 644–57

— 1981, 'Ideology and Material Culture', in R. Gould and M. Schiffer (eds.), *Modern Material Culture, the Archaeology of Us*, New York: Acdemic Press

— 1983, 'The Antiquity of Man and the Development of American Archaeology', *Advances in Archaeological Method and Theory* 6, 1–51

Fowler, D. D., and Sabloff, J. A. (eds.), 1986, *American Archaeology Past and Future*, Washington: Smithsonian Institution Press

Merleau-Ponty, M., 1962, *Phenomenology of Perception*, trans. C. Smith, London: Routledge and Kegan Paul

Merriman, N., 1987, 'An Investigation into the Archaeological Evidence for "Celtic Spirit"', in I. Hodder (ed.), *Archaeology as Long Term History*, Cambridge University Press

— 1989a, 'Museum Visiting as a Cultural Phenomenon', in P. Vergo (ed.), *The New Museology*, London: Reaktion Books

— 1989b, 'The Social Role of Museum and Heritage Visiting', in S. Pearce (ed.), *Museum Studies in Material Culture*, Leicester University Press

— 1991, Beyond the Glass Case, Leicester University Press

Meskell, L., 1995, 'Goddesses, Gimbutas and "New Age" Archaeology', *Antiquity* 69, 74–86

— 1996, 'The Somatization of Archaeology: Institutions, Discourses, Corporeality', *Norwegian Archaeological Review* 29, 1–16

— 1998a, 'Intimate Archaeologies: The Case of Kha and Merit', *World Archaeology* 29, 363–79

— 1998b, 'Twin Peaks. The Archaeologies of Çatalhöyük', in L. Goodison and C. Morris (eds.), *Ancient Goddesses: The Myths and the Evidence*, London: British Museum Press

— 1999, *Archaeologies of Social Life*, Oxford: Blackwell

— 2002, *Private Life in New Kingdom Egypt*, Princeton: Princeton University Press

Miller, D., 1982a, 'Artifacts as Products of Human Categorisation Processes', in I. Hodder (ed.), *Symbolic and Structural Archaeology*, Cambridge University Press

1982b, 'Structures and Strategies: An Aspect of the Relationship between Social Hierarchy and Cultural Change', in I. Hodder (ed.), *Symbolic and Structural Archaeology*, Cambridge University Press

1983, 'Things Ain't What They Used To Be', *Royal Anthropological Institute Newsletter* 59, 5–7

1984, 'Modernism and Suburbia as Material Ideology', in D. Miller and C. Tilley (eds.), *Ideology, Power and Prehistory*, Cambridge University Press

1985a, 'Ideology and the Harappan Civilization', *Journal of Anthropological Archaeology* 4, 34–71

1985b, *Artifacts as Categories*, Cambridge University Press

1986, *The Limits of Dominance: Comparative Studies in the Development of Complex Societies*, edited by the World Archaeological Congress, London: Allen and Unwin

1987, *Material Culture and Mass Consumption*, Oxford: Blackwell

(ed.), 1995, *Acknowledging Consumption*, London: Routledge

(ed.), 1998, *Material Cultures: Why Some Things Matter*, Chicago: University of Chicago Press

Rowlands, M., and Tilley, C., 1989a, 'Introduction', in D. Miller, M. Rowlands, and C. Tilley (eds.), *Domination and Resistance*, London: Routledge

Rowlands, M., and Tilley, C. (eds.), 1989b, *Domination and Resistance*, London: Unwin Hyman

and Tilley, C. (eds.), 1984, *Ideology, Power and Prehistory*, Cambridge University Press

1984, 'Ideology, Power and Prehistory: An Introduction', in D. Miller and C. Tilley (eds.), *Ideology, Power and Prehistory*, Cambridge University Press

Mithen, Steven, 1996a, 'Ecological Interpretations of Paleolithic Art', in R. Preucel and I. Hodder (eds.), *Contemporary Archaeology in Theory*, Oxford: Blackwell

1996b, *The Prehistory of the Mind: A Search for the Origins of Art, Science and Religion*, London and New York: Thames and Hudson

1998a, 'Introduction', in S. Mithen (ed.), *Creativity in Human Evolution and Prehistory*, London: Routledge

1998b, 'A Creative Explosion? Theory of Mind, Language and the Disembodied Mind of the Upper Paleolithic', in S. Mithen (ed.), *Creativity in Human Evolution and Prehistory*, London: Routledge

2001, 'Archeological Theory and Theories of Cognitive Evolution', in Ian Hodder (ed.), *Archaeological Theory Today*, Cambridge: Polity

Monaghan, John, 1998, 'Dedication: Ritual, or Production?', in Shirley Mock (ed.), *The Sowing and the Dawning*, Albuquerque: University of New Mexico Press

Moore, H., 1982, 'The Interpretation of Spatial Patterning in Settlement Residues', in I. Hodder (ed.), *Symbolic and Structural Archaeology*, Cambridge University Press

1988, *Feminism and Anthropology*, Oxford: Polity Press

1990, 'Paul Ricoeur: Action, Meaning and Text', in C. Tilley (ed.), *Reading Material Culture*, Oxford: Blackwell

1994, 'Gendered Persons: Dialogues between Anthropology and Psychosis', in S. Head and A. Deluz (eds.), *Anthropology and Psychoanalysis: An Encounter through Culture*, New York: Routledge

Moore, J. A., and Keene, A. S., 1983, 'Archaeology and the Law of the Hammer', in J. A. Moore and A. S. Keene (eds.), *Archaeological Hammers and Theories*, New York: Academic Press

Moran, Paul, and Hides, David Shaun, 1990, 'Writing, Authority and the Determination of a Subject', in I. Bapty and T. Yates (eds.), *Archaeology after Structuralism*, London: Routledge

Morgan, Charles G., 1973, 'Archaeology and Explanation', *World Archaeology* 4, 259–76

Morris, Ian, 1999, *Archaeology as Cultural History*, Oxford: Blackwell

Muller, J., 1971, 'Style and Culture Contact', in C. L. Riley (ed.), *Man Across the Sea*, Houston: University of Texas Press

Naroll, R., 1962, 'Floor Area and Settlement Population', *American Antiquity* 27, 587–8

Nash, Ronald J., 1997, 'Archetypal Landscapes and the Interpretation of Meaning', *Cambridge Archaeological Journal* 7, 57–69

Neiman, Fraser, 1995, 'Stylistic Variation in Evolutionary Perspective: Inferences from Decorative Diversity and Interassemblage Distance in Illinois Woodland Ceramics', *American Antiquity* 60, 7–37

1997, 'Conspicuous Consumption as Wasteful Social Advertising: A Darwinian Perspective on Spatial Patterns in Classic Maya Terminal Monument Dates', in G. Clarke and M. Barton (eds.), *Rediscovering Darwin: Evolutionary Theory in Archaeological Explanation*, Arlington: American Anthropological Association

Nelson, Margaret C., Nelson, Sarah. M, and Wylie, Alison (eds.), 1994, *Equity Issues for Women in Archaeology*, Archaeological Papers of the American Anthropological Association 5, Washington: American Anthropological Association

Norwegian Archaeological Review, 1989, 'Discussions', *Norwegian Archaeological Review* 22, 1–54

Okely, J., 1979, 'An Anthropological Contribution to the History and Archaeology of an Ethnic Group', in B. C. Burnham and J. Kingsbury (eds.), *Space, Hierarchy and Society*, Oxford: British Archaeological Reports International Series, 59

Olsen, Bjornar, 1990, 'Roland Barthes: From Sign to Text', in Christopher Tilley (ed.), *Reading Material Culture: Structuralism, Hermeneutics and Post-Structuralism*, Oxford: Blackwell

O'Neale, L. M., 1932, *Yurok-Karok Basket Weavers*, University of California Publications in American Archaeology and Ethnology 32

Orser, C. Jr., 1991, 'The Continued Pattern of Dominance: Landlord and Tenant on the Postbellum Colonial Plantation', in R. H. McGuire and R. Paynter (eds.), *The Archaeology of Inequality*, Blackwell: Oxford

Ortner, S., 1995, 'Resistance and the Problem of Ethnographic Refusal', *Comparative Studies in Society and History* 37(1), 173–93

Paddaya, K., 1981, 'Piaget, Scientific Method, and Archaeology', *Bulletin of the Deccan College Research Institute* 40, 325–64

Pader, E., 1982, *Symbolism, Social Relations and the Interpretation of Mortuary Remains*, Oxford: British Archaeological Reports International Series, 130

Palkovich, Ann M., 1988, 'Asymmetry and Recursive Meanings in the 18th Century: The Morris Pound House', in Mark Leone and Parker Potter, Jr (eds.), *The Recovery of Meaning: Historical Archaeology in the Eastern United States*, Washington: Smithsonian Institution Press

Parker Pearson, M., 1982, 'Mortuary Practices, Society and Ideology: An Ethnoarchaeological Study', in I. Hodder (ed.), *Symbolic and Structural Archaeology*, Cambridge University Press

1984a, 'Economic and Ideological Change: Cyclical Growth in the Pre-state Societies of Jutland', in D. Miller and C. Tilley (eds.), *Ideology, Power and Prehistory*, Cambridge University Press

1984b, 'Social Change, Ideology and the Archaeological Record', in M. Spriggs (ed.), *Marxist Perspectives in Archaeology*, Cambridge University Press

1996, 'Food Fertility and Front Doors: Houses in the First Millennium', in Timothy Champion and J. R. Collis (eds.), *The Iron Age in Britain and Ireland: Recent Trends*, Sheffield: Sheffield Academic Press

Bibliography

1999, 'Food, Sex and Death: Cosmologies in the British Iron Age with Particular Reference to East Yorkshire', *Cambridge Archaeological Journal* 9, 43–69

Parkington, J., 1989, 'Interpreting Paintings without a Commentary: Meaning and Motive, Content and Composition in the Rock Art of the Western Cape, South Africa', *Antiquity* 63, 13–26

Patrik, L. E., 1985, 'Is there an Archaeological Record?', in M. B. Schiffer (ed.), *Advances in Archaeological Method and Theory*, vol. 8, New York: Academic Press

Patterson, T. C., 1986, 'The Last Sixty Years: Toward a Social History of Americanist Archaeology in the United States', *American Anthropologist* 88, 7–26

Pauketat, T., 2000, 'The Tragedy of the Commoners', in M.-A. Dobres and J. Robb (eds.), *Agency in Archaeology*, London: Routledge

Paynter, R., 1988, 'Steps to an Archaeology of Capitalism: Material Change and Class Analysis', in M. Leone and P. B. Potter (eds.), *The Recovery of Meaning*, Washington: Smithsonian Institution Press

1989, 'The Archaeology of Equality and Inequality', *Annual Review of Anthropology* 18, 369–99

and McGuire, R. H., 1991, 'The Archaeology of Inequality: Material Culture, Domination and Resistance', in R. H. McGuire and R. Paynter (eds.), *The Archaeology of Inequality*, Oxford: Blackwell

Piggott, S., 1959, *Approach to Archaeology*, Harvard: McGraw Hill

1965, *Ancient Europe*, Edinburgh: Edinburgh University Press

Pittman, C., 1998, 'If Bones Could Speak', *Transforming Anthropology* 7, 59–63

Plog, S., 1978, 'Social Interaction and Stylistic Similarity', in M. B. Schiffer (ed.), *Advances in Archaeological Method and Theory*, vol. 2, New York: Academic Press

Preucel, R. (ed.), 1991, *Between Past and Present: Issues in Contemporary Archaeological Discourse*, Carbondale: Southern Illinois University Press

1995, 'The Post-Processual Condition', *Journal of Archaeological Research* 3, 147–75

and Bauer, Alexander A., 2001, 'Archaeological Pragmatics', *Norwegian Archaeological Review* 34(2), 85–96

Pyburn, K. A., Dixon, B., Cook, P., and McNair, A., 1998, 'The Albion Island Settlement Pattern Project: Domination and Resistance in Early Classic Northern Belize', *Journal of Field Archaeology* 25, 37–62

Raab, L. M., and Goodyear, A. C., 1984, 'Middle-Range Theory in Archaeology: A Critical Review of Origins and Applications', *American Antiquity* 49, 255–68

Rahtz, P., 1981, *The New Medieval Archaeology*, York: University of York

Randsborg, K., 1982, 'Rank, Rights and Resources: An Archaeological Perspective from Denmark', in C. Renfrew and S. Shennan (eds.), *Ranking, Resource and Exchange*, Cambridge University Press

Rappaport, R. A., 1971, 'Ritual, Sanctity, and Cybernetics', *American Anthropologist* 73, 59–76

Rathje, W., 1978, 'Archaeological Ethnography ... Because Sometimes It Is Better to Give than to Receive', in R. Gould (ed.), *Explorations in Ethnoarchaeology*, Albuquerque: University of New Mexico Press

1979, 'Modern Material Culture Studies', *Advances in Archaeological Method and Theory* 2, 1–27

and Schiffer, Michael B., 1982, *Archaeology*, New York: Harcourt Brace Jovanovich

Read, Dwight, 1989, 'Intuitive Typology and Automatic Classification: Divergence or Full Circle?', *Journal of Anthropological Archaeology* 8, 158–88

Renfrew, A. C., 1969, 'Trade and Culture Process in European Prehistory', *Current Anthropology* 10, 151–69

1972, *The Emergence of Civilisation*, London: Methuen

(ed.), 1973a, *The Explanation of Culture Change*, London: Duckworth

1973b, *Social Archaeology*, Southampton: Southampton University

1976, 'Megaliths, Territories and Populations', in S. J. de Lact (ed.), *Acculturation and Continuity in Atlantic Europe*, Bruges: de Tempel

1977, 'Space, Time and Polity', in J. Friedman and M. J. Rowlands (eds.), *The Evolution of Social Systems*, London: Duckworth

1982, 'Discussion: Contrasting Paradigms', in C. Renfrew and S. Shennan (eds.), *Ranking, Resource and Exchange*, Cambridge University Press

1983a, *Towards an Archaeology of Mind*, Cambridge University Press

1983b, 'Divided We Stand: Aspects of Archaeology and Information', *American Antiquity* 48, 3–16

1985, *The Archaeology of Cult*, London: Thames and Hudson

1989, 'Comments in Archaeology into the 1990s', *Norwegian Archaeological Review* 22, 33–41

1993, 'Cognitive Archaeology: Some Thoughts on the Archaeology of Thought', *Cambridge Archaeological Journal* 3, 248–50

1994a, 'Towards a Cognitive Archaeology', in C. Renfrew (ed.), *The Ancient Mind: Elements of a Cognitive Archaeology*, Cambridge University Press

1994b, 'The Archaeology of Religion', in C. Renfrew (ed.), *The Ancient Mind: Elements of a Cognitive Archaeology*, Cambridge University Press

1998, 'All the King's Horses: Assessing Cognitive Maps in Later Prehistoric Europe', in S. Mithen (ed.), *Creativity in Human Evolution and Prehistory*, London: Routledge

2001, 'Symbol before Context: Material Engagement and the Early Development of Society', in Ian Hodder (ed.), *Archaeological Theory Today*, Cambridge: Polity

Richards, C., and Thomas, J., 1984, 'Ritual Activity and Structured Deposition in Later Neolithic Wessex', in R. Bradley and J. Gardiner (eds.), *Neolithic Studies: A Review of some Current Research*, Oxford: British Archaeological Reports British Series, 133

Ricoeur, P., 1971, 'The Model of the Text: Meaningful Action Considered as a Text', *Social Research* 38, 529–62

Rindos, D., 1986, 'The Evolution of the Capacity for Culture: Sociobiology, Structuralism, and Cultural Selection', *Current Anthropology* 27, 315–32

Rosaldo, M., 1980, 'The Uses and Abuses of Anthropology: Reflections on Feminism and Cross-Cultural Understanding', *Signs* 5, 400

Rountree, K., 1999, 'Goddesses and Monsters: Contesting Approaches to Malta's Neolithic Past', *Journal of Mediterranean Studies* 9, 204–31

2001, 'The Past is a Foreigners' Country: Goddess Feminists, Archaeologists, and the Appropriation of Prehistory, *Journal of Contemporary Religion* 16, 5–27

2002, 'Re-inventing Malta's Neolithic Temples: Contemporary Interpretations and Agendas', *History and Anthropology* 13, 31–51

Rowlands, M., 1984, 'Conceptualising the European Bronze Age and Early Iron Ages', in J. Bintliff (ed.), *European Social Evolution*, Bradford: Bradford University Press

1993, 'The Role of Memory in the Transmission of Culture', *World Archaeology* 25, 141–51

and Seagraves, B., 1982, *Theory and Explanation in Archaeology*, New York: Academic Press

Russell, James, 1995, 'At Two with Nature: Agency and the Development of Self-World Dualism', in J. L. Bermudez, A. Marcel, and N. Eilan (eds.), *The Body and the Self*, Cambridge, MA: MIT Press

Sahlins, M., 1972, *Stone Age Economics*, Chicago: Aldine

    1981, *Historical Metaphors and Mythical Realities*, Ann Arbor: University of Michigan Press

    1996, 'The Sadness of Sweetness: The Native Anthropology of Western Cosmology', *Current Anthropology* 37, 395–428

Saxe, A., 1970, *Social Dimensions of Mortuary Practices*, unpublished Ph.D thesis, University of Michigan

Scheper-Hughes, N., and Lock, M., 1987, 'The Mindful Body', *Medical Anthropological Quarterly* 1(1), 6–41

Schiffer, M. B., 1976, *Behavioural Archaeology*, New York: Academic Press

    1987, *Formation Processes of the Archaeological Record*, Albuquerque: University of New Mexico Press

    1991, *The Portable Radio in American Life*, Tucson: University of Arizona Press

    1995, *Behavioral Archaeology: First Principles*, Salt Lake City: University of Utah Press

    1996, 'Some Relationships between Behavioral and Evolutionary Archaeologies', *American Antiquity* 61, 643–62

    1999, 'Behavioral Archaeology: Some Clarifications', *American Antiquity* 64, 166–8

    2000, 'Social Theory in Archaeology: Building Bridges', in M. B. Schiffer (ed.), *Social Theory in Archaeology*, Salt Lake City: University of Utah Press

    and Skibo, James, 1997, 'The Explanation of Artifact Variability', *American Antiquity* 62, 27–50

Schmidt, P., 1997, *Iron Technology in East Africa: Symbolism, Science, and Archaeology*, Bloomington: University of Indiana Press

Schnapp, A., 1984, 'Eros en chasse', in *La Cité des images*, Paris: Fernand Nathan

Schrire, C., 1980, 'Hunter-Gatherers in Africa', *Science* 210, 890–1

Scott, J. C., 1985, *Weapons of the Weak*, New Haven: Yale University Press

    1990, *Domination and the Arts of Resistance*, New Haven: Yale University Press

Searle, J., 1970, *Speech Acts: An Essay in the Philosophy of Language*, Cambridge University Press

Bibliography

Shackel, Paul, 2000, 'Craft to Wage Labor: Agency and Resistance in American Historical Archaeology', in M.-A. Dobres and J. Robb (eds.), *Agency in Archaeology*, London: Routledge

Shanks, Michael, 2001, 'Culture/Archaeology: The Dispersion of a Discipline and Its Objects', in Ian Hodder (ed.), *Archaeological Theory Today*, Cambridge: Polity

and Hodder, I., 1995, 'Processual, Postprocessual and Interpretive Archaeologies', in I. Hodder, M. Shanks, A. Alexandri, V. Buchli, J. Carman, J. Last, and G. Lucas (eds.), *Interpreting Archaeology: Finding Meaning in the Past*, London: Routledge

Shanks, M., and Tilley, C., 1982, 'Ideology, Symbolic Power and Ritual Communication: A Reinterpretation of Neolithic Mortuary Practices', in I. Hodder (ed.), *Symbolic and Structural Archaeology*, Cambridge University Press

1987a, *Re-Constructing Archaeology*, Cambridge University Press

1987b, *Social Theory and Archaeology*, Cambridge: Polity Press

Shennan, S., 1983, 'Monuments: An Example of Archaeologists' Approach to the Massively Material', *Royal Anthropological Institute News* 59, 9–11

2001, 'Demography and Cultural Innovation: A Model and Its Implications of the Emergence of Modern Human Culture', *Cambridge Archaeological Journal* 11, 5–16

and Wilkinson, J. R., 2001, 'Ceramic Style Change and Neutral Evolution: A Case Study from Neolithic Europe', *American Antiquity* 66, 577–94

Sherratt, A., 1982, 'Mobile Resources: Settlement and Exchange in Early Agricultural Europe', in C. Renfrew and S. Shennan (eds.), *Ranking, Resource and Exchange*, Cambridge University Press

Silliman, Stephen, 2001, 'Agency, Practical Politics and the Archaeology of Culture Contact', *Journal of Social Archaeology* 1(2), 190–209

Small, D., 1987, 'Toward a Competent Structuralist Archaeology', *Journal of Anthropological Archaeology* 6, 105–21

Smith, Adam, 1999, 'The Making of an Urartian Landscape in Southern Transcaucasia: A Study of Political Architectonics, *American Journal of Archaeology* 103, 45–71

2001, 'The Limitations of Doxa: Agency and Subjectivity from an Archaeological Point of View', *Journal of Social Archaeology* 1(2), 155–71

Sørensen, M. L. S., 1987, 'Material Order and Cultural Classification: The Role of Bronze Objects in the Transition from Bronze Age to Iron Age in Scandinavia', in I. Hodder (ed.), *The Archaeology of Contextual Meanings*, Cambridge University Press

1988, 'Is there a Feminist Contribution to Archaeology?', *Archaeological Review from Cambridge* 7, 7–20

2000, *Gender Archaeology*, Cambridge: Polity Press

Spector, Janet, 1993, *What This Awl Means*, St. Paul: Minnesota Historical Society Press

Spriggs, M. (ed.), 1984, *Marxist Perspectives in Archaeology*, Cambridge University Press

Stacey, J. and Thorne, B., 1985, 'The Missing Feminist Revolution in Sociology', *Social Problems* 32, 301–16

Strathern, A., 1996, *Body Thoughts*, Ann Arbor: University of Michigan Press

Swidler, N., Dongoske, K., Anyon, R., and Downer, A. (eds.), 1997, *Native Americans and Archaeologists: Stepping Stones to Common Ground*. Walnut Creek, CA: Altamira

Tanner, N., 1981, *On Becoming Human*, Cambridge University Press

Tarlow, Sarah, 1999, *Bereavement and Commemoration*, Oxford: Blackwell

Taylor, C., 1985, *Philosophy and the Human Sciences*, Cambridge University Press

1999, 'To Follow a Rule...', in R. Shusterman (ed.), *Bourdieu: A Critical Reader*, Oxford: Blackwell

Taylor, W., 1948, *A Study of Archaeology*, New York: Memoirs of the American Anthropological Association 69

Thomas, J., 1988, 'The Social Significance of Cotswold-Severn Burial Practices', *Man* 23, 540–59

1995, 'Reconciling Symbolic Significance with Being-in-the-World', in I. Hodder, M. Shanks, A. Alexandri, V. Buchli, J. Carman, J. Last, and G. Lucas (eds.), *Interpreting Archaeology: Finding Meaning in the Past*, London: Routledge

1996, *Time, Culture and Identity*, London: Routledge

1998, 'The Socio-Semiotics of Material Culture', *Journal of Material Culture* 3, 97–108

and Tilley, C., 1993, 'The Axe and the Torso: Symbolic Structures in the Neolithic of Brittany', in C. Tilley (ed.), *Interpretative Archaeology*, Providence: Berg

Thompson, J. B., 1981, *Critical Hermeneutics*, Cambridge University Press

Bibliography

Thorpe, I., 1984, 'Ritual, Power and Ideology: A Reconstruction of Earlier Neolithic Rituals in Wessex', in R. Bradley and J. Gardiner (eds.), *Neolithic Studies*, British Archaeological Report 133

Tilley, C., 1984, 'Ideology and the Legitimation of Power in the Middle Neolithic of Southern Sweden', in D. Miller and C. Tilley (eds.), *Ideology, Power and Prehistory*, Cambridge University Press

1989a, 'Discourse and Power: The Genre of the Cambridge Inaugural Lecture', in D. Miller, M. Rowlands and C. Tilley (eds.), *Domination and Resistance*, London: Unwin Hyman

1989b, 'Archaeology as Sociopolitical Action in the Present', in Valerie Pinsky and Alison Wylie (eds.), *Critical Traditions in Contemporary Archaeology*, Cambridge University Press

(ed.), 1990a, *Reading Material Culture*, Oxford: Blackwell

1990b, *The Art of Ambiguity: Material Culture and Text*, London: Routledge

1990c, 'On Modernity and Archaeological Discourse', in I. Bapty and T. Yates (eds.), *Archaeology after Structuralism*, London: Routledge

1991, *Material Culture and Text: The Art of Ambiguity*, London: Routledge

1993, 'Introduction: Interpretation and a Poetics of the Past', in C. Tilley (ed.), *Interpretative Archaeology*, Oxford: Berg

1994, *A Phenomenology of Landscape*, Providence: Berg

Tolstoy, P., 1966, 'Method in Long Range Comparison', *Congreso Internacional de Americanistas* 36, 69–89

1972, 'Diffusion: As Explanation and as Event', in N. Barnard (ed.), *Early Chinese Art and its Possible Influence in the Pacific Basin*, New York: Intercultural Arts Press

Treherne, P., 1995, 'The Warrior's Beauty: The Masculine Body and Self-Identity in Bronze Age Europe', *Journal of European Archaeology* 3, 105–44

Trigger, B., 1978, *Time and Tradition*, Edinburgh University Press

1980, 'Archaeology and the Image of the American Indian', *American Antiquity* 45, 662–76

1984, 'Marxism and Archaeology', in J. Maquet and N. Daniels (ed.), *On Marxian Perspectives in Anthropology*, Malibu: Undena

1989, 'Hyperrelativism, Responsibility, and the Social Sciences', *Canadian Review of Sociology and Anthropology* 26, 776–97

Tringham, Ruth, 1991, 'Men and Women in Prehistoric Architecture', *TDSR* 3(1), 9–28

1994, 'Engendered Places in Prehistory', *Gender, Place, and Culture* 1(2), 169–204

and Conkey, M., 1998, 'Rethinking Figurines. A Critical View from Archaeology of Gimbutas, the "Goddess" and Popular Culture', in L. Goodison and C. Morris (eds.), *Ancient Goddesses: The Myths and the Evidence*, London: British Museum Press

Trubitt, M. B. D., 2000, 'Mound Building and Prestige Goods Exchange: Changing Strategies in the Cahokia Chiefdom', *American Antiquity* 65, 669–90

Tuggle, H. David, Townsend, Alex, and Riley, Thomas J., 1972, 'Laws, Systems, and Research Designs: A Discussion of Explanation in Archaeology', *American Antiquity* 37, 3–12

Turner, B. S., 1994, *Orientalism, Postmodernism and Globalism*, London: Routledge

Van de Velde, P., 1980, *Elsloo and Hienheim: Bandkeramik Social Structure*, Analecta Praehistorica Leidensia 12, Leiden: University of Leiden

VanPool, C. S. and VanPool, T. L., 1999, 'The Scientific Nature of Postprocessualism', *American Antiquity* 64, 33–54

Voss, Barbara, and Schmidt, Robert (eds.), 2000, *Archaeologies of Sexuality*, New York: Routledge

Walker, William, 1998, 'Where Are the Witches of Prehistory?', *Journal of Archaeological Method and Theory* 5, 245–308

Washburn, D. (ed.), 1983, *Structure and Cognition in Art*, Cambridge University Press

Watkins, J., 2000, *Indigenous Archaeology*, Walnut Creek, CA: Altamira

Watson, P.J., 1986, 'Archaeological Interpretation, 1985', in D. J. Meltzer, D. D. Fowler and J. A. Sabloff (eds.), *American Archaeology Past and Present*, Washington: Smithsonian Institution Press

Leblanc, S. J., and Redman, C. L., 1971, *Explanation in Archaeology: An Explicitly Scientific Approach*, New York: Columbia University Press

Weber, M., 1976, *The Protestant Ethic and the Spirit of Capitalism*, London: George Allen and Unwin

Weiner, Annette, 1992, *Inalienable Possessions: The Paradox of Keeping-While-Giving*, Berkeley: University of California Press

Bibliography

Wells, P. S., 1984, 'Prehistoric Charms and Superstitions', *Archaeology* 37, 38–43

    1985, 'Material Symbols and the Interpretation of Cultural Change', *Oxford Journal of Archaeology* 4, 9–17

Whallon, R., 1974, 'Spatial Analysis of Occupation Floors, II: The Application of Nearest Neighbour Analysis', *American Antiquity* 39, 16–34

Wiessner, Polly, 1983, 'Style and Information in Kalahari San Projectile Points', *American Antiquity* 48(2), 253–76

    1985, 'Style or Isochrestic Variation? A Reply to Sackett', *American Antiquity* 50(1), 160–6

Wilk, R. R., 1985, 'The Ancient Maya and the Political Present', *Journal of Anthropological Research* 41, 307–26

Wilkie, L., and Bartoy, K., 2000, 'A Critical Archaeology Revisited', *Current Anthropology* 41, 747–77

Willey, G., 1980, *The Social Uses of Archaeology*, Murdoch Lecture (unpublished typescript), Harvard University

    1984, 'Archaeological Retrospect 6', *Antiquity* 58, 5–14

Williamson, T., and Bellamy, L., 1983, *Ley Lines in Question*, London: Heinemann

Willis, P., 1977, *Learning to Labour*, Saxonhouse: Westmead

Wittig, M., 1985, 'The Mark of Gender', *Feminist Issues* 5(2), 1–10

Wobst, M., 1976, 'Locational Relationships in Palaeolithic Society', *Journal of Human Evolution* 5, 49–58

    1977, 'Stylistic Behaviour and Information Exchange', University of Michigan Museum of Anthropology, Anthropological Paper 61, 317–42

    and Keene, A., 1983, 'Archaeological Explanation as Political Economy', in J. M. Gero, D. M. Lacy, and M. L. Blakey (eds.), *The Socio-Politics of Archaeology*, Research Reports 23, Department of Anthropology, University of Massachusetts Amherst

Woodburn, J., 1980, 'Hunters and Gatherers Today and Reconstruction of the Past', in E. Gellner (ed.), *Soviet and Western Anthropology*, London: Duckworth

Wright, Rita, 1995, 'Technological Styles: Transforming a Natural Material into a Cultural Object', in Stevan Lubar and W. David Kingery (eds.), *History from Things: Essays on Material Culture*, Washington: Smithsonian Institution Press

    (ed.), 1996, *Gender and Archaeology*, Philadelphia: University of Pennsylvania Press

Wylie, M. A., 1982, 'Epistemological Issues Raised by a Structuralist Archaeology', in I. Hodder (ed.,), *Symbolic and Structural Archaeology*, Cambridge University Press

1985, 'The Reaction against Analogy', in M. Schiffer (ed.), *Advances in Archaeological Method and Theory*, New York: Academic Press

1989a, 'Archaeological Cables and Tacking: The Implications of Practice for Bernstein's "Options beyond Objectivism and Relativism"', *Philosophy of the Social Sciences* 19, 1–18

1989b, 'Introduction: Sociopolitical Context', in Valerie Pinsky and Alison Wylie (eds.), *Critical Traditions in Contemporary Archaeology*, Cambridge University Press

1992a, 'The Interplay of Evidential Constraints and Political Interests: Recent Archaeological Research on Gender', *American Antiquity* 57, 15–35

1992b, 'On "Heavily Decomposing Red Herrings": Scientific Method in Archaeology and the Ladening of Evidence with Theory', in Lester Embree (ed.), *Metaarchaeology*, Dordrecht: Kluwer

1993, 'A Proliferation of New Archaeologies: "Beyond Objectivism and Relativism"', in Norman Yoffee and Andrew Sherratt (eds.), *Archaeological Theory: Who Sets the Agenda?*, Cambridge University Press

1994, 'On "Capturing Facts Alive in the Past" (or Present): Response to Fotiadis and to Little', *American Antiquity* 59, 556–60

2000, 'Questions of Evidence, Legitimacy, and the (Dis)Union of Science', *American Antiquity* 65, 227–38

Wynn, T., 1979, 'The Intelligence of later Achenlian Hominids', *Man* 14, 371–91

Yates, T., 1989, 'Habitus and Social Space: Some Suggestions about Meaning in the Saami (Lapp) Tent ca. 1700–1900', in I. Hodder (ed.), *The Meanings of Things*, London: Unwin Hyman

1990, 'Archaeology through the Looking Glass', in I. Bapty and T. Yates (eds.), *Archaeology after Structuralism: Post-Structuralism and the Practice of Archaeology*, London: Routledge

1993, 'Frameworks for an Archaeology of the Body', in C. Tilley (ed.), *Interpretative Archaeology*, Providence: Berg

Yellen, J. E., 1977, *Archaeological Approaches to the Present*, New York: Academic Press

Yentsch, Anne, 1991, 'The Symbolic Dimensions of Pottery: Sex-Related Attributes of English and Anglo-American Household

Pots', in Randall H. McGuire and Robert Paynter (eds.), *The Archaeology of Inequality*, Oxford: Blackwell

and Beaudry, Marilyn, 2001, 'American Material Culture in Mind, Thought, and Deed', in Ian Hodder (ed.), *Archaeological Theory Today*, Cambridge: Polity

Young, T. C., 1988, 'Since Herodotus, Has History Been a Valid Concept?', *American Antiquity* 53, 7–12

Index

Index

organization in tombs 95
residues and prehistoric sites 127
boundedness 69
Bourdieu, P. 106
   child's understanding 122
   historical knowledge 147
   theory of practice 90, 92, 93, 94
Boy George 62
Bradley, R. 140
Braithwaite, M. 229
Braudel, F. 136
British public
   attitudes to archaeology 232
   involvement in archaeology 233
British public opinion
   past in relation to present 220–1
   value of past 221
Brück, J. 120, 121
building identification 70–1
burial 2–3
   conceptual transformation of society
      73
   function 28, 126
   ideology in 81, 85
   megalithic in Neolithic Europe 81
   mound function 28
   Western 138
Butler, J. 100, 109
Butzer, K. 170

Cahokia, Changes in economy and
   society 22, 23
c-transforms 2
Calvinism 132, 133
Cambridge burials 3
capitalism
   emergence 131
   spirit of 131, 133
   Western 132
Case, H. 171, 193
catastrophe theory xii, xvi
categories of objects 17
Catholicism 132, 133
causality 21
cause and effect 15–16
cave paintings, Palaeolithic 57, 70,
   80–1
Celtic style 138
Chaco Canyon 56
chaos theory xvi
chevron design analysis 50
Childe, V. G. 14, 95, 149
   European culture 137
   processes 214

children
   habitus 92
   Ilchamus tribe
Clark, Grahame 214
Clarke, D. L. xi, 69, 243
class struggle 76
cloth production, Inca 137
Coe, M. D. 137
coherence in historical method 148
Collingwood, R. G. 125
   coherence 148
   Hadrian's Wall 150–2
   historical data interpretation 147
   historical idealism 129
   historical method and theory
      145–50
   meaning content reconstruction 149
   meaning of terms 176
   theory of social action 145
   universality 148
Conkey, M. W. 18, 228–9
context 187–91, 204–5
   analogy 194
   archaeological 170
   artifacts 171
   cultural 6, 244
   description of 193
   excavation procedures 171
   explanation and description 170
   and horizons 198
   material culture 5
   systemic 171
   text and symbolic meaning 172
Contexts for Prehistoric Exchange 170
contextual analysis 195
contextual archaeology 171, 193
contextual boundaries 198
contextualism xvi
continuity patterns 140
control, central 210, 211
Cook, Captain James 135
covering law 42
   of causation 21
   individuals 30
   normative 31
Critical Theory 218–23
   new enlightenment 219
   philosophy of history 219
   presentation of archaeological
      past 218
critical thought and action 235
cultural context 6, 244
cultural development, temporal phases
   31

Index

Index

formal analysis 46, 47–51
  chevron design 50
  nature 51
  subjectivity 51
formal gardens 82, 87, 210
Foucault, M. 13, 84, 85, 99
Frankenstein, S. 208
Frankfurt school 218
Freud, S. 13, 115
Friedman, J. 76, 79
Fritz, J. 45, 55
function 24
  and symbolic meaning 174
functional meaning 71
  contextual relationships
  and environmental factors 72
functionalism xi

Gadamer, H.-G. 160, 195, 198
Gailey, C. W. 229
gardens, formal 82, 87, 210
Gellner, E. 21, 42
gender dominance 230
gender relations
  cultural constructions 229
  material culture 230
  meaning 230
generative grammars 47–50
Georgian gardens 82, 88
Gero, J. 228
Gibson, J. 114
Giddens, A. 84, 85, 86, 90, 92, 94, 96, 106,
  135
Gilman, A. 77, 78, 80
Glassie, J. 70
Glastonbury
  Iron Age site 69
  study 243
Gosden, C. 119
Greene, G. 210
Gregory, T. 231, 233

Habermas, J. 219
habitus 90, 92, 215
  body in 94–5
  child's understanding 92
  conditions of existence 134
  conflict of opposing 135
  enculturation process 94
  links with structure and practice 135
Hadrian's Wall 150–1
Hall, R. L. 140, 183
Hamann, B. 142
  Chan Kom 142

Handsman, R. 18, 220
Hardin, M. 47
Harraway, D. 202
Harries, Mags 246
Hastorf, C. 229
Hawaii 135
Hawkes, C. 43, 138, 145
head-dress function 28–9
hearth, activity area 175
Hebrides, 54
Heidegger, M. 117
Hegel, G. 219
Held, D. 218, 219, 221
helix of interaction 38
henge monuments 59
hermeneutics 195–202
  data interpretation 241
Heuneberg (Germany) wall 151
Hillier, B. 49
historical imagination 147, 149
historical insight validation 148
historical meaning
  reality 217
  reconstruction 149
historical process 136, 214
history
  archaeology, links with 125
  contextual 182
  continuity and meaning assignation 70
  data interpretation 147
  generalization in 131, 135
  human action 128
  and idealism 129, 217
  as ideology 220
  inside of events 155
  interpretation 125, 134
  knowledge 147
  of the long term 130–45, 247
  method and theory 145–52
  particularist dimension 125
  phases 130–1
  philosophy of 219
  reconstruction of long-term 247
  relationship with archaeology 145,
    243–7
  scales of 136
Hodder, I.
  analogy 148
  analytical techniques 170
  Annales School 136
  archaeologists' writing 220
  axe exchange 152
  British public attitudes 233
  function of decoration 230

287

Index

Index

Longacre, W. 14
Lozi pottery 8

McCafferty, G. A. 19
McCafferty, S. D. 19
McGhee, R. 57–9, 71, 174
McGuire, R. H. 87
male domination 97, 142
  activities 228
male strategies 238
male/female relationship 95
mana 135, 145
Marxist archaeology 75–9
  class division 76
  criticisms of ideology 83–8
  cross-cultural methods 86
  false consciousness 84
  generation of ideology 87
  historical context 86
  ideology 79–83
  individual in 88–9
  links with structuralism 94
  social structure 215
  structure 79–80
Marxist theories, symbolic meanings 184
mass genocide 226
material culture
  activity 80
  and behaviour 14–15
  boundaries 24
  context 5, 204
  distinction from language 167
  gender relations 230
  interpretation 173–83
  manipulation by positioned subjects 10
  meanings relationship 36
  meanings 173, 210
  meanings analysis 72
  role in ideology 83
  similarities and differences 173–83
  social effects 9
  as texts to read 172
material culture distinctiveness 1–2
  material survival questions 4
  and New Archaeology 3
material objects
  context 245
  meaning 242
materialism 126
  Marxist archaeology 75, 127
materialist analysis 234
materialist systemic explanation 25, 126
matrilocal residence hypothesis 14
Mauss, M. 108

meaning 157–66
  abstract analysis 60
  of archaeological terms 176
  constitutive 158
  and context 70, 188, 189
  contextual 166, 173, 203, 204, 209, 215
  cross-cultural application 70
  cultural 126
  dispersal on chains of signifiers 222
  fixing of 210
  frameworks of 156
  internal 144
  interpretation 159, 209
  materialisation 66–7
  similarities and differences in
    interpretation 173–6
  and structuralism 126
  structures 95
  subjective 126, 129
  subjectivity 126
  symbolic 174, 184, 189
  systemic 184
  verbal reasons 209
meaning content 96, 216
  historical particularism 216
measurement 17
  independent instruments 17
megaliths (European) 29
Meltzer, D. J. 206
men
  dominance in Palaeolithic 81
  symbolism in Palaeolithic art 80–1
  see also male
mentalité 136, 142
Merleau-Ponty, M. 117
Merriman, N. 151, 232
Meso-American culture 137
metal-detector enthusiasts 231, 233
metallurgy, tools and weapons in New
    World and Old World 136–7
Mickey Mouse Laws 155
Middle Range Theory 4, 14, 17, 146,
    234
  non-cultural processes 240
Mill, J. S. 7
Miller, D. 87
mind
  concepts 38
  natural science model 38
Mcthen, S. 40, 41, 123
Moore, H. 73, 230
Moore, J. A. 206
motifs 47, 189
  bow-tie 48

Index

Index

Index

Index